Brand *Manners*

Reviews for *Brand Manners*

'This is the single best book that helps us understand the Holy Grail of marketing: the "supreme customer experience", and how corporations and their brands can achieve that hallowed goal.'

Warren Bennis, Distinguished Professor of Business Administration at the University of Southern California, USA. Author of Managing The Dream *and* Organizing Genius

'*Brand Manners* puts up a strong challenge to the "command and control" school of management and I found the authors' arguments for the "self-confident" organisation compelling at both the academic and commercial levels.'

Professor John Quelch, Dean of London Business School, UK

'The study of brands has come a long way since the seminal paper by Gardner and Levy, published in 1955. This book by Gordon and Pringle moves us measurably forward in blending consumer and corporate lifestyles, and it is the brand which is the entity that connects the two. This is a significant piece of work.'

John Philip Jones, Professor, Syracuse University, New York, USA
Author of When Ads Work

'*Brand Manners*, a book on organisation which emphasises "the true potential of employees", is refocusing the aims and values of enterprise in a radically new way. Pringle and Gordon widen the agenda to include the spiritual and challenge readers to take a more realistic and fulfilling world view.'

The Rt Revd David Urquhart, Bishop of Birkenhead, UK

'A refreshingly accessible perspective on branding. Marketers have waited for a long time for a common sense book that acts as a bridge between brand theory and practice.'

Dr Jonathan Reynolds, Director, Oxford Institute of Retail Management, Fellow of Templeton College & Lecturer in Management Studies, Saïd Business School, University of Oxford, UK

'*Brand Manners* is an excellent reminder of one of the nearly forgotten truths of marketing, that in most industries, people buy from people, and even when computers buy from computers, people affect how well it is done. If your people have poor brand manners, then your customers will feel it, and some of the best of them will leave you. *Brand Manners* tells you how to avoid this.'

Merlin Stone, IBM Professor of Relationship Marketing, Bristol Business School, UK

Brand
Manners

How to create the self-confident organisation to live the brand

Hamish Pringle and William Gordon

JOHN WILEY & SONS, LTD

Chichester · New York · Weinheim · Brisbane · Singapore · Toronto

Other Wiley Editorial Offices

John Wiley & Sons, Inc., 605 Third Avenue,
New York, NY 10158-0012, USA

WILEY-VCH GmbH, Pappelallee 3,
D-69469 Weinheim, Germany

John Wiley & Sons Australia Ltd, 33 Park Road, Milton,
Queensland 4064, Australia

John Wiley & Sons (Asia) Pte Ltd, 2 Clementi Loop #02-01,
Jin Xing Distripark, Singapore 129809

John Wiley & Sons (Canada) Ltd, 22 Worcester Road,
Rexdale, Ontario M9W 1L1, Canada

British Library Cataloguing in Publication Data

A catalogue record for this book is available from the British Library

ISBN 0-471-49606-5

Typeset in Goudy by MHL Typesetting Limited, Coventry, Warwickshire
Project managed by Macfarlane Production Services, Markyate, Hertfordshire
Printed and bound in Great Britain by Biddles Ltd, Guildford and King's Lynn
This book is printed on acid-free paper responsibly manufactured from sustainable forestry, in which at least two trees are planted for each one used for paper production.

Dedications

To Victor Gordon and Margaret Maxwell, my parents, with heartfelt thanks, and to Joëlle Pineau and Antoine Pineau–Gordon, with love.

William Gordon

To Vivienne Pringle, mother of Sebastian, Benedict, Tristan and Arabella, and co-founder of Blooming Marvellous and Girl Heaven – with love and in admiration.

Hamish Pringle

Contents

Now, each of us has his own special gift
And you know this was meant to be true,
And if you don't underestimate me,
I won't underestimate you.

'Dear Landlord', Bob Dylan

Acknowledgements

Brand Manners has been created by a core team effort, with the support of family, close friends and associates, and by the contributions of many helpful individuals at the companies we have used as examples or case histories, which are acknowledged in the publisher's notes.

But in particular we must thank Accenture, previously Andersen Consulting, for sponsoring the project: we literally could not have produced the book without the outstanding efforts of Laura Jones and Philip Doherty, the two researchers the firm provided for us.

There are many others each of us must thank.

First of all our team at John Wiley & Sons, led by our editor Claire Plimmer and ably supported by Karen Weller, Viv Wickham, Stuart Macfarlane, Michelle Long and Julia Lampam.

Secondly our colleagues at Accenture, Terry Corby, Jennifer Garland, Stacey Jones, Julie Stibich and Julia Wright.

For advice and comment: Vernon Ellis, David Frankel, Gavin Fraser, Stephen Goodchild, John Stopford and Michael Wemms.

For assistance with the IPA Data Bank and its case histories: Lesley Scott and Natalie Swan.

For help with the text: Helena Lenehan, Maria Oddy, Thomas Sfounis and Roger Ingham.

For education: Hugo Brown, headmaster of Croftinloan School, Pitlochry; Ronald Craig, Noel Barrington-Prowse, Alan and Heather Elliott, David Graham-Campbell and Hugh Price of Glenalmond College, Perth; Sandy Ogston, Roderick Martin and Bede Rundle of Trinity College, Oxford; and Charles Handy, David Norburn and Will McWillan of London Business School.

For professional development: Charles Fiero, Bill Dinsmore and Ian Sym-Smith of the Hay Group; James Kelly and Dan Valentino of Gemini Consulting; and Tim Breene, Joe Forehand, Mary Tolan, Bob Willett and Adrian Lathja of Accenture; Richard Venables of Ogilvy & Mather; John McCormick of McCormick Richards; Martin Boase of BMPDDB; Michael Conroy of Publicis; Peter Mead of AMV.BBDO; John Madell of MWP; Tim Delaney of Leagas Delaney; Stuart Bull of KHBB; Charlie Scott of Cordiant; John Ayling of The Lord's Taverners; Andrew Wilkinson of music3w/com, and Nick Phillips of the IPA.

For friendship and stimulation: Charles Blakeney, Didier Bonnet, Richard Demarco, Jonathan Mueller, Louise Grant, Bruce Haines, Michael Hockney, Steven Hurwitz, David King, Kit Molloy, Alan Morgan, Simon Pringle, Simon Prior, Mark Robinson, Bertrand Siguier, Marjorie Thompson and David Urquhart.

Publisher's Note

The publisher wishes to thank the following who have kindly given permission for the use of copyright material.

BP for Figure 25.
Consumer Insight for Figure 32.
The Co-operative Bank for Figure 34.
Frank Dick for Figures 39, 40 and 41.
Forrester for Figure 37.
Future Foundation/Consumers' Association for Figure 30.
Gateway for Figures 42 and 43.
Girl Heaven for Figures 56 and 57.
Henley Centre for Figure 29.

IPA for Figures 19, 20, 46 and 53.
Kogan Page for Figures 61, 62 and 63.
London Business School for Figure 59.
MORI for Figure 33.
Ronseal for Figure 54.
Private Eye for cartoons.
Saatchi & Saatchi for Figure 24.
Tesco for Figures 8, 9, 10 and 11.
Vauxhall for Figures 48, 49 and 50.
WRCS for Figures 17, 18 and 21.

Preface

It's always puzzled the two of us that the disciplines of advertising communications and management consulting occupy such separate parallel universes in the provision of professional services to clients. Obviously they have their different skills and expertise, and the qualities and characters of the protagonists vary widely, but their common goal of delivering customer-focused strategies and executions for clients means they actually have a great deal in common.

In conversations over a quarter of a century working in our separate areas, we often found ourselves operating in the same markets and once, albeit briefly, for the same client. The same thought recurred often: surely there must be a benefit in closer collaboration between the 'upstream' world of corporate strategy and the 'downstream' one of brands.

We also believed that a more holistic approach could ensure that the internal organisation and its human capital were not only better aligned behind the external brand values and promises that a company delivers to its customers, but actually enhance the quality of working life of employees too.

Finally, we felt that the time was right as we entered the new century, to take an ambitious look at the core personality of the business we would like to work in ourselves and define its character in such simple terms that everyone could understand the notion from executive suite to shop floor, and be inspired and motivated by it. We wanted to articulate the process whereby a company could evolve into this management and cultural space.

Thus *Brand Manners* was born with the intention of helping move companies into the new world of the 'self-confident organisation'.

Hamish Pringle and William Gordon

Foreword

Brand Manners may be a book whose time has come. It's a novel contribution to the never-ending search for business improvement.

The approach taken by Bill Gordon and Hamish Pringle is surprising – it certainly surprised me! No-one can accuse them of recycling old ideas, but I do recognise the central tenet of their argument. There can be a huge improvement in business performance by applying the incredibly simple principle that good manners – good conduct, good behaviour – motivate everyone; staff, of course, but also customers, suppliers, communities – everyone. And the improvement lasts – it's self sustaining. It may be a simple principle, but in my experience it's far from easy to apply, and *Brand Manners* teaches through case study 'how to' do it.

I commend this book. It offers the prospect of achieving business success by making work a better place to be.

Terry Leahy
CEO, Tesco

PART I
The Brand Manners Book of Life

1

'Manners Maketh Man'

This book is about you and me. It is about us as individuals, and how we behave towards one another. Nearly all of us are employed in producing and consuming branded products and services and these brands have become an inextricable part of our working and leisure lives. Thus in order to understand ourselves fully in this modern branded culture, we need to appreciate the behavioural relationship we have with brands and the companies which create them.

Brands represent promises about what we can expect from a product, a service or a company. This actually boils down to what we expect of the people involved in delivering us their brand. Manners mean good habits, in terms of the way people behave towards each other, based on a code of how things should be done properly and with mutual respect.

Thus 'brand manners' are the way in which an organisation can manage its promise to customers and ensure that they are happily surprised as often as possible. These 'manners' occur in every encounter which takes place between the customer and the organisation offering a branded product or service.

Each of our experiences, as customers, is an intensely personal event. It involves four different dimensions:

1. The rational experience – what goes on.
2. The emotional experience – how we feel.
3. The political experience – why it is right for us.
4. The spiritual experience – where it leads us to or, 'whither'.

By managing these four dimensions explicitly, both the customer and the employee can benefit enormously.

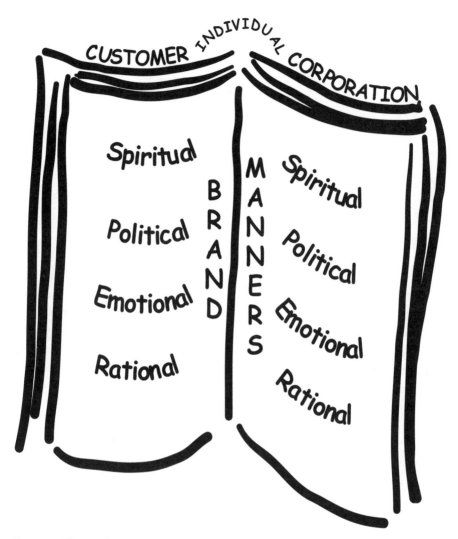

Figure 1 *The Brand Manners Book of Life.*

The Brand Manners Book of Life (Figure 1) sets out this framework, with the Customer and the corporation meeting in the customer experience through brand manners.

We call this a 'Book of Life' because brand manners should make life better for customers and provide more enjoyment and satisfaction for those in work. By learning how to relate better to one another, we hope that not only will customers and employees be happier but also by seeking out a higher purpose in our often frenetic existence, we may all be able to live more fulfilling lives. The contents of the book are set out at a high level in 'Feeling good' (Figure 2).

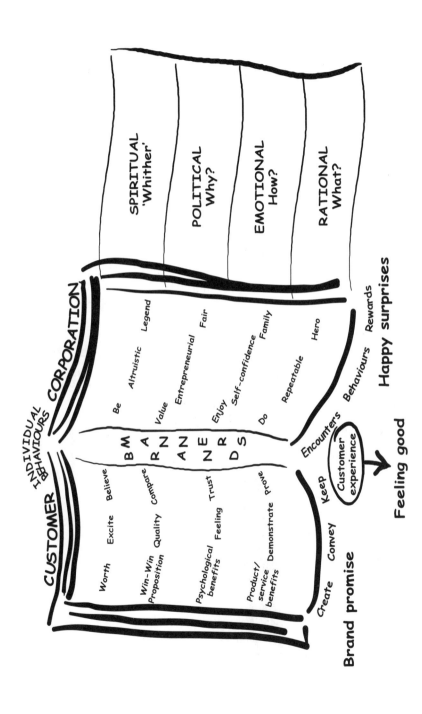

Figure 2 *Feeling good.*

2

Customers – The Brand Promise and Individual Brand Manners

The left-hand side of the book (Figure 3), which relates to the Customer, focuses on the brand promise: how it is created, how it is conveyed, and how it is kept. Brands in the new millennium have functional and rational attributes, and they also have emotional and psychological imagery.

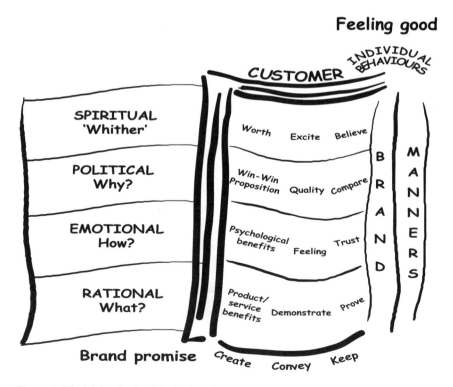

Figure 3 *The left-hand side of the book – the Customer.*

Increasingly they also need higher-order values in terms of political attitudes; ethical codes or even spiritual attributes as customers ask questions about corporate governance and the role of the company or brand in society.

At the rational or functional level, these three ingredients of 'create, convey and keep' are about bringing the product or service benefits to life, demonstrating that they are real, and proving that the promise is being kept. The emotional and psychological benefits of the brand need to be created, felt, and generate trust. The political dimension is about creating a win-win proposition for the buyer and the seller, demonstrating quality and providing appropriate comparisons to justify the purchase. Finally, the spiritual level concerns the inherent worth of the brand promise in terms of its contribution to society and individuals, how that excites people and what resulting beliefs and degrees of trust it produces.

The rational customer

It is essential that the product or service brand has some rational or functional benefits to offer its customers. In the history of modern communications there have been times, especially early in the 20th century, when brands were almost entirely rational in their propositions. The era of Rosser Reeves and the Unique Selling Proposition was at its height in the 1950s. Rational or functional brand benefits are best conveyed by means of product or service demonstrations, or side-by-side comparisons. They can be measured easily by means of competitive benchmarking, and this reveals the degree to which the brand has kept its promise at the rational level.

The emotional customer

Since the advent of commercial television and the arrival of behavioural psychologists such as John Watson, advertisers have used emotional and psychological attributes to add more layers of imagery to brands. This trend started in the USA in the late 1960s and the approach was aptly defined in the UK as the ESP, or emotional selling proposition, by the advertising agency Bartle Bogle Hegarty.

Emotional and psychological brand values can be created by the tone, style and user imagery of the creative communications for the product or service. These attributes and values can be measured using both qualitative research in the form of focus group discussions or depth interviews, and quantitative tracking studies which can be used to monitor the degree to which marketing communications establish and maintain the promised brand values and identity.

The political customer

As customers have become more sophisticated, they have become accustomed to exercising the power of their wallet in support of, or as a veto against, companies which have policies or standards with which they approve or disapprove. Green environmentalism, oil spills, third-world labour, product purity and tampering scares, GM and organic foods, and BMW's sale of Rover are all examples of areas in which a political dimension has come into play. The brand can establish values in this area both defensively and proactively, through politically sensitive management and the use of public customer charters and guarantees. These elements of the brand's promise can be measured through the use of customer satisfaction studies, mystery shopping programmes and social and economic risk assessments.

The spiritual customer

More recently, and as argued in *Brand Spirit*, a new dimension has emerged which relates to people's desire for higher-order values in life and in the brands they buy. Some corporations such as Body Shop, The Co-operative Bank, Virgin and Orange have managed to create brand positionings, which in themselves speak to this emerging consumer need. Those brands, which do not have an intrinsic ethical or spiritual dimension, can embark on a long-term social or cause-related marketing campaign. The results for companies such as American Express and Tesco have demonstrated the power of linking corporations to good causes or charities with whom they have an affinity or 'fit'. These values can be measured by quantitative research into employee morale and customer trust.

Brand manners

The central spine of the Book focuses on the fundamental 'Individual Behaviours' which create 'Brand Manners' (Figure 4). These form the linkage between the customer and the employee of the corporation that generate the total 'Customer Experience', giving both the reward of

Feeling good

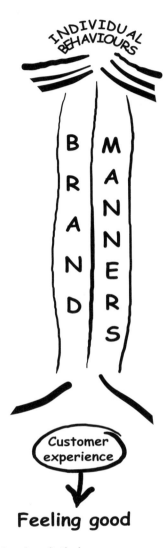

Figure 4 *The spine of the book – the individual.*

'Feeling Good'. 'Brand Manners' are the synthesis of all the behaviours which enable the board, management and staff alike to align the internal values of the company with the external values of the brand.

As employees we're all customers now, and we're all customers of the brand, whether we work for it or buy it. A customer's perception of the quality of service received in a given situation is almost entirely a function of their pre-existing expectations created by the brand. Perceived brand performance depends upon the degree to which these were, or were not, satisfied as a result of customer's interaction with the company. Therefore it is essential for an outstanding customer service organisation to have a clearly defined and robustly created set of 'Brand Manners' in order to manage these expectations successfully.

Individual behaviours

The leadership must enable the creation of a brand, which fulfils their business dream or vision. It must codify the appropriate employee behaviours and must ensure that rewards and penalties are aligned with them. In creating the brand itself, the leadership must ensure that it contains a full set of attributes and values relevant to its customers, that these virtues are convincingly conveyed to the market, and that the promise that the brand represents is actually kept in terms of its performance.

However, there is often a significant disconnect between General Management and Marketing Departments, mirrored by high-end consulting firms focusing on the 'upstream' elements of corporate strategy, organisation and e-commerce, whilst advertising agencies and marketing services groups focus more on the downstream aspects of new product development, brand positioning and brand communications. This militates against a holistic branded delivery from within the organisation to the world outside. Brand manners are either inconsistent, non-existent or downright contradictory.

Customer experience

Whilst brand marketers and communicators have become increasingly sophisticated during the last half of the 20th century, so have their customers. Practitioners have realised that it is essential to have a convincing and totally integrated brand positioning, manifested through all the channels of communication. This situation is being exacerbated by 'disintermediation', and the creation of direct buyer-seller links in so many markets, where there used to be at least one intermediary, if not two or three.

This means that managers can no longer avoid direct contact with their customers that the digital era not only enables, but demands. Accepting this collective challenge will create bonds between operational divisions in companies, which can no longer survive in their previous silos. It will also remove the buffer between company and customer that has been effectively erected by the sub-contracting of responsibility for this core relationship to a level below the main board. It will require the measurement and reporting of key metrics that in the majority of companies never reach the Chief Executive, according to research by Tim Ambler at The London Business School.

All the good work done on brand positioning, marketing and communication can be easily undone by a poor interaction between a customer and a brand representative. How often has a telephone response to an advertisement or direct mailing turned out to be a turn-off? How often has a customer–employee 'moment of truth' turned into a relationship killer, rather than a loyalty builder? How many buyers are now locked up in 'help line hell'?

The challenge for general management is to ensure that the whole company, and in particular its customer-facing employees, actually 'live their brand' and convey its essence in everything they do on its behalf for customers and other stakeholders.

3

Corporations – Happy Surprises

The right-hand side of the Book, the 'Corporation' (Figure 5) shows how the company can create 'happy surprises' for the customer, relative to the 'brand promise'.

The mirror image of Figure 3, the 'Customer' page of the Book, is Figure 5: the 'Corporate' page. This is about the 'Encounters' with customers, the 'Behaviours' involved, and the 'Rewards' that result. As with the left-hand page, there are four levels at which these need to be developed.

The rational part concerns what is done, or happens, during the customer experience. Good behaviours need to be repeatable and rewarded: the individual who performs well should be a hero in the organisation. At the emotional level, both the customer and the employee should enjoy the experience, boosting the self-confidence of each (in a non-egotistical way), and creating a sense of belonging or family both inside the organisation and with customers. The political is all about real value being created, through entrepreneurial behaviour (taking measured risks for customers), and resulting in a sense of fairness all round. The spiritual level concerns being (as opposed to having or doing), altruism, and creates myths or legends of great experiences for the customer.

The rational corporation

In terms of the rational – the 'what', aspect of the brand delivery, this is all about the practical, functional or rational components of production or service processes. This happens through the internal organisation which creates the customer experience and which is involved in any transaction through any of its representatives, agents or intermediaries. These basic

Feeling good

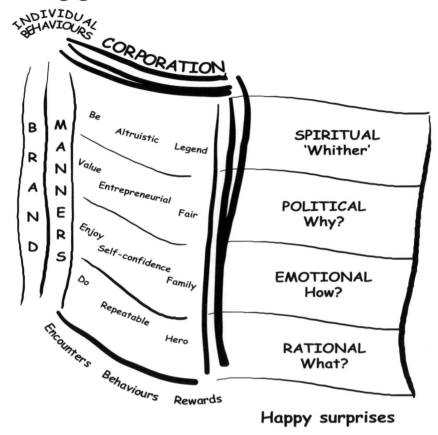

Happy surprises

Figure 5 *The right-hand side of the book – the corporation.*

service or support behaviours should be clearly describable and repeatable. Fulfilment of them should be closely linked to remuneration.

The emotional corporation

Regarding the emotional, the 'how' of the experience, people should be recruited for best fit with the core brand values. Their manners should be designed to reinforce the emotional and psychological values created for the brand by all its image aspects: name, logo, packaging and marketing communications.

In terms of the nature of the behaviour, it should be that of self-confident people who enjoy the support of their team and management. These employees prefer to relate to colleagues and customers alike in the 'adult-to-adult' mode, but are quite capable of recognising the appropriateness of 'adult-to-child' or even 'child-to-adult' interactions in certain situations. The reward for success in this key area is simply psychological; the feeling of 'closeness' and family membership within the organisation, colleagues and the brand engendered with the support of management.

If the corporation is to compete effectively for the attention of its people against all the attractions of the outside world in terms of non-working leisure activities, it will have to embrace the emotional world and make it come alive inside the organisation. The management of emotion is vital to conveying the brand promise to customers. All the evidence suggests that those internal communications, which are limited to mainly rational content, are the least effective. They are boring and do little to fire the imagination of their various audiences. Employees and customers alike are much more susceptible to rich, complex appeals based on a powerful mix of the emotional and the rational together, with the former in preponderance.

Most people's tangible connection between work and financial reward has been diluted over time. Bank accounts and payments direct to them, taxes deducted at source, the widespread usage of credit and debit cards, standing orders, direct debits, and all the other sophistication of contemporary financial services, means that tangible, personal financial links between employer and employee have all but disappeared.

At the emotional level, companies should surround the invisible process of remuneration with visible reinforcement that it is indeed taking place. The placebo effect in medicine confirms how powerful the behaviour surrounding a physical prescription can be. So too can corporate behaviour be around the process of remuneration. Rewards need to be closely linked to the satisfaction of customers. In particular they should acknowledge self-confident behaviour and those people who are prepared to take the right risks on behalf of their customers, to the extent that even failure can be celebrated if the attempt was made in the right spirit. By the same token, selfish or ineffective actions should be sanctioned.

The political corporation

The 'why', or political dimension of the internal and external customer experience, relates to the human need for a 'win' in virtually any transaction. This can be achieved by enabling employees at whatever level to adopt sensible risk-taking behaviour of an entrepreneurial nature. The reward for taking such risks within agreed financial parameters, nearly always results in outstanding customer service. This should trigger performance-related bonuses, and promotion, hedged with clear penalties for irresponsibility or malfeasance, all administered in a firm but fair manner.

At every twist and turn of the corporate saga, there will be winners and losers. In a corporate culture which is largely governed by the rational, and lacking in emotional and spiritual attributes, it is far more likely that people will act with narrow and calculated self-interest. By contrast, in an environment imbued with a motivating corporate vision, supported by a code of behaviour or brand manners, which values the emotional and spiritual as much as the rational, it is much more likely that a greater degree of altruism will come into any personal political equation. This doesn't mean to say that top management will not have to take, or indeed themselves be victims of, tough decisions which go against their own political agenda. It simply means that the criteria for those decisions will be apparent to all, for the greater good of the organisation.

The political dimension is also a vital one in customer relationships. Brand ambassadors have daily to weigh up customer situations and take calculated risks for the benefit of their brand. They cannot do this purely on the basis of the rational facts alone. They have to have the self-confidence to make emotional and ethical judgements too, based on their code of brand manners and in the knowledge that their company will support them in their interpretation.

The spiritual corporation

Finally, with regard to the 'whither', or spiritual aspects of the brand, the ultimate fulfilment of every company's dream is that customers gain an extra level of experience, which is over and above the other three, more tangible aspects. This relates to their own sense of self-worth and self-realisation as human beings. It works for both the customers and the employees who serve them through their brand. This behaviour is intrinsically altruistic and set by example from the very top of the organisation where the chief executive and the members of the executive board have to act as the role models. The reward for this most valuable of behaviours is to become part of the corporate 'legend', the company history of great deeds in the service of others and the brand.

The organisation should put considerable effort into rewarding those who truly fulfil their leadership's vision and ideal behaviour in their brand. So often 'employee of the month' or 'sales person of the year' feels like a formulaic and relatively empty accolade. How many corporations present these awards at their annual shareholder meetings, let alone invite their employees to attend? When do they get wider exposure than in the in-house magazine? Corporations, which lionise their employees in their advertising and marketing communications, not only sell their brand to customers, they sell it to their people too.

Modern management should embrace the newly powerful spiritual or ethical dimension of corporate leadership. Customers, employees, government, pressure groups, journalists and opinion formers, suppliers, alliance partners, consumers – all of the stakeholders in a company are increasingly concerned with its position in the community. They question the contribution it is making to society, not just in the usual terms of profit and loss, but in the much wider sense of what it is putting back, in relationship to what it is taking out. Hence the rise in importance of social and community programmes, company-sponsored volunteering schemes and cause-related or social marketing campaigns.

Employees, faced with increasing divergence in attractiveness between their working environment and their leisure one which awaits them beyond 'the factory gate', need better and better reasons for getting out of bed in the morning and going to work. They need greater opportunities to define and assert their individuality, to take control over their own lives and to express themselves in a way which will achieve recognition and self-fulfilment. Thus, employers need to give their people more than material reasons to be, and a much greater sense that doing what they do in their working life makes the world a better place, and in so doing gives more meaning to their own life.

Natural laws

Brand manners are experienced between individuals through the customer experience, which should result in all parties feeling good about the encounter. Brand manners are all about how we live and behave as individuals. Around these are the natural laws which govern our lives. The laws which most affect brand manners are:

- trust
- responsibility
- self-confidence
- habits
- boundaries

- the four dimensions of manners: the rational, emotional, political and spiritual.

These are set out in 'The Brand Manners Improvement Cycle'.

When we understand these laws and learn how to channel them – go with the flow – we can unlock our real potential as individuals. The book comes back to this time and time again. Brand manners cannot be achieved without personal development.

'The Tesco Story' (Chapter 4) provides an excellent example of the creation of brand manners and the 'Self-confident Organisation'. This is followed by 'The Brand Manners Way' (Part II) which provides a framework and approach for creating brand manners. 'The Orange Story' (Chapter 8) is another fine example of bringing brand manners to life.

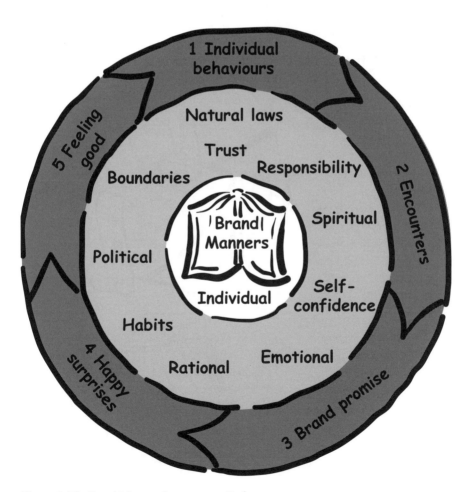

Figure 6 *The Brand Manners Improvement Cycle.*

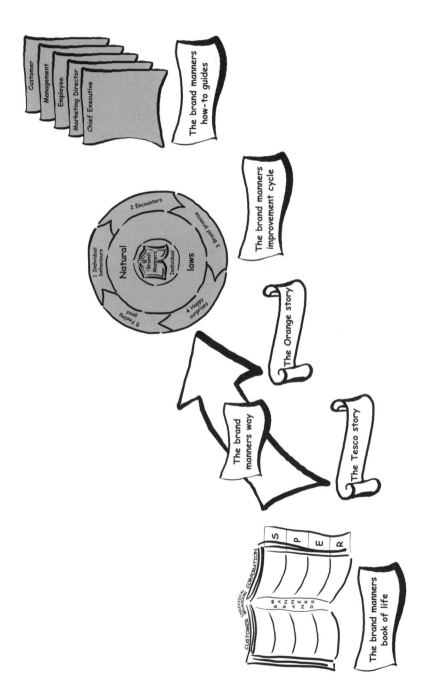

Figure 7 *The brand manners summary.*

Part III, 'The Brand Manners Improvement Cycle' covers the following sections, and provides an in-depth look at brand manners theory and practice:

1. individual behaviours – how we interact with one another
2. encounters – between customers and employees
3. the brand promise – which sets the expectations of customers
4. happy surprises – resulting from delighting the customer
5. feeling good – the results of successful brand manners.

The five form a cycle, with 'Feeling good' (Figure 2) translating into learning for individuals and continuously improving behaviours, resulting in the virtuous circle, shown in Figure 6.

The contents of the book, set out in 'Feeling good', are sprinkled throughout the chapters of the five sections, providing real-life examples and case histories and implications for customers and employees alike.

Brand manners – from theory into practice

In Part IV, 'The Brand Manners How-to guides' are then turned into a series of personal and practical guides for:

- The Chief Executive Officer
- The Marketing Director
- The employee
- Management
- The customer.

The resulting structure of the book is set out in the brand manners summary (Figure 7).

The purpose of this book is to explain the concept of 'brand manners' and to show how a salesforce, a call centre, a shop floor and, perhaps most importantly, management and the entire boardroom can be enlisted for the benefit of the brand and the company. All these individuals who collectively constitute the culture that creates the brand, can each be seen as internal customers of each other and as the deliverers of the brand to the customers outside, amongst whom they number.

4

The Tesco Story

Tesco is an excellent example of brand manners. Over the last five years or so, the company's leadership has succeeded in creating a 'self-confident' organisation, which is winning in the marketplace. Once a self-confident organisation emerges in a sector, traditional 'command and control' competitors begin to flounder, and blue water appears between them and the leader.

This is demonstrated by the relative evolution of Tesco's market share in comparison to its competitors, shown in Figure 8. Let's look at the antecedents to this great transformation.

In the highly competitive, commodity food retailing business how do you change from a brand known as a joke to the leading position in the UK retail marketplace? In the 1970s one reporter equated doing a 'Tesco' with

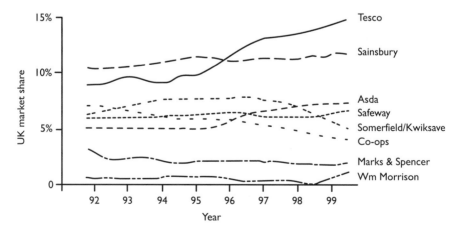

Figure 8 *UK market share for supermarkets.*

taking a headlong decline. An advertising agency stated the brand imagery conjured by Tesco's red colour was the 'exit sign' on the door. In 1998, Tesco became the leading food retailer, the most admired retailer in the *Financial Times* annual survey and the most admired company in the UK.

Terry Leahy, the Chief Executive since 1997, is the current leader of the Tesco transformation, but would be the last to claim all the credit. They say Leahy has two passions in life – Tesco and Everton Football Club. He shares his passion for the latter with half the population of his native Liverpool. He shares his passion for Tesco with earlier CEOs. Under 'Slasher' Jack Cohen and, in the 1980s, under Sir Ian (later Lord) MacLaurin (Chairman) and David Malpas (Managing Director), Tesco has enjoyed the sort of high-profile leadership that is commonplace in retailing around the world. But Terry Leahy is a very different proposition from both Cohen and MacLaurin/Malpas (whom he succeeded). His is 'A new style for a new era in Tesco's development' he might point out – actually he wouldn't as he is careful never to personalise or claim any credit for the recent success of a business that now is the UK's leading food retailer, having overtaken J. Sainsbury in the mid 1990s.

Tesco's rise to leadership in the UK

The success of Tesco in the 1990s owes much to the legacies of earlier managements in earlier years, as Leahy would admit. The most obvious asset that has been passed on is the underlying portfolio of stores and sites. Tesco has 370 superstores (stores of 20,000 sq. ft and above) in the UK, more than any other operator. Good people who have been with the business a long time and know it inside out are also another legacy. In the 1990s how many other major, industry-leading UK corporates can claim a record of not having had a single Executive Main Board Director leave for a better offer from elsewhere?

The people legacy is central to Leahy's personal self-confidence and to his understanding of Tesco's core capabilities as demonstrated by many of his comments:

I had a good advantage to grow up in the business. I know how it ticks, was well prepared for my role and am well settled in my responsibilities. This makes it easy to change Tesco from within.

Tesco has an unsurpassable strength in people and organisation. We have deep retailing skills in serving people and managing staff. Our people know how to empathise with customers and have terrific optimism.

One of the least obvious, but arguably more important, assets handed down the years is the corporate culture. Years of pursuing Sainsbury under MacLaurin and Malpas in the 1980s taught the business never to rest on its laurels, to strive always to better itself – a habit that continues to stand it in good stead even now market leadership is secured. 'We are never complacent. Tesco people come from humble origins and have been through ups and downs many times. This safeguards against complacency and makes it possible to make step changes in the business – 50%, 100% better – not just small incremental steps', asserts Leahy.

Not that Tesco hasn't made mistakes over the years. At the start of the 1990s, Tesco was a strong business – like Leahy's beloved Everton, a big club with a proud history. But, like today's Everton, Tesco was also a club in crisis. Tesco was not alone amongst the UK superstore operators to be slow to respond to changed consumer conditions. Used to the Thatcher years of never-ending trading up, in 1989–1991 the superstores tried jealously to guard their margins, either through avoiding any move to lower prices (which created the headroom into which came the European limited-range discount formats like Aldi), or through constantly re-engineering their business and in-store processes, eliminating cost (even if this eliminated elements of customer service). Tesco and the other superstores were not listening to their customers. The resulting loss of custom wasn't great – the UK shopper has long appreciated the one-stop shopping service that their superstore can offer. But it was sufficient to set alarm bells ringing. In the City, share prices in the food retail sector slumped, falling by over 40% in 1993 against the market. And Tesco was hardest hit – both in business and share price terms. In late 1993, Tesco was capitalised at just £3.5 billion.

The 1990s surge

Looking back, the turning point came perhaps a year before the share price reached its nadir with Leahy's appointment to the main board as Marketing Director in late 1992. It was Leahy who was given the task of re-creating the sales-led growth of the 1980s and in essence, he set about it in an old-fashioned way. 'The customer is always right' they say in retailing and Tesco's post-1993 revival has been founded on getting back in touch with customers and putting them first – or as Leahy prefers to call it 'Investing in the Shopping Trip'.

Figure 9 outlines how Leahy and Tesco set out to create a marketing edge. The modern Tesco philosophy is to stick to the customer through

Core purpose The core purpose of Tesco, is 'to create value for customers in order to earn their lifetime loyalty'. Customers and value are repeatedly mentioned in many conversations with Terry Leahy.

Marketing The leading edge of Tesco's success is marketing. Their approach to marketing starts with 'what you've got because you'll find in there some gem you can build on'. In Tesco's case the gem was and is a reputation for giving value to customers.

Market research Value is created by understanding the customer better than anyone, and this requires relentless research. One campaign in 1992 involved interviewing 250,000 customers. Customers are interviewed daily, customer panels convene regularly (often attended by Leahy). A Clubcard is used to understand real-life behaviour driving 30 segments of customers based on lifestyle such as 'shoppers on budgets'. Tesco doesn't mass market. It picks up on special needs so that 'one or two don't slip away' leading eventually to a flood of lost customers.

Innovate and invest Based on research-driven customer understanding, Tesco innovates and invests. This includes new ranges such as the value line range, new formats such as metro store, superstore, hypermarkets and home shopping. Innovation has taken Tesco into financial services and involvement in a range of e-commerce. International is another dimension of innovation and investment designed to keep Tesco ahead of the best retailers, not just in the UK, but in the world.

Look after staff Staff look after customers. Those who understand the customer in the local marketplace will succeed. Local staff are the key to making this happen and are the focus of Tesco's 'Every little helps' values.

Figure 9 *How to achieve (and maintain) a marketing edge.*

extensive market research and with the help of the market-leading Clubcard loyalty card and its database. Management's role is to interpret what customers want – the assumption is that if Tesco keeps customers happy then sales growth is assured. If management and staff deliver to customers and then work hard to drive out costs in order to yield profit/ justify better remuneration, and if this successful formula is communicated to the stock market, then all interested parties – customers, staff, management and shareholders – will be happy. Tesco lives by this 'Steering Wheel' – a circle in which all four interested parties in the business have an equal role to play and deserve an equal share of the rewards. It is a strategy that has clearly worked.

Managing the brand promise

*"Father, I've got an Asda loyalty card and
I shopped at Tesco"*

Cartoon 1 *'Card Loyalty'.*

Since 1993, Tesco has enjoyed a steady stream of marketing 'firsts' – the
first nation-wide superstore loyalty scheme with Clubcard, the first
superstore to promise to minimise checkout queues, the first to offer
widespread 24-hour shopping, the first to begin a nation-wide roll-out of a
home shopping service. Alongside these has come a series of price-cutting
initiatives – from 'Unbeatable Value' in 1994 to 'We've cut Prices Again' in
1999 – £100 million of price cuts having been announced in the last year
alone. Finally, this has all been communicated in an open way to customers
– the 'Every Little Helps' marketing strapline continues to underline
Tesco's appreciation of the need to be close to its customers.

Building the self-confident organisation – happy surprises for customers

Concurrent with these strides in marketing, Tesco was quietly building the
self-confident organisation, through 'better, simpler, cheaper' work

processes, systems recalibrated to make them easier to use, and the development of individuals through core skills which helped them do their jobs better. This was underpinned by measures and rewards guided by tailored balanced scorecards (known as Steering Wheels in Tesco), and a series of on-going mobilisation events to energise tens of thousands of people behind the company's goals and values. Tesco believes its future success will be based on values, leading to the continuous improvement of the 'Tesco Way'. Terry Leahy has publicly stated:

> I regard Values as one of the most important ways of working in Tesco today. They will shape and sharpen the way we do things for our customers in the years to come. The values are Tesco – the way we work, the way we manage – it's everything we do and always will be. Creating a culture where everyone is encouraged to make the most of their talent for the benefit of customers has never been more important.

Responding to such comments, staff quotes include:

- 'I like to say I work for Tesco.'
- 'We are a retail business, and proud of it.'
- 'There are no right and wrong answers.'
- 'Without customers, none of us would have jobs.'
- 'If staff are happy, customers will be, too.'

By taking a holistic approach to understanding its customers and putting in place the capability to deliver consistently, Tesco has reaped the benefits of true Brand Manners. Profit has risen by over 70% to £955 million last year: the share price has more than trebled. Today, Tesco is capitalised at almost £20 billion.

Tesco in the 21st century: more than a food retailer...

So, in the last six years Leahy has taken Tesco from the bottom to the top of the UK superstore pile – from the bottom to the top of the Premier League. However, it is typical of the business that it continues to try to prove and improve itself. Tesco know that the UK food retail market is highly dynamic and competitive; Tesco cannot rest on its laurels, nor can it concentrate solely on its existing markets. Whilst it is big and by no means ex-growth, the UK food retail market offers relatively limited growth opportunities for a business of this size. New growth is being sought in two ways – both of which have come to the fore under Leahy, both of which pose new challenges to this business.

The first opportunity lies within the UK – Tesco is seeking to break down the traditional boundaries between retail markets. The logic runs as follows: why should a business, whose brand name and sites are so widely trusted that over 10 million people a week visit the stores to spend, limit itself to food? Leveraging the sites and brand are the next steps. This can be as obvious as adding a much more authoritative range of non-food in carefully chosen sub-markets into existing superstores – Tesco is aiming to become a general merchandise as well as a food retailer. But leveraging can be as esoteric as developing a financial arm. Leahy has a strong sense of how to stretch Tesco's brand and retail capabilities:

> The essence of the Tesco brand is customer trust. If customers trust you, they will take you with them. Follow the customer. If they spend more on services and trust Tesco, they will take you through traditional barriers. Our restlessness and insecurity is borne from our people. They are not arrogant or complacent. There is no safe place, no steady state. We must keep moving, testing natural limits as long as we can do things better. We put our brand on a whole range of products.

More than just a UK food retailer

The business development of the last five years that has grabbed the most headlines has been the one which, with hindsight, Tesco was certainly not in a position to undertake six years ago when Leahy joined the board. These days, Tesco is seen as one of the coming pan-European, even global food retailers, but back in 1993 things were very different. Not only was the UK business in need of attention, but Tesco was trying to enter the already well-developed French food retail market through Catteau, a small private supermarket chain that was acquired in mid-1993. The French food retail market may be a big market (slightly bigger than that of the UK) and Tesco was certainly right to predict that the market would see consolidation amongst the leading players. However, in the home of the hypermarket, Tesco struggled to persuade itself, never mind shareholders, that it was adding value. Consequently, when the major moves in the consolidation process came (notably when Auchan acquired Docks De France in 1996) Tesco could not justify joining in. Leahy did not inherit an international legacy but international did become a mandate of his management team. Catteau was sold in late 1997. This was the beginning, not the end of the international expansion as outlined in Figure 10.

- Poland entry in 1995 through merger with Savia. Investing £400 million to grow from 4 supermarkets to 20 by 2001.

- Operating 9 hypermarkets and 30 smaller outlets in Hungary. Opening 5 new hypermarkets in 2000.

- Operating 13 stores in Czech Republic and Slovakia and planning 4 more in 2000.

- Ireland entry in 1997 by purchase from ABF. Operating 76 supermarkets, building central warehousing and opening 4 new stores.

- In Thailand, operating 15 stores and opening 12 more in the next 4 years. Operating 2 stores in Korea, taking over Samsung distribution centres in 1999. Moving into Thailand and researching Malaysia.

- Clubcard, a store loyalty card launched in 1995, now has 10 million cardholders with free internet service available to them.

- Internet sales in UK to 2,000,000 customers through 100 stores. Becoming largest on-line grocer in the world.

- Adding on-line banking in 1999 in partnership with Royal Bank of Scotland. Originated financial services for retail customers in 1996.

- Starting cyberzone in stores for items not sold in store ranging from books to refrigerators. Extending to all 639 stores in UK. Considering internet cafes in stores.

Figure 10 *Investing to become a world class retailer – pushing the edge.*

Tesco had been busy opening stores in underdeveloped retail markets, notably in Central Europe – The Czech Republic, Hungary, Poland and Slovakia. This was virgin territory – not just for Tesco, but for organised retailing in general. There were no established retail chains to acquire as in France: no established retail formats to copy, just adapt and improve on. Tesco – a multi-billion pound UK employer of well over 150,000 just had to experiment and hope for the best. Tesco – a company whose only international experience had been less than auspicious with Catteau – had to create a business from scratch in a new market. No wonder the outgoing Chairman, Ian MacLaurin, described the opening of Tesco's first large store in Central Europe – in the Polus Centre in Budapest in Spring 1996 – as the single most important move by the company in over a decade, even though he personally was a domestic UK man.

It is taking time as the markets are still forming, but the Tesco formula is working, according to Leahy:

> We play our international cards as well as possible by focusing on emerging growth. We must find the right way to enter. This is what led us into hyper-stores and eventually enabled us to export this format back into the UK.

Anyway why shouldn't it work? In essence the Tesco formula of putting customers first and not taking them for granted is retailing at its best and it should work whether it is applied in Budapest or Basingstoke. The Tesco Way, driven from the company's goals and values, provides the common framework so that the company can share knowledge and learning, while leveraging its scale and technology.

Tesco goes global

Of course, it doesn't end there. Central Europe is relatively close to home compared to Thailand and South Korea (which Tesco has developed over the last few years), and to Taiwan and Malaysia (markets which Tesco is researching with a view to opening stores soon). This all brings challenges for management. Within ten years, from being a UK-only business with all the centralised control that allowed and that came with a semi-automated supply chain and the like, Tesco's management is now having to learn to devolve power to the periphery of the group. Tesco is no longer trading against just Sainsbury: it is having to trade and benchmark itself against the likes of Wal-Mart, Carrefour, Ahold and Auchan. These are world leaders not just UK leaders: they are new, less predictable competitors whose resources and vision present new challenges for Tesco. But according to Leahy they serve an important purpose:

> We must be the best, must set high standards for ourselves. This is difficult when you become the number one in the UK. Tesco's people are better at being at the bottom looking up than being on the top. Therefore, focusing on world competition sets a new standard and puts us at the bottom again, when we are at our strongest. Dealing with new and different competition is good for you, like in a sports league, competition is the answer. This is still a regional business but slowly economic scale is moving up and we must move up with it.

Leahy has taken his club away from the relegation zone to the brink of European and even world success. If only, he might add wistfully, someone could do the same for his beloved Everton. However for Leahy, Everton serves a purpose – 'it shows you know you can get worse'. His assessment of

	Leahy's current evaluation			Leahy's future priorities		
	Just starting 1	5	Excellent performance 10	Ignore 0	Sustain 10	Special focus 20
Mobilisation: We harness the mental energy of our people		5				20
Vision: We have clear, powerful widely understood vision and values		7				15
Measurement: We have balanced performance measures to implement vision	3				6	
Economic model: We manage our business portfolio based on shareholder value		4				15
Infrastructure: Our physical investment is aligned with strategic objectives		4			8	
Work architecture: We capture best practice and continuous improvement in processes	3				4	
Market focus: We have clear external focus on key market segments and value propositions		7			10	
New business: We use core competence and alliances/acquisitions to create new businesses		4 5			15	
Change rules through IT: Our IT priorities support strategy and create new business opportunities	4					15
Reward system: Our incentives are tied to strategic objectives and promote learning and improvement		4			4	
Individual learning: We make significant investment in the development of critical skills of people	3				4	
Organisation development: We use organisation design and knowledge management to achieve vision and strategy		4			4	

Source: 12 part questionnaire based upon the book *Transforming The Organisation.* Gouillart and Kelly, 1995.

Figure 11 *Terry Leahy's evaluation of his organisation.*

where Tesco stands in the continuous process of transformation is outlined in Figure 11.

Regardless of the current evaluation, Leahy has a very clear sense of what's important in the future and it fits with the entire sense of what Tesco stands for:

> We have 220,000 staff. Their *mobilisation*, their commitment, is our most important resource. We want to be at the bottom of the mountain looking up and therefore our *vision* is also critical, even though we already have a good sense of it.

> *New business* is also critical. We must follow the customer. We saw e-tailing as an opportunity 5 years ago. Most said, 'it won't work'. We said we can make it work. We are using *technology* to transform our business before someone else does. We want to be the lead dog in technology, seeing things first before others do in supply chain or database management.

> Within all of this the *economic model* is also important. Our thinking in e-tailing, international, vision, etc. must be grounded in an economic model that works. We must be grounded in reality, even if it is a new format in the UK.

> We have an antipathy to bureaucracy. Thus many of the low-rated ingredients in my future priorities are the enablers, the infrastructure that must be there but that should be an integrated package, not over baked into a bureaucratic nightmare.

In the future, Terry Leahy and Tesco will be there, following the customer with humility from the bottom of the mountain.

PART II
The Brand Manners Way

5

The Self-confident Organisation

Top executives will realise that 'management by walking about' is not just some trendy guru mantra, but is a key way to coach and up-skill individuals, and ensure that the company vision – which we call the dream to reinforce emotional and spiritual imagery – can not only be kept alive, but also continually relevant and fresh. Keeping this sensitive 'hand on the tiller' is crucial to maintaining employee and customer loyalty, and the repeat purchase habit.

We believe that self-confident staff lead to happy customers. This implies the need for a code of 'brand behaviour', which makes the brand's world a happier place to work in. As people work better when they are self-confident, they are more likely to over-deliver on customer expectations, as well as enjoy themselves more. Finding a way to inform this management style and ensure that everyone in a company genuinely 'lives the brand' according to a clear code of behaviour is the key to success and is the purpose of this book. This set of corporate behaviours evolves according to market circumstances, whilst remaining true to the core vision or dream of the company.

The requirement for effectively 'living the brand' means companies have to move beyond the traditional, fear-based mode of 'command and control' into a new management space, which we call the self-confident organisation, in order to over-deliver on consumer expectations by creating and enabling a happy, and participative employee environment. Many employees go to work with their tails down and return home every night with them down. Imagine what would happen if they had their tails up!

Our conviction is that the key to this new environment will be the degree to which it can be described as 'self-confident'. This means that employees fully understand the parameters within which they operate and can trust their employers to stand by these criteria. By the same token, customers of the product or service brand, which these employees make or deliver, can also trust that it will fulfil the complete promise that the manufacturer or provider makes in public on its behalf.

These same employees can enjoy an ever-richer leisure environment outside working hours. The multiplicity of choice of programmes available through terrestrial, cable and satellite channels is dazzling. The infinity of options accessible via the internet, the escalating standard of movies, the bewildering variety of music and the plethora of printed magazine formats, are all contributing to a richness of media that was unimaginable a decade ago.

Meanwhile higher disposable incomes, the explosion in in-home entertainment, out-of-home eating, and the massive increase in foreign travel are making huge impacts on everyday life. The development of hi-tech theme parks, allied to the growth in niche museums and cultural attractions, to say nothing of the wealth of sporting events, means that in the third millennium citizens of the developed economies have quite extraordinary leisure opportunities.

All this represents enormously increased competition for the attention and affections of employees. The days when an employer could offer its staff genuine benefits simply by providing central heating, a works canteen and in-house hair cutting, have long gone. How can a corporation hope to compete with the range of excitements on offer at the end of the working day, and which are more than likely to have preoccupied its employees for much of the time during it?

The corporate dream and the corporate drama

The answer is that the corporation has to develop its own dream and create its own drama, with the chief executive not only writing the script, directing the action, designing and building the set, but also acting as narrator, giving a running commentary on how the story is unfolding. The CEO becomes the brand author. Thus employees become dramatis personae in their own play and one which is as compelling and exciting as their favourite soap opera. As in the real theatre, in the corporate world it is the simple compelling story line which captures the imagination and retains the attention. Top management need to identify, focus on and reiterate their obsession with the single driving issue, which means commercial life or death.

In order to be successful actors, each must know their part and their relationship to others. Because this is a living drama, it is much more like an extended improvisation than a set-piece four-act play, and therefore the underlying code of behaviour, or set of brand manners, is much more important than slavish attention to a predetermined script.

In a total sense then, the chief executive can be recast as manager of expectations, both internally and externally, and the skills to conceive, communicate and make concrete these expectations become paramount. Driving this is the will to achieve the corporate vision and the capability to do so. In the era of 'internet time' fleetness of foot, and the ability to make a high percentage of right decisions in a given period is crucial. Moving forward with sufficient velocity and critical mass to achieve unstoppable momentum is more important than worrying about the minority of mistakes that may be made on the way.

Key principles

While customer expectations of service have increased over the years, the ability of organisations to deliver, and indeed exceed, the promises inherent in most brands, has seldom kept up. In fact, whereas technological innovations could have delighted the customer, in reality, the customer has been increasingly cut off from rewarding purchasing experiences. In addition, many organisations are increasingly losing touch with the heartbeat of their customers, as they sub-contract out most of the direct contact and discussions with customers to marketing services firms. Even when rich customer insights are sensed by the front line of the organisation in question, the message often gets warped or diluted as it rises up the organisation. With the average tenure of Marketing Directors and CEOs dropping significantly, many companies are operating in the dark relative to where their existing and potential customers are today and where they will be tomorrow. On the other hand, the folks in Finance tend to stay!

The true test of delivering on promises to customers occurs at the interface between the customer and the organisation in question. The heart of this delivery lies in the interaction between individuals, in terms of the four key dimensions set out below.

1. The rational quality of the transaction: 'It's even better than I expected!'
2. The emotional benefits springing from the feelings generated on both sides: 'I would like to do that again.'
3. The political realities of perceptions of 'win-win': 'Was this a good deal for me?'

4. The spiritual experience in terms of its inherent worth: 'I really believe that I am better off as a person for that, and the world may be benefiting, too!'

The ability to deliver what we call brand manners rises exponentially as the customer moves through these four dimensions. You can break into the progression at any level, depending on the circumstances, but, at the end of the day, all four in combination create greater potential and all four should therefore be worked on in harmony. Communications around the brand and its inherent promises should be built around them. Even more important, and more difficult to deliver, is the organisation, which operates effectively across these four dimensions.

The implications of this for the marketing world are profound. The opportunity to go beyond the rational attributes into the emotional has already been recognised to some extent. Going beyond this to tackle the political elements and the spiritual ones requires a new mindset and approach to marketing in its fullest sense.

The implications for the corporate world, as a whole, are also profound. Most companies, even those regarded currently as being the best run, typically operate in a 'command and control' way, where pressure and risk increases as you go down the organisation. These are the cultures where the 'get the person who can' mentality (hire on apparent capability, leave them to sink or swim, then if they sink, fire them, and get another), means that politics undermines teamwork, and the people serving the customer are merely a means to an end.

In these organisations, the vast majority of people don't look forward to going to work, as they are not enriched personally by their efforts or experiences. They therefore only give the 80% required to satisfy their way through the day, rather than the 120%, which their full potential could deliver. Moving beyond the fear-based command and control model is tough, requiring vision, will and capability. When these are applied effectively, the corporation can break into the new space which we call the 'self-confident organisation', the one required to deliver consistently the brand manners needed for the long-term success of the individual, the company and the well-being of the customer.

6

Brand Manners Approach

The Chief Executive of any organisation has the opportunity to create the environment whereby brand manners can flourish for customers and employees alike. We believe that there are natural laws, which apply to business and organisations, just as they exist for people and the world in which we live. Embracing these laws and following their impetuses is more likely to lead to success than fighting against them. There are some key areas where this new approach can be applied:

- right dream
- right team
- right programme
- right improvements
- right involvement.

These are set out in Figure 12, the brand manners approach.

Creating the right dream

A dream in this context is about setting a vision for the organisation, which will result in the customer being delighted by the performance of every employee. We use 'dream' as it encapsulates the power of the four dimensions of brand manners – rational, emotional, political, and spiritual. Individuals, and therefore organisations, respond to each of these and each can contribute to unleashing the full potential of each person.

We have to look at the difference between the excitement that many people get outside work and compare this to what is available to them, or what can be created for them, in the workplace. The CEO needs to create

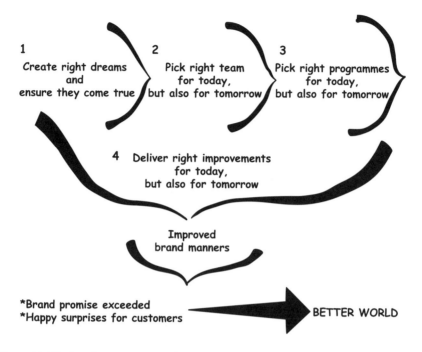

1
Create right dreams
and
ensure they come true

2
Pick right team
for today,
but also for tomorrow

3
Pick right programmes
for today,
but also for tomorrow

4   Deliver right improvements
for today,
but also for tomorrow

Improved
brand manners

*Brand promise exceeded
*Happy surprises for customers   BETTER WORLD

Figure 12 *The brand manners approach.*

and communicate an on-going 'corporate drama', which captures the imagination of each individual so that they become intimately involved in the story as it unfolds.

One of the exciting opportunities opened up by the digital world, is the ability to refine strategy and build capability at the same time. Gone are the days where one could set strategy and then drive through implementation. This takes too long to work. It needs to be replaced by action learning, whereby direction is set sufficiently to move forward; 'directionally correct' has become one of the great liberating concepts of modern management. It is better to be 80% correct on direction so long as the organisation moves forward as fast as possible: 'Act-Review-Learn' replaces or complements 'Plan-Do-Review'.

Just as important is the recognition that the operational variables can today be changed massively by the fast development of capability. So the traditional strategy paradigm (forget what I have; what *should* I do to be successful?) and the capability paradigm (forget what I should do; what *could* I do?) need to exist together, feeding on each other to produce continuous improvement in brand manners. 'Could' and 'Should' become as one! This provides management with lots of food to nourish the corporate drama.

This new definition of strategy has another important aspect – one where not only 'why' and 'what' questions are addressed, but also 'whither', the spiritual dimension. For whom are we doing this? What meaning does it have? Providing a higher-order vision for the organisation will capture people's imagination, and encourage them to achieve things they might otherwise consider impossible. Once the higher-order vision has been created, the task of senior management is to translate it into reality through a series of managed programmes.

Enlisting the right team

The drama needs the right actors. To have this, the CEO has to pick not only today's top team, but also that of tomorrow. The management model of picking 'someone who can' is no longer sufficient. This approach assumes that success is in the hands of one individual, who must succeed or be fired. It is fatally flawed in the modern world, as success requires two new ingredients – speed (accelerated, but not only driven by the digital or 'e' world), and leverage (whereby the knowledge, technology and other assets of the corporation are fully deployed to help each individual in the organisation). The individual approach also assumes that the best can be achieved by a top-down approach, primarily by setting targets and letting people 'get on with it'. What is the value added of the management of the layer above in this case? Limited we think.

What is required, and will be even more so in the future, is teamwork across the organisation ('horizontal working'), a holistic approach (where all the bits fit together), and a relentless focus on the 'how' in order that the higher-order vision can be achieved. The 'how' and the 'whither' are the two key ingredients required to complement the traditional 'why' and 'what' of the vertically managed, accountability-led organisation. The 'why' and 'what' are still essential, but they are not sufficient to create a complete set of brand manners.

The keys to unlocking horizontal teamwork, the holistic approach, and the 'how' lie in choosing the right team and leading the team through a series of capability-building programmes which deliver increasingly the longer-term goals implicit in the higher-order vision. The choice of the right team may seem blindingly obvious, but it is not. The underlying question to be answered is what is the most appropriate balance between managing today's operations and building tomorrow's capabilities. Can and should the existing executive team take on both tasks? How can new blood be brought into the existing team, in a way that leverages the strengths that exist, while preparing the next generation of leaders?

In some cases, a young management team can take on today and tomorrow. This can be difficult for many top teams who have grown up managing operations tightly, by focusing downwards; their board agendas are already overflowing with today's tasks. How can they take on more, particularly when more may require two days a week and diaries are already full for the next three months? These issues need to be identified in each case and the right balance struck.

The choice is essentially between the existing team (in which case, is it the right team with the right skills and aspirations for the job?), and a combination of the existing folk and new blood. This blend can often be best managed through a steering group, whose job is to create the future, leaving the executive board to manage current performance. Getting the right team(s) and governance structure in place for managing today and tomorrow, simultaneously, is essential and indeed is one of the natural laws. Those responsible for human resources and recruitment should bear this in mind and ensure that the right skills and attitude are being brought into the organisation, so that they can evolve into true ambassadors for the brand.

Choosing the right programme

We have found that a great way to do this is for the CEO and the top team(s) to identify the single driving issue which they will focus on for, say, 20 months. Why 20 months? Firstly, because the world is changing so fast, many assumptions we make today are unlikely to be valid beyond this timeframe. Secondly, because in our experience it still takes at least six months to build significant organisational capability. So the choice is between some six and twenty months. For the smaller firm, and those in the 'e' world, six months will be possible. For larger organisations, with 1,000 employees or more, the effort will take longer, and depend on the diversity of the businesses being managed. A time scale, which either falls well within or straddles the standard twelve-month financial year, can help ensure completion by avoiding short-term budgetary cuts.

The single driving issue provides an opportunity for the top team(s) to focus attention on a topic, which will have a significant impact on the customer experience, and thereby, the company's competitive position. They can use this issue to galvanise the energies of the organisation behind the holistic programme, which will build capability significantly.

The identification of the single driving issue requires a creative combination of all of the four dimensions. The rational: will the issue deliver sufficient shareholder value? The emotional: will the issue ignite the imagination of the vast majority of the people employed by the organisation? The political: will the issue harness the momentum and potential available through aligning the personal and business agendas of the most powerful people in the organisation? And, finally, the spiritual: will the issue contribute significantly to the sense of purpose of the organisation, and provide a higher-order sense of purpose for individuals to feel they are living their lives in a meaningful way?

The 'brand manners logic' provides the framework for correctly identifying the single driving issue. Even executive boards made up of people who have known each other for years often struggle to distinguish between symptoms and causes. This is particularly true when the team

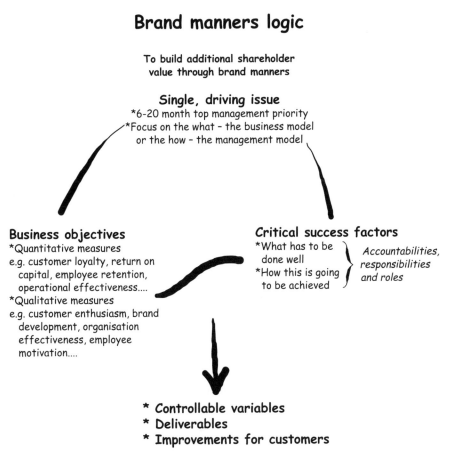

Brand manners logic

To build additional shareholder value through brand manners

Single, driving issue
*6-20 month top management priority
*Focus on the what – the business model or the how – the management model

Business objectives
*Quantitative measures
e.g. customer loyalty, return on capital, employee retention, operational effectiveness....
*Qualitative measures
e.g. customer enthusiasm, brand development, organisation effectiveness, employee motivation....

Critical success factors
*What has to be done well
*How this is going to be achieved
} Accountabilities, responsibilities and roles

* **Controllable variables**
* **Deliverables**
* **Improvements for customers**

Figure 13 *The brand manners logic.*

needs to adapt to a new way of working: not only will individuals have differing 'mental maps', but the same words will mean different things to different people. The brand manners logic framework, in Figure 13, includes the single driving issue: focusing on the what – the business model, or the how – the management model, depending on the situation. It also addresses the underlying business objectives – ways of measuring progress against the issue, both quantitative and qualitative, and the critical success factors. In addition the framework covers the things that have to be done well, both the 'what' – the programme elements, and, more importantly, the 'how' – the way the programme needs to be managed, with corresponding accountabilities, responsibilities and roles.

In our experience, discussions around the 'issue', the 'objectives', and the 'success factors' quickly unravel the symptoms from the causes and provide a means of building understanding and alignment amongst the team. Clarity on these three top topics is essential before turning to the remaining three items of the brand manners logic. These are the controllable variables or the 'levers' which management can pull to change things, the 'deliverables' required from the programme, and the 'benefits' which flow naturally from the resulting improvement in the customer experience through enhanced brand manners.

The CEO and the top team can use the brand manners logic to conduct a diagnosis using large populations of the organisation to identify the opportunities for improvement in the business related to the single driving issue. It is vital to involve large numbers of people so that both the rational ('the opportunities exist') and emotional ('I believe in these opportunities as I have been involved'), dimensions are enlisted.

The output of the diagnosis can then be translated into a programme to address the single driving issue. This works by combining the work which needs to be done to deliver the improvements, and the existing initiatives (and their ownership), thus embracing the political agendas of not only the most powerful people, but also right down to those of the customer-facing employee. When people see individuals they respect, and whom they regard as real leaders, getting behind the programme, they will swing in behind with their support, thus addressing the political issues which so often undermine otherwise sound initiatives.

This leaves the CEO with the opportunity to relate the programme to the corporate drama and the higher-order vision, thus adding the spiritual dimension, which truly amounts to leadership of the brand. Finally, the programme can be led through a governance structure based on the top-team dynamics set out in the previous section.

Picking the right improvements

The improvements in the company's brand manners need to be viewed from the customer's perspective. This seems obvious, but organisations with more than say 500 people have many dimensions: the functions – marketing, sourcing, supply chain, production, finance, etc., and the different businesses or formats, often with both common as well as different customers and different geographies. Knitting these together in a coherent way, so that brand manners are actually delivered is no easy task.

The real test of business improvement is that it flows through to cash and thence to shareholder value. Improvements must drive the numbers, and not the other way round, otherwise, results will not be sustainable. The starting point is often projections of shareholder value based on market position, competitor and benchmarking comparisons. This is the 'top-down' business case, which should provide the organisation with a directionally correct set of targets, in terms of revenues, cost and capital.

We find the gold-mining analogy often helpful in explaining all of this. Management believe that 'there is gold in the hills', the top-down business case suggests that there is enough gold to justify the cost of mining, and the organisation has some firm hypotheses about where the gold may lie. The diagnosis must identify where the gold actually is, the opportunities, and validate that the gold is real – with front-line operations, as well as with the local finance function. The programme is designed to dig out the gold, with a bottom-up, i.e. opportunity by opportunity, validated business case to measure progress transparently, through the chosen governance structure, and the active support of the 'Robber-Barons'! This is shown in Figure 14.

Remember, re-invention involves a lot more than just a series of projects – they have to fit together, should be mutually reinforcing, and need the full and continuous backing of the top team. The danger is to commit just enough resources, in both quality and quantity, to fail. Every organisation has lots of initiatives going on, which each have a sensible rationale, although only the minority will have a proper business case. The question is, how do all of these fit together, do they enhance each other and where are the white spaces where something is missing? The top team must ensure that adequate resources are committed and that the steering group, or whatever governance body is in place, relentlessly removes the barriers that inevitably occur, with the most difficult ones being political.

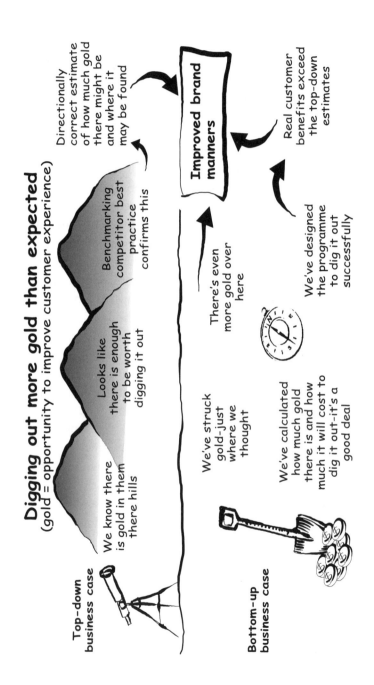

Figure 14 *Digging out the gold.*

Delivering the right involvement

So far, we should have identified the right dream, team, programme and improvements. While important, in terms of creating the optimal conditions for success, the difficult part is still to come – delivery. Many of the people involved in the diagnosis of the improvements need to be involved in the delivery programme, not only for reasons of continuity, but also to ensure that the programme can be delivered. It is easier to sell the attributes of a flying saucer, but it is somewhat difficult to build one! So people involved in the design need to have their 'skin in the game' when it comes to turning it into reality (the emotional and political dimensions).

The number and quality of resources deployed on both diagnosis and delivery is critical to the success of the result. Choosing the best people in the organisation to work full time on the programme offers many benefits as the probability of success will be much higher than otherwise as they will deliver the emotional and political dimensions. The results will be nearer 120% versus the conventional 80% at the rational level and more sustainable as the individuals will grow immensely and become more rounded general managers. Further, the spaces opened up in the organisation by their secondment to the programme will be quickly filled by people who previously did not have the opportunity for rapid growth.

Although plucking the best people out of day-to-day operations may seem hard, even foolhardy at the time, it pays off very quickly. One caveat: the processes for moving people around the organisation must be fair, robust and transparent. If people take risks by leaving their day jobs, it is essential that the organisation as a whole sees that they are treated appropriately, indeed they should advance their careers faster than would have otherwise been the case. If this is done well, the organisation will develop fluidity where people are keen to work on the leading-edge projects, which are necessary to create the future lifeblood of the firm.

Not putting some of the corporation's best talent into play because of concerns about the continuity of the day-to-day running, is likely to result in an 80% achievement with the regret being the lingering sense that another 50% improvement could have been secured. The 120% will be missed, sadly. Bear in mind that it is within the gift of each and every employee to work 80% or up to, say 120% of potential. The authority for this flows upwards, and not down.

7

Brand Manners in Action

Having got the right programme with the right resources, the role of the governance body or steering group, is to ensure that the correct objectives are in place and that barriers are removed as they develop. Calling this leadership body by the name of the overall programme, which should be chosen to reflect the higher-order agenda and therefore capture hearts and minds, is a powerful communications device and an opportunity not to be missed.

Meetings should report progress on an exception only basis; things that are going well do not need time spent on them unless there are best-practice lessons being learned which could be of use to other parts of the organisation. The team should concentrate on making decisions and working issues through to action.

Mobilisation is the way to breathe oxygen into the work thus ensuring people feel constantly that they have wind in their sails. The CEO should assign accountabilities to ensure the executive board are actively managing the critical success factors, and are constantly seen to be supporting the programme and even taking personal risks themselves as individuals. The CEO should split the extended top team, comprising the existing managers and future leaders of the firm, which might number up to one hundred souls, into manageable groups of, say, thirty. At the outset of the programme, the CEO should spend three to four hours with them, setting out the agenda and answering tough questions in open forum.

This reinforces credibility and builds intimacy. It also lowers people's perception of risk. These are the three key ingredients necessary to build the trust, which will become the muscles of the future organisation. The concept of the 'town meeting' can be hugely energising for the organisation. The whole executive board should meet with all of the managers twice a year, in groups of less than 300.

The four quadrants of the balanced scorecard – Customer, People, Operations and Finance – can provide a great framework for discussing how the company will make an operational reality of its aggressive plans, and put the conditions in place for brand manners to flourish. After a decent break, so that people can socialise and discuss what they have heard, the CEO should engage in a shepherded discussion with the floor, starting with questions, but ending in a dialogue with individuals at their tables. It helps for the directors to be sprinkled around the room, encouraging people to ask the hard questions which are normally left to the washrooms and corridors.

Successful delivery of the programme depends on the right mixture of ingredients, a focus on the 'how' as well as the 'what', and collaborative horizontal working across organisation boundaries. In terms of the ingredients, these must be focused on improving the customer experience through enhanced brand manners. The route to this lies in the front-line employees who deal with customers on a day-to-day basis. The triad of simplified work to do, IT systems which are up to the job and easy to use, and core skills make the job both easier to do and more rewarding. Combined with guidance through balanced measures, which is tailored to the job environment, can go a long way to delivering the self-confident organisation necessary for improved brand manners, as shown in Figure 15.

Focusing on the 'how' is full of powerful nuances. The most important are 'show', versus 'tell', and 'consult', versus 'inform'. It is essential for roles and authorities to be clear, so that people understand where the buck stops for what, and how each person is expected to, or can, contribute. Avoid people trying to do the job of the person below them. Once these are in place, clarity as to who should be consulted and who should be informed about a key activity can avoid frustration and increase energy levels.

Consultation is a massively powerful tool, as we all respond well to being asked our view on something we care about and this engages us in the emotional and often the political dimension. The very word 'communication' implies a simple, one way, 'inform'. This can feel very disempowering and can undermine people's commitment. Hence the importance of mobilisation, as well as communication. Communication is the minimum required so that, at least, people have some idea of what is transpiring in the corporate drama. Imagine the theatre where the actors just read the script – the curtain would come down rather quickly!

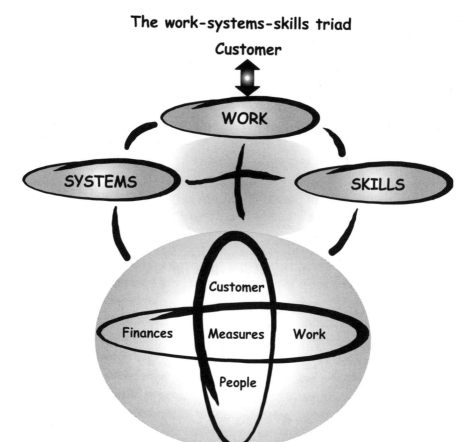

The work-systems-skills triad

Balanced measures

Figure 15 *Serving the customer better.*

This brings us to the second topic of the 'how', or 'show' versus 'tell'. How many times do executives tear their hair out, asking: 'Why don't they understand? I have told them three times ... why don't they just do it?' A lot of the answer lies in how individuals react to stimuli and how we learn. Lots of 'Best Practice' initiatives fail in companies because they attempt to tell people what to do and, even, how to do it! Human beings often respond badly to being 'told'. Much better to show them, and allow them to draw their own conclusions so that they have the space to learn, and, if one thinks about it, to be, in the fullest sense of the word.

The results from an approach which says: 'Here is what other people have found works – have a go and adapt it to your situation ... if it works well, you may be able to share your learning with others' can be spectacular. The final part of the 'How' jigsaw, horizontal working, as shown in Figure 16, is about

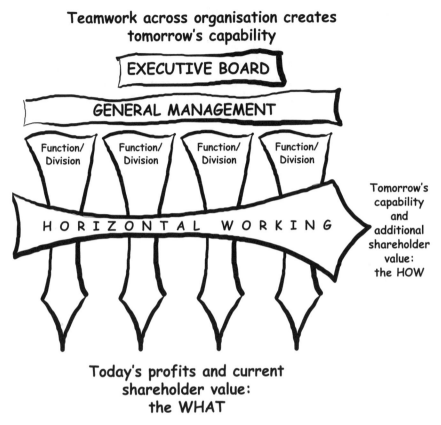

Figure 16 *Horizontal working.*

involving the people who will be affected by any changes in the organisation in the identification of opportunities, and the construction of new and better ways of working. This is best done through the creation of natural work teams, that is, collections of people who would naturally be right to address the opportunity. Frequently, these natural work teams need the oversight of an operational steering group, to ensure that the emotional and political buy-in is in place; membership comprising senior managers from across the units/ functions concerned.

The brand manners approach: summary

The landscape described above for putting the brand manners way into practice can be applied to small as well as large organisations, by focusing on the lessons suggested by the natural laws, which we have outlined. With respect to the 'New Economy', brand manners applies equally well, and particularly in the focus on the customer experience and the capability consistently to over-deliver on expectations.

In The Tesco Story (Chapter 4), we concentrated on the right-hand side of the Brand Manners Book of Life – The Corporation. With Orange, Chapter 8, which was the fourth entrant to the UK mobile telephony market, we focus of the left-hand side of the book – The Customer.

8

The Orange Story

The Orange story is about one of the most exciting brand-building successes in recent years. The company's market value has gone from nothing in 1994 to £28 billion in the year 2000. No doubt some great deal-making, shrewd distribution-building and technological development have been key contributors to this astonishing achievement, but most observers, including their CEO, Hans Snook, attribute the lion's share of it to the power of the Orange brand. This story shows how customers can be engaged by a highly creative and motivating brand promise, which addresses all four key needs: rational, emotional, political and spiritual.

This Story draws heavily on the 1996 and 1998 papers written by Charles Vallance, and Don Izbicki and Cameron Saunders, respectively, of Orange's agency WCRS for the IPA Advertising Effectiveness Awards. We are indebted to the Institute of Practitioners in Advertising (IPA) for permission to use excerpts from these cases, the full versions of which can be accessed via warc.com or obtained via the IPA at www.ipa.co.uk. We are also grateful to Stephen Woodford, CEO of WCRS, for his recollections of the history of the Orange account with which he and Chairman Robin Wight have been closely associated since its inception.

The genesis of the brand promise

The Orange name, logo (Figure 17) and corporate identity was created by Wolff Olins, with Doug Hamilton, their Creative Director being then and still today the key person for the company at the brand consultancy remaining absolutely critical to the spirit of the Orange brand. Under the leadership of Robin Wight, WCRS worked very closely with Wolff Olins

Figure 17 *The Orange logo.*

on the future-orientated strategy, and it was they who came up with the line 'The future's bright, the future's Orange'. Both agencies believed passionately that the new company would fail miserably if they were just the fourth entry into the market and argued strongly for a radical approach to the problem. It's indicative of their success in this, and in Hans Snook's courage as a client, that the new baby was christened with the name 'Orange' over fifteen years before brands called 'Egg' or 'Cahoot' had become quite common. Indeed Hutchison had originally intended to launch as Hutchison Microtel, a name redolent of potential disaster.

The inspiration for the whole Orange vision for the future world came from one of the many concepts that WCRS researched in qualitative focus groups. They tested all sorts of different propositions and there was one concept that was based on reports of a test community in the United States, where an organisation was experimenting with having a digital town without wires, and where you could call people and not places. Larry Barker, Creative Director of WRCS at the time, attended these group discussions. He saw that the agency had come up with seventeen worthy concept statements that were essentially lots of meaningless waffle about the future being better, and then there was this eighteenth one about the experimental community, which absolutely set the focus groups alight in terms of interest. People really sat up and started talking and became very animated for the first time in the research. This concept was the real germ of Barker's visionary brand positioning, 'The future's bright the future's Orange'. Inspired by this idea of a wire-free future, WCRS developed the mantra that they were not going to be forced into an old market, they were going to be first into a new one, and that was going to be the wire-free market. This copy line and thinking became the basis of a compelling 'future narrative', a vision of the future which stood in stark contrast to the spirit of the times in the dog days of the Conservative Government under John Major.

The language of Orange

As a result, the agency never talked about mobile and never used the language of the existing category; they have always used the new visionary language of the wire-free future which has had such a strong emotional, even spiritual appeal for customers. 'Wire free' became an important part of the corporate vocabulary and essential in Hans Snook's. It was also a driving force behind the corporate strategy, linked as it was to core organisational ideas such as the crucial need for coverage. 'It's about coverage, coverage, coverage' repeated Snook as he built the infrastructure and roaming agreements that were the essential underpinning of a wire-free future, where data transmission would be as important, if not more so than speech.

It is also almost 100% true that, in the same radical spirit, WCRS have never shown a mobile phone in an Orange advertisement. On one occasion there was a joint-funded campaign with Motorola where they were pressurised into showing a phone, but actually just used an x-ray of one! WCRS certainly never showed a phone in a TV commercial and always worked on the assumption that people knew what a mobile was and what to do with it. Indeed not showing an actual handset avoided the risk of potential customers getting hung up on the aesthetics or features of a particular model. Instead, the campaign always talked much more about the potential of wire-free communication and what the benefits of that were: the fact that you could call people not places, that you never need to be out of touch, and all the things that you can do with your phone other than just talk on it, such as send messages and data. Orange have always talked about much much more than just being a telephonic device.

Perhaps most important of all has been the manner in which Orange has communicated. WCRS has always had a very clear idea of what is Orange and what is not Orange in terms of the brand's way of talking. For example, there has literally been a consistent voice in the sound of voice-over artist Paul Vaughan. Further, the viewer has always been able to tell an Orange ad by the art direction. There is never a set character; it is always multi-racial, old, young, male, female, but it is always beautifully photographed, with the characteristically optimistic 'sunset glow', so there is always a feeling of huge space and tranquillity.

Honeymoon and after

Faced with this radical, visionary and potentially highly controversial package of brand identity and positioning, Chris Moss, then Marketing Director, bought into it straight away, and to his eternal credit Hans Snook immediately endorsed it too. The advertising campaign was presented in November 1993, shot in February and went on air in April 1994. Everybody at the top of Orange saw the potential and everyone knew they had to be involved.

Nevertheless, there was a distinctly wobbly period 4–6 months after launch when sales were beginning to pick up, but they weren't as high as had been hoped. There was also confusion with people saying they didn't know what Orange was. Indeed, it took a long time before the whole company was as passionate about the advertising as the agency and the marketing people. The campaign was seen as eccentric and the sales people were saying, 'Why aren't we showing phones?' and because it broke many of the conventions in the market, a lot of people felt uncomfortable about it. Perhaps the defining moment was when Orange took on Vodafone and Cellnet and did comparative advertising. They then went to the High Court when Vodafone sued. The case was provoked by the claim that, on average, Orange users could save £20 a month compared to Cellnet and Vodafone users. This was based on an analysis of 300,000 accountancy records of Orange customers, which were then put against the tariffs of Vodafone and Cellnet prevailing at the time. On this comparison it worked out that an Orange user would save on average £20 a month. The WCRS Account Director at the time endured days of aggressive cross-examination by Vodafone's QC, but in the end their case was thrown out and they had costs awarded against them, which was most unusual in a commercial libel case of this sort.

As a result of the publicity surrounding the case and the advertising campaign getting into its stride, Orange suddenly seemed to capture the imagination. People were taken by the political nature of the legal battle, and also had their eyes opened to the practical, rational benefits of Orange – significantly better value – and understood what the brand was all about. The press started talking it up rather than talking it down and it just went from strength to strength from there. The lawsuit also really got the whole company behind the campaign, which was starting to win industry creative awards and Orange was beginning to be regarded as a potential world-beating brand with a high degree of emotional content. In addition the company had its eye on a stock market flotation and realised that the value of the brand would form a major part of the valuation of the company. In addition, the 'other worldly' quality of the thematic Orange TV commercials created an uplifting, almost spiritual, feeling of optimism regarding the future. This meant that the Orange brand was built on all of the four brand manners dimensions – the rational, the emotional, the political and the spiritual.

Market context at launch

In the light of Orange's subsequent success, it is now difficult to appreciate fully the immense problems which the brand faced when it was launched in April 1994. Conditions could hardly have been more hostile. Cellnet and Vodafone had ten years of market dominance behind them, with full national coverage and millions of captive subscribers on their analogue networks. Both had also successfully developed low-user tariffs as part of a pre-emptive strategy to block entry into the consumer market and had assiduously strengthened their dominance of the business market through the development of their digital (GSM) networks (Figure 18).

The old duopoly, therefore, represented a hugely formidable opponent, more than capable of squashing a fledgling network at birth. Which is why, six months before Orange's launch, Mercury One2One also decided to adopt an entirely different approach. With an infant network of approximately 30% coverage, it recognised the impossibility of competing with Cellnet and Vodafone directly and, instead, developed the famous free-call strategy alongside a regionalised approach to coverage build. The strategy was to prove immensely successful in gaining connections.

Orange, which launched with approximately 50% coverage was, therefore, faced with a daunting challenge. From the old and the new it

Network coverage at time of Orange launch (April 1994)

Orange	c 50%
Cellnet Analogue	98%
Cellnet GSM	c 95%
Vodafone Analogue	98%
Vodafone GSM	c 95%
One2One	c 30%

c = approximately
Source: Network Coverage Maps

Figure 18 *Network coverage.*

had seen most of its competitive opportunities closed off. It was late, had an eccentric name and came from Hutchison, the warren which had bred the unlucky Rabbit. Commentators queued up to write it off:

> 'Hutchison Whampoa's billionaire owner Li Ka-Shing is reported to be under pressure to quit the UK telecommunications business ...' *The Times*, 5 April 1994

> 'It would be a brave man who would bet on the Hong Kong company seeing to the end of the decade.' *Investor's Chronicle*, June 1994

> 'Andrew Harrington, telecommunications analyst at Salomon Brothers is adamant that Orange will not be a success in Britain.' *South China Morning Post*, 16 October 1994

Getting the strategy right

One consideration dominated the launch and strategic development process. How could Orange overcome, or minimise, the huge disadvantage of being last? BSB's experience of being last into the UK satellite market was hardly a reassuring precedent. But all was not doom and gloom. Orange did have a number of important competitive features. Most notably, it offered per-second billing and inclusive minutes, which for most users would save 20% to 40% per month versus Cellnet and Vodafone. Given this cost advantage, a value for money/'we're cheaper' strategy was superficially the obvious route. For a variety of reasons it would also have been a disastrous one. Firstly, Orange was not the cheapest (One2One was). Even if it had been, a lower cost of usage argument would have pitched Orange directly against one of Cellnet and Vodafone's greatest strengths, namely exceptionally low entry costs. Whereas most of Vodafone or Cellnet's analogue handsets fell into the £49.99–£99.99 price range, Orange's cheapest handset at launch was £249.99. Above all, however, a cost-led strategy would have been disastrous because it would have squandered the one advantage of being last, the opportunity to avoid the mistake the others had made.

The category mistake and Orange's opportunity

This 'mistake' was to allow what should have been a highly popular and exciting category to become both commoditised and compromised. With the partial exception of One2One, the mobile phone category was more or less devoid of branding and brand values. Cellnet and Vodafone's duopoly mentality had resulted in a mobile phone 'ghetto', characterised by confusion, distrust and a tangle of complicated tariffs, deals and price claims. The last thing Orange should have done was emphasise its similarities by focusing on cost. Instead, its opportunity was to escape the ghetto by being the first to develop a fully rounded brand identity. This brand identity, moreover, could be built on the market high ground, which had been left so conspicuously unoccupied by the competition. Once the high ground was secure, Orange would then be able to deliver its price-based message from a position of brand strength rather than commodity weakness.

High ground positioning research

The task, therefore, was to find an expression of these benefits that would allow Orange to position itself well above the limitations of the existing market. Through an iterative process of concept development, the following expression was arrived at by WCRS and was to become the Orange brand vision:

> There will come a time when all people will have their own personal number that goes with them wherever they are so that there are no barriers to communication; a wirefree future in which you call people, not places, and where everyone will benefit from the advances of technology.

Being first rather than last

The two key words in Orange's brand vision are 'wirefree' and 'future', since they enabled Orange to distance itself entirely from the vocabulary and associations of the existing market. Indeed, psychologically, they allowed Orange to create a new category away from the two existing types of telephony. By defining its own category, Orange could be first rather than last: the first mobile phone company to benefit from the advantage of a fully rounded brand identity.

Media strategy

Given the doubts which surrounded Orange at launch, the most important task for media was to imbue the brand with as much confidence as possible. This core strategic requirement was translated into a highly assumptive multimedia schedule. Rather than dominate one medium, Orange would dominate them all with posters heralding each new campaign theme, TV communicating core brand benefits and press providing detailed messages in the information-led environment of newspapers. This integrated approach has been rolled out across five phases of activity. The efficiency of the chosen media solution is emphatically demonstrated by Millward Brown's tracking survey which showed how advertising helped Orange achieve a position of enviable pre-eminence in the public consciousness, so much so that, after only two years, Orange enjoyed greater awareness than either Cellnet or Vodafone.

More remarkably still, the combined impact of Orange's multimedia strategy resulted in higher overall advertising awareness than BT, whose vast £90 million advertising budget dwarfed that of Orange. These remarkable levels of awareness enabled the campaign to achieve the rare distinction of becoming a public property. From the *Sun* to the *Telegraph* it became a part of journalistic currency, further enhancing the value of the advertising investment.

Expert opinion

Bit by bit, as Orange's success became more and more inescapable, scepticism gave way to admiration, even from direct competitors:

> 'Orange's advertising has made its mark. It has served Hutchison well by helping to establish a distinctive brand personality.' Sholto Douglas-Home, BT, *Marketing Week*, 6 October 1995

> 'One of the great strengths of the Orange campaign has been its consistency.' William Ostrom, Cellnet, *Marketing Week*, 1 March 1996

More importantly, Orange's advertising success was enthusiastically endorsed by the trade. This was to represent a very important secondary contribution of advertising:

> 'The image and advertising of Orange is very, very powerful and it is part of what helped build the brand. It's a really aspirational product and service.' Charles Dunstone, MD, Carphone Warehouse, *Money Programme*, 10 December 1995

The net result was that, even before flotation, Orange was hailed as an unqualified success. The turnaround had been remarkable:

> 'It is one of the most dramatic transformations in modern British corporate history. One moment Orange appeared to be an eccentrically marketed also-ran. The next, it was revealed as a big-time winner racing towards a flotation value of about £2 billion.' *Sunday Times*, 3 May 1995

Econometrics and value added

In conjunction with the Orange market planning department, research agency Millward Brown constructed an econometric sales model designed to isolate all key variables, having defined and accounted for three key constraints – and thus attribute a statistical value to advertising. Overall, the total number of connections attributable to the short-term effects of advertising was calculated by the Millward Brown model to be 61,000. Allowing for cost of acquisition, and assuming network average revenue of £37 per month, the net value of these additional 61,000 connections amounted to £128 million. This was more than four times in excess of payback on the cost of the advertising campaign.

The plc era and the drive for shareholder value

Over the subsequent period from April 1996 to April 1998, which was the first two years of Orange in its new guise as a FTSE 100 plc, the *raison d'être* of the company fundamentally changed. The sole rationale for its existence was now to provide its shareholders with a profit, to create shareholder value. The imperative of shareholder value resulted in a very different corporate strategy for Orange plc, as opposed to Orange in its launch years. Prior to flotation, the focus had been on volume share in order to gain critical mass. Following flotation, Orange plc's business plan resolved that value share would be the key determinant of success. Unlike its competitors, Orange could not sacrifice margin for the sake of volume. It could not trade quality for quantity:

> 'Customer loyalty and usage breeds shareholder value. This means we do not chase market share at any cost.' Hans Snook, Group Managing Director, 1997 Preliminary Results, 12 March 1998

In light of its business plan, Orange plc was precluded from the two hard-hitting strategies pursued by the competition, namely price cuts and distribution growth. The former would compromise both short- and long-term subscriber values. The latter would either involve high fixed cost (building or buying a national network of wholly owned shops), or would endanger short- and long-term revenues (increased dealer incentives). Instead, to achieve *value share*, the Orange plc had three core objectives: earnings growth, earnings security and risk diversification. In order to achieve these objectives, Orange continued to commit itself to an unequivocally brand-led strategy. If Orange could exert enough brand pull, this would prove the most value-enhancing insulation against its relative weakness in terms of price and distribution. Heightened brand desirability would prove to be Orange plc's core competitive advantage.

Intensifying competition

Over the recent period, there had been three key trends in UK mobile telecoms. Between 1996 and 1998, the average cost of using a mobile phone had fallen by 25%. This fall was solely attributable to tariff changes amongst Cellnet, Vodafone and One2One. Instead of price-cutting in line with the market, Orange's core tariff proposition remained unchanged. The result was that Orange was approximately 5% more expensive than Vodafone and Cellnet, and 20–35% more expensive than One2One. This price premium inevitably impacted on volume share, but it did not impact on Orange plc's value share of the market, the key driver for shareholder value.

Meanwhile there had been significant changes in the distribution strategies of Orange's rivals. In advance of their October 1997 brand relaunch, Vodafone spent millions buying up distribution channels. By the third quarter of 1997, Vodafone had by far the strongest distribution of any of the four mobile networks, with over 250 wholly owned shops, effectively one on every key high street in the country.

One2One's distribution had also grown at a speed to mirror their network expansion. Between April 1996 and April 1998 the One2One network grew from 45% to 95% population coverage (compared to equivalent figures for Orange of 90% to 96%). Cellnet took ownership of The Link group throughout the UK, and leading mobile phone retailer DX Communications in Scotland. This significantly improved Cellnet's distribution strength in addition to their nation-wide chain of BT Shops. In contrast, between April 1996 and April 1998, Orange opened just 13 own branded shops and there were no other changes to their distribution strategy.

Further compounding the competitor's breadth of distribution, was its quality. For the networks this quality equated to the likelihood of a dealer recommending their network to a customer. This likelihood was driven by two factors, firstly an assessment of customers' needs and future satisfaction with a network, secondly, the dealer incentives being offered by all four networks. In a context where price and coverage were converging, the latter was of growing importance:

'We estimate that other operators (than Orange) increased their dealer incentive payments in Q4 ('97), thus encouraging some dealers to recommend other networks above Orange, even if Orange was the customer's initially favoured network.' Dresdner Kleinwort Benson Analysts Report, March 1998

Nor had the success of the Orange advertising campaign during its first two years gone unnoticed. The result was heavy investment by all the competitive networks in brand advertising, with significant media support. The result of these increases in spend was a curtailment in Orange's share of voice.

Holding to the brand promise and vision

Through all this intense competitive pressure, the Orange company and WRCS, its agency, continued to hold to the brand's powerful communications mix of visionary brand promise and hard-hitting transparency in its financial offers and tariffs. As Hans Snook confirmed:

'The way you define a brand is as a promise deliverer. And we've always delivered – to our staff, our customers and our shareholders'. *Sunday Times*, 4 June 2000.

Proving the contribution to shareholder value

WCRS also continued to innovate in terms of the evaluation of the campaign's effectiveness, building on the econometric modelling that had been so persuasive in their 1996 IPA paper. They embarked on a more radical calculation of advertising's contribution based on the actual working practices used by City analysts to determine the value of UK stocks. To this end, they enlisted Lehman Brothers to apply the sophisticated spreadsheet methodology by which they calculate an implied value per share. The difference between this implied value and the real value is the basis on which they base their notices to buy, sell or hold. At the time Lehman Brothers equity market valuation showed Orange to be a 'buy' stock with an implied value per share of 528p, compared to the current market value of 443p (Figure 19).

WCRS then asked Lehman Brothers to re-work their valuation on the assumption that advertising's effects on net subscriber growth, customer revenue and churn had not applied over the course of the plc's history (Figure 20). In this way, they were able to arrive at a surrogate for Orange's

EBITDA Terminal Multiple	13.2
Discount rate	9%
NPV cash flows	1035
PV terminal value (£m.)	6396
Enterprise value Orange PCS	7432
Value per population	**$209**
Other businesses	459
Asset/Enterprise value	7891
Net debt (projected end 1998)	−1571
Equity value	6320
Implied value per share	**528**
Current share price	443
Current discount/premium	16%
Implied in perpetual growth rate	4%

Assumes £:US$ exchange rate of 1.6294

Figure 19 *Lehman Brothers current equity market evaluation.*

implied value per share, excluding advertising. The results were an emphatic confirmation of Orange advertising's contribution.

On this basis, the implied value per share would have plummeted from 528p to 279p, suggesting that without advertising, Orange plc would have underperformed the FTSE 100 index by 19%. So not only did the visionary advertising campaign enable Orange plc, on a budget of £43.6 million to create a conventional payback in excess of £276.34 million – over six times

EBITDA Terminal Multiple	13.6
Discount rate	9%
NPV cash flows	328
PV terminal value (£m.)	4,172
Enterprise value Orange PCS	4,500
Value per population	**$126**
Other businesses	459
Asset/Enterprise value	4,959
Net debt (projected end 1998)	(1,616)
Equity value	3,343
Implied value per share	**279**
Current share price	443
Current discount/premium	**−59%**
Implied in perpetual growth rate	4.0%

Assumes £:US$ exchange rate of 1.63

Figure 20 *Lehman Brothers equity market evaluation removing advertising contribution.*

the advertising investment – but Lehman Brothers' calculation also suggested advertising's capacity to increase Orange plc's implied value per share by £2.49. This is equivalent to an increased Market Capitalisation of £3 billion.

Takeover fever

Since this analysis was done, the Orange company's changes of ownership have rendered these sorts of calculation pretty meaningless and the valuation in the market has gone way beyond the wildest expectations. In October 1999, having made a pre-tax loss in the previous year of £98 million, Orange was acquired by Mannesmann for £19.8bn. Then in May 2000, as a result of a disposal required by the EC competition authority ruling as a condition of the take-over of Mannesmann by Vodafone, Orange was acquired by France Telecom for £31.6bn.

The penultimate word should go to Hans Snook, who commented as follows in the *Sunday Times* of 4 June following this epoch-making deal:

> Advertising and marketing are very advanced here (the UK). If we had launched Orange in the US, which is considered the home of branding, it would never have worked.

However, the last word should go to WCRS. In a sad ending to this success story they lost a competitive review of the Orange business to another agency in August 2000. Their CEO Stephen Woodford had this to say:

> The thing is that as a brand Orange is like an open book. You could write the book of Orange very easily from just looking at the ads. Watch a reel of Orange commercials, read the press ads, and you have got the mantra. It is one of the benchmark campaigns in terms of actually wearing its heart on its sleeve. It tells people what it believes, and what it thinks. Because of this honesty, integrity and transparency, it's trusted. Orange is the best-placed brand to capitalise on the explosion in wirefree digital services by far.

The WCRS 'house ad' (Figure 21) which appeared in *Campaign* after their loss of the Orange account in August 2000, said it all.

It will be very interesting to see how the new owner, France Telecom, handles its Orange acquisition and thus how the brand fares in future. In corporate history, there have been many examples where big multinationals take over bright, entrepreneurial firms and tensions develop between the new owners and the original management. There is also the prospect that the many Orange managers made very wealthy on paper may cash in their share options, and thus there could be a considerable change in senior

Figure 21 *WCRS house ad.*

personnel. A further challenge may be represented by Wolff Olins's resignation of the Orange account whilst key player Doug Hamilton has become committed to the creation of the identity for the new H3G brand following Hutchison's successful acquisition of their third-generation mobile franchise.

However, our view is that the legacy of WCRS is a visionary brand ethos and advertising campaign so powerful and demonstrably global in its appeal – 'The future's bright, the future's Orange' – that it should survive any of these short-term hiccups. Orange can go from strength to strength as mobile, internet and computing technologies converge and Orange becomes the universal personal service provider. Besides, France Telecom have paid enough for the brand and that should guarantee they'll look after it.

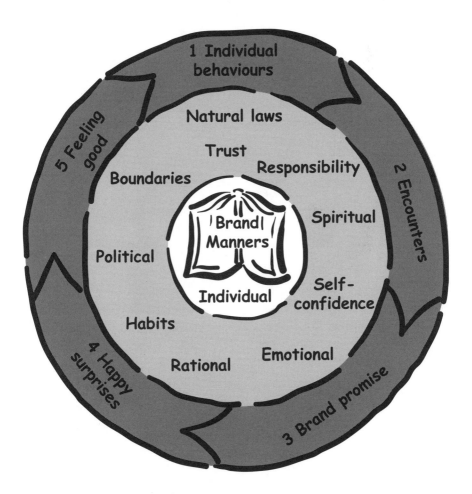

Figure 22 *The Brand Manners Improvement Cycle.*

The Orange story is an excellent example of developing brand manners on the rational, emotional and spiritual dimensions, through creating, conveying and keeping the Brand Promise. While we have focused on the customer (left-hand side of the book of life) in The Orange Story, the company also has done a great job of delivering the promise (the right-hand side of the book of life), resulting in Happy Surprises for customers, and everyone feeling good.

Having illustrated the Brand Manners Book of Life and Way through the Tesco and Orange stories, we now turn to Part III: The Brand Manners Improvement Cycle (Figure 22), which starts with 'Individual Behaviours', moves through 'Encounters', 'The Brand Promise', and 'Happy Surprises', to 'Feeling Good'. Each of the five sections takes theory and practice from real life and signposts the lessons learned in terms of their implications for Management.

PART III
The Brand Manners Improvement Cycle

Section One
Individual Behaviours

The first section of the cycle concerns our behaviour as individuals. As brand manners occur during the interactions between people, it is vital to get to the heart of the issues involving behaviour concerning conditioning, boundaries, habits and stress.

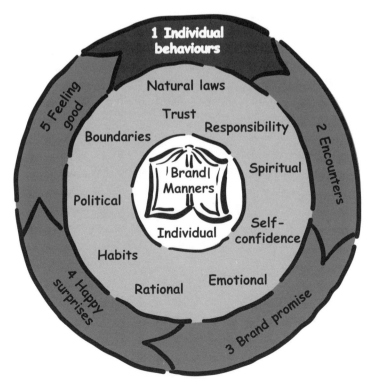

Figure 23 *Section One: The Brand Manners Improvement Cycle – individual behaviours.*

9

Conditioning Creates Brands

Physical experience remains the most powerful way in which we learn. Corporations and brands have underestimated the power they have in teaching their employees and customers about their product and service values through personal interaction. It's not enough to just talk about visions, missions, roles, values, objectives, strategies and measures. These elements have to be manifested in the concrete reality of individual interactions between customers and representatives of the brand if they are to have their true force.

We learn about ourselves, and the environment in which we live, through a process of trial and error. We also learn about brands and companies in exactly the same way. If brands are effectively a set of expectations in our minds, then it is clear that these expectations have been created through a whole series of interactions between us, as customers, and the product or service brands, which we purchase and use. Thus one can see that companies and brands evolve in the same way as people do in their relationships with their stakeholders such as employees, customers, suppliers and stockholders. To a large degree a brand represents a complex series of conditioned reflexes. These are created whenever a stakeholder comes in contact with the brand: each time we are conditioned and our expectations change for the better or worse.

Up until quite recently the main inputs to this learning process have come from practical usage, conditioned by the advertising, packaging, and public relations imagery, which surround the particular product or service brand in question. Whilst companies and brands in the service sector have always had a direct interface with customers on a regular basis – retailers for example – the new digital interactive era is creating a situation in which virtually every consumer product can now have a direct customer interface.

Brands are coming to terms with the fact that, through their websites and call centres, they have opened up a channel of dialogue and direct customer service to which they have hitherto not been exposed. This means that companies, which have long been able to rely on highly controlled customer communications, through carefully contrived advertising campaigns, now have to grapple with much more variable and unpredictable communications. The physical and emotional experiences which result from large numbers of *ad hoc* contacts with customers via the telephone, e-mail and direct contact are much more complex, and more powerful in their formative effects. These lead the brand to develop emotional assets whenever the brand behaviour is executed well.

In very simple terms, companies and brands, which used to have trade customers and wholesalers acting as a buffer between them as manufacturers and ultimate end users, are now at the sharp end of customer contact. On the one hand this has increased massively the exposure to customers, and can be seen as potentially threatening, with much greater chances of failures in communication and misunderstanding. The advent of this new technology means that it is easy to alienate customers by over-reliance on interactions with answerphones and automated response mechanisms, which can so easily detract from the positive emotional and feelings needed to reinforce the brand. On the other hand this new intimacy with customers offers the opportunity to build much deeper and more meaningful relationships which leverage the power of the organisation to deliver the brand one-to-one, via direct personal interaction and communications between customers and employees imbued in the appropriate brand manners.

If companies and brands seize this new opportunity to create much more intensive relationships with customers then they should be able to teach those customers much more about their brand ideal. Those companies, which do not take advantage of this new situation may lose out to competitors through the sheer lack of focus on this key area of interpersonal interaction in communications. They may also be at risk of undermining their investment in conventional brand-building activity via advertising, direct marketing, sales promotion and all the other traditional tools in the marketing communications mix.

How often are we, as customers ourselves, disappointed by the brand's representative at the point of purchase, or on the help desk? All the carefully laid pieces of the marketing jigsaw may have led the horse to water, but the final piece, namely appropriate brand behaviour on the part of its employee 'ambassadors' is missing and prevent it from drinking!

The increasingly detailed customer records that brands own are being used for very sophisticated 'data mining' analysis and subsequent communications of a highly targeted and personalised nature. The goal must be to evolve products and services, which are in effect mass customisations corresponding to the smallest economically viable human niches. A crucial adjunct to the delivery of these brands will be personal behaviour and communications, which reinforce their values in the most potent manner.

However, a parallel set of thinking has evolved over the last century or so which makes an equally powerful claim to the influence of environment and setting on acquired human behaviour. This dichotomy is of course the basis of the 'nature v. nurture' debate. It is clear in principle, but occurs in ways which we still do not fully understand. There is clearly some complex interaction between genetically inherited characteristics and predispositions, and acquired beliefs, attitudes and behaviours, which modify them in significant ways, and may perhaps be inherited themselves.

To extend this thinking to the nature of a brand, we can say that at base a brand is made up of its physical attributes – its genetic makeup – but it can also have powerful imagery – its acquired characteristics. Increasingly we can see these acquired values extending into new areas such as social conscience and ethics. These acquired characteristics exist in the minds of potential or actual customers but clearly have a strong connection with and indeed arise out of the brand's 'genetics' and its perceived behaviour. These also interact and develop just like our human characteristics, and it is this development, which should be carefully constructed and monitored.

The father of the 'nurture' school is Pavlov who was able to show that animals can be taught to react in certain ways. He thus proved that innate behaviour is only part of the explanation of animal, and by extension, human actions. His work was followed up by the likes of John Watson, Edward Thorndike and Burrhus Skinner who developed the idea of the conditioned reflex. Although the language used seems old-fashioned, it's worth reading in the original how Thorndike defined his psychological law of effect:

> Of several responses made to the same situation those which are accompanied or closely followed by satisfaction to the animal will, other things being equal, be more firmly connected with the situation, so that, when it recurs, they will be more likely to recur; those which are

accompanied or closely followed by discomfort to the animal will, other things being equal, have their connections to the situation weakened, so that, when it recurs, they will be less likely to occur. The greater the satisfaction or discomfort, the greater the strengthening or weakening of the bond. *Laws of Psychology*, Edward Thorndike, 1910.

In the contemporary context what this means for the company or brand is that reinforcing the brand message, for example through positive personal interaction by committed 'brand ambassadors' amongst the firm's employees, is likely to have a massively enhancing effect. By contrast, a negative experience, through a poor customer interaction, will inevitably undermine the brand. A company can transform its product or service by a conditioning process. That is to say by moving the undifferentiated, unconditioned stimulus, or commodity item, associated with purchasing on price and availability alone up to the status of conditioned response, or higher level. This is achieved by using naming, logo styling, packaging, marketing communications and behaviour to make promises about delivery to satisfy customer needs at a number of different levels.

If these promises are fulfilled in practice by the brand's delivery, then these brand communications become an external stimulus, which eventually, with repetition, create a conditioned reflex in customers. These brand values can therefore create the 'benefit of the doubt' and in a marginal situation add significant and differential benefits. Thus there will always be a place for codes of practice in company-to-customer relationship building. Developing, and endlessly refining, appropriate, repeatable and measurable sequences of interactive brand manners will condition reactions to the products or services more powerfully than many other forms of customer communications.

It's fair to say that much of this early work, based on the 'rats in mazes' type of experimentation, inevitably focused on physical stimulation. For many this did not easily translate to the human situation and indeed provoked negative reactions comparable to the religiously based anti-Darwinism from those who could not accept the implication that man was in some way descended from animals. The linkage to the human situation only became clearer through the work of Dr John Watson, the founder of Behaviourism. Watson joined the J Walter Thompson advertising agency in 1920. He often spoke on the correlation between advertising, selling and behaviourist psychology. In one particular speech in 1935 he said:

Since the time of the serpent in the Garden of Eden influenced Eve and Eve in turn persuaded Adam, the world has tried to find out ways and means of controlling human behaviour. In advertising, we call the process selling.

Watson believed that at birth, infants possessed an inventory of only three basic reactions – love, fear, and rage. Beyond these emotions, the environment was responsible for individual habits. Thus advertising's job was simply to tap into fear, rage or love and thus strike at a deep psychological need. He found that the best way to reach the consumer was to understand them at a profound level, and that was only possible through research.

At a time when the prevailing philosophy of advertising was heavily based on 'salesmanship in print' and rational approaches, there is evidence that he wished to 'dispense with rational copy almost entirely' (Coon 1994).

It certainly appears as if Watson was a contributor to the growing theory that advertising should be more aesthetically pleasing and appeal more to non-rational emotions rather than reason. This radical approach was eventually to come to fruition in the 1960s with the pioneering work by agencies such as Doyle Dane Bernbach.

The business lesson from this is clear: Management must focus on how their organisation's collective behaviour, and its communication to its customers, is conditioning the response from them. Actions do speak so much louder than words, and so often it is the rhetoric that has the attention, rather than the action. Brand manners, which reinforce the core positioning of the company's product and service brands are vital in conditioning positive responses from customers. The digital interactive era provides the opportunity to build more direct relationships with customers while managing the attendant risks. Target the smallest, economically viable niches, customise the brand positioning for them and develop living codes of practice whereby employees can continually develop their brand manners.

10

How Boundaries Create Self-confidence

Corporations are increasingly questioning the 'command and control' philosophy of management and enthusiastically embracing the notion of the 'empowered' organisation. However, there is a great danger in swinging too far in this direction. The need for boundaries and parameters is deeply inculcated in us as children, and throughout their lives people perform better when they are in an environment with structure. Indeed, it is that very structure, which may appear to be limiting, which is in fact the springboard to creativity and self-expression. CEOs should view their companies as families and not abrogate their responsibility for 'parental control' and the exercise of 'tough love' when need be.

Perhaps the famous Jesuit saying 'give me the child at seven and I shall give you the man' was right. There is no doubt that a significant minority of late developers do exist in society, and many of us know people who are literally different persons from their teenage years to the way they present themselves in adulthood. Nevertheless, most people would probably accept that the majority have their character formed at a remarkably early age. Whether it's eleven or seventeen probably doesn't make much difference as far as the employer is concerned. The fundamental point is that some very important attitudes have become pretty ingrained by the time that the majority of people go into employment.

This argument should not be construed as implying that large numbers of the working population are 'childish' in their attitudes and behaviour. On the contrary, there is an increasing body of evidence to suggest that actually children are remarkably sophisticated in their attitudes, in respect of the marketing environment and commercial communications.

What purchases do kids influence?

	%
Breakfast cereals	73
Clothes	70
Soft drinks	60
Day-to-day meals	54
Stationery/School materials	54
Holidays	44
Schools	35
Computer	33
Restaurants	30
House	22
Car	17

Source: Saatchi & Saatchi/Taylor Nelson AGB Omnimas.
Base: All housewives with children aged 0–15 years

Figure 24 *Saatchi & Saatchi Kid Connection data.*

Research conducted amongst mothers by Saatchi & Saatchi Kid Connection (Figure 24) in 1998 showed that children have a significant influence on parental purchase, not only in the areas that one would expect, such as confectionery and toys, but also in some surprising market sectors such as cars, houses, schools, and holidays.

Attitudes to life, other people, social behaviour, authority, the work ethic, honesty, integrity, morality, indeed the whole catalogue of virtues and vices, is likely to have become relatively fixed during their childhood years. The implications for this are quite simple: employers need to understand the educational context of childhood in order to create a working environment that is effective in delivering appropriate behaviour to support the enterprise and the brand. With this knowledge it should also be possible to understand much better how people will behave in the work context from a detailed study of their background. This information will enable employers to recruit people who will have the desired brand behaviour more naturally.

CEOs will need to ensure that those responsible for Human Resources and Personnel do not rely simply on recruiting by competencies alone. This will lead to a population of employees, which is generically opposed to 'branded' behaviour. The organisation that wishes to 'live the brand' needs to develop tailor-made proprietary tests, which match human performance and attitudes to the brand's mission and values.

As we all know there have been dramatic changes in social attitudes towards education and the bringing up of children over the last century and a half. We have moved from the era of an authoritarian parental style where manners and education were rigidly enforced to the extent that 'children should be seen and not heard' to the era of 'child as fashion accessory' where extremes of *laissez-faire* are the order of the day. It's not uncommon for very young children to be seen out in top restaurants late at night, tired, crying and therefore dominating proceedings and annoying neighbouring tables with their bad behaviour, whilst the parents look on in adoring puzzlement and do nothing.

The classroom has evolved from the blackboard jungle to the group table, and all right-thinking people abhor any form of physical punishment. Certainly there could not be a starker contrast between the liberal teachings of Dr Benjamin Spock and the attitudes expressed by the Gradgrind of Dickens's novel, *Hard Times*:

> NOW, what I want is, Facts. Teach these boys and girls nothing but Facts. Facts alone are wanted in life. Plant nothing else, and root out everything else. You can only form the minds of reasoning animals upon Facts: nothing else will ever be of any service to them. This is the principle on which I bring up my own children, and this is the principle on which I bring up these children. Stick to Facts, sir!

There are still many senior people in the top executive positions in major corporations on both sides of the Atlantic who were educated in institutions that were governed by the quasi-Victorian, 'public' boarding school regime (called 'private' Stateside). This highly influential cadre was responsible for the dominance of the 'command and control' style of management. This is typified by a highly pyramidal and authoritarian management process, in which the ultimate leadership gains an intimidating form of dominance through distance from the vast majority of employees. Even at the very top of such organisations the board of directors is essentially deferential to the ultimate leader (whilst things are going well). More lowly employees go about their business in fear and woe betide them if they accidentally find themselves sharing the executive elevator.

The problem is that this 'command and control' approach has been out of kilter with the prevailing educational approach for certainly 30 or perhaps 40 years. Hardly surprisingly this means that the vast majority of company employees have been brought up, both within their families, and within their schools, under a completely different philosophy, the philosophy of *laissez-faire*, of Spock.

During the last decade and a half of the last century, corporations began to make the necessary adjustment to their corporate style moving from 'command and control' to a new-age culture. There are direct parallels between this and the ideas of educationalists, which came to fruition during the 1960s and 1970s. It looks as if there could be a very simple time lag between the educational regime that was in place during the formative years of senior management and that which obtains during the same period for their younger employees.

The danger now is that we see a pendulum swinging from one polar opposite to the other; from authoritarianism to *laissez-faire* with neither really providing the desired results. A better system of management would be to achieve an environment where staff are self-motivated, tuned into structured company beliefs and with a dedication to achieve its goals and dreams through appropriate behaviours.

Studies of children growing up are pretty well unanimous that one of the key dynamics is that of attachment and separation between parent and child. Quite literally from birth we are separated from our mothers and then immediately rushed back to the breast. Childhood seems to be a successive series of steps forward and steps back. With increasing confidence and experience the steps get longer, the distance gets further and the invisible underlying connections between parent and child get stretched until they finally break in the teenage years and the bridging into adulthood.

A problem with the authoritarian school is that the reins are kept so tight that the child literally has no chance to explore the boundaries of its own personality and no room to develop its own ideas and sense of self. The problem with the *laissez-faire* approach is that the lack of boundaries makes it impossible for self-definition to take place; literally there are no limits and therefore no indication of where self begins or ends.

Human creativity seems to thrive on limitations. We are an innate problem-solving species. There are many examples where the extreme difficulty of circumstance and the paucity of materials have actually led to some of the most extraordinary demonstrations of human ingenuity. Look at the sheer creativity of the prisoners in Colditz. How on earth did they build a working glider inside there?! Perhaps Lord Rutherford, who led the development of science's understanding of atomic structure in 1911, which in itself was a precursor of the discovery of atomic energy, got it right when he said: 'we haven't the money, so we've got to think'.

There is a fond belief about the creative industries such as advertising, design, and film, that a blank sheet of paper is the ideal stimulus for great work. Nothing could be further from the truth. In reality creative people like to receive what they describe as 'a tight brief'. Indeed, much of the work of the majority of people, working in these so-called creative industries is actually far removed from the public perception of airy-fairy flights of fancy and blue-sky thinking. Most of the time, most of the people, and much of the energies are devoted to specifying in great detail the precise parameters within which an idea might be deemed to be creative.

The analytical process produces the 'tight brief' which becomes a springboard for a creative leap, which flips the rational analysis into a piece of emotional communications magic. The point about this is that both components are necessary to the outcome. Unstructured thinking very rarely leads to great creativity. The contention is that in childhood and education the same is true. Children need structure because it gives them some boundaries to bounce against. On the other hand, they need the freedom to get to those boundaries, occasionally to go over them and be able to return with impunity and some valuable experience.

Managing this requires a delicate touch from parents. They need to have a sense of proportion, of what really matters and what can be left aside, then using this as a framework to provide a structure, which also has room for manoeuvre. There need to be points of principle, which are unshakeable and points of view, which are flexible. Contrary to what a vocal minority have argued, children enjoy a greater sense of security if they have a greater sense of place. That is to say, a fuller understanding of 'where they stand', rather than being left stranded in no man's land.

In order to present a coherent culture, brand positioning, company ethic or any other distinctive and defining characteristics that will produce competitive advantage, it is obvious that there will have to be structure, rules, guidelines and lines of authority. But by now we know that if this adds up to a repressive regime, redolent of the educational mores of an earlier century it is, if not doomed to failure, certain to be less than effective.

Thus the task of management, the leaders who have to define the code of manners for the company and their brand, is to decide what really matters, and to be really tough about those things. Equally they need to be clear about what doesn't really matter and where large degrees of freedom should be allowed or indeed actively encouraged. People need to know where their boundaries are and also what the vision is to create a sense of inclusion and security.

As with parenthood, corporate management benefits enormously from consistency. One of the great benefits of having some clearly defined boundaries is that it enables individuals to discover and define themselves.

The problem is that many of those boundaries are constantly shifting! Much of the cause of friction within families is that children perceive their parents to have differing standards, varying tolerance levels, or even plain and simple disagreements, all of which add up to a lack of consistency in the growing-up environment. This lack of consistency can lead to the breakdown of the child's perception of parents as the secure base for them, as the child grows to realise that the parent is changeable, not all-knowing or infallible and loses confidence in them accordingly.

The same thing happens within companies; conflicting signals transmitted from rival factions within an organisation very quickly reduce it to impotence, if not outright internecine warfare. Quite rightly, very few corporations have joint managing directors and increasingly there is a focus on a singular leader, or Chief Executive. This gives clarity of direction and a sense of authorship to the company culture and *modus operandi*, which is hard to achieve by a duopoly or collective.

The skill in the new style of leadership, which perhaps embodies the mediaeval notion of the 'iron hand in the velvet glove', is to strike a consistent balance between passionate intolerance of anything that threatens the core values of the company, and a welcoming enthusiasm for freedom of innovation which will lead to their next iteration. This creates a corporate culture which can truly be described as 'self-confident' and enables everyone to maximise themselves and their contribution to the enterprise within the parameters set by the leadership.

Truly dynamic organisations have the ability to challenge themselves constantly from a position of their own strength, to ask the awkward questions of themselves before the market does, and to engage their employees in a dialogue which can oscillate from the 'parent to child' to the 'adult to adult' mode with fluency and sensitivity. Indeed, to be truly successful, management needs to work with all Freud's three ego states. In employees there is the need for the 'natural child', with playful discovery aiding innovation and leading to discovery; 'adult', to enable discussion, the ability to weigh the pros and cons of a given situation and make rational decisions on the facts and the 'parental' role to guide all of the others in the right direction.

The lesson to be learned is that people need to feel an overwhelming sense of belonging and love, but in a context where they have a clear sense of self and place. They need boundaries that flex and respond to their push, and in the parental and environmental 'push back', they learn more about themselves and the outside world.

So too, with the people in companies. Through every element of their manner, CEOs and top managers must show they love their employees, and their customers. In wrapping them in this security blanket they will thrive, but they must also love them enough to be tough on occasion. Doing this will create a culture which will enable people to be self-confident in their individual behaviours to the benefit of themselves, their colleagues and their customers.

Managers should try to understand the ingrained attitudes of their employees (often related to life stage), and set clear boundaries – decide what matters and be tough. This should be combined with a respect for each person as an individual and the continuous development of trust. Top management need to ensure the same boundaries and guidelines are set for everyone so that people do not receive conflicting signals from different political empires within the organisation.

11

Making the Most of Habits

One of the most difficult challenges facing CEOs is the management of change and this means changing habits. Routinised or habitual behaviour can be very useful; customers continue to repeat purchase when on an objective assessment they should have long since defected to other brands. Employees stay loyal when they could be earning more elsewhere. Familiarity amongst top executives can create great teamwork. However, habits can also be very dangerous. Senior management can get into a too comfortable consensus about how the business should be run. Employees become hidebound in their working practices and inflexible in response to new technologies. These bad habits can effectively insulate the company from the changing market reality around them. When they wake up to the new situation it's often too late to rectify.

We are creatures of habit. After the coffee break in a seminar, we return to exactly the same seat we sat in before. We go on holiday and establish our 'territory' by the pool, and on the beach. We then spend a fortnight guarding it against all comers. Commuters know exactly where to stand on the platform in order to get onto their train, their bus or the underground at the most convenient point from which to alight at their destination. We know the best route by car from home to the shops or to the office. Even walking in the park we have preferred circuits and pathways.

Two things seem to be at work here. Firstly, it is simply easier and more convenient to follow a tried and tested approach to virtually everything we do in life. Secondly, it takes more effort to do things differently, to explore a new route, to stand at a different part of the platform, or even to walk down an unaccustomed supermarket aisle. It takes a conscious effort to break a habit; security advisers and bodyguards have to prevail upon their charges to vary their routine in order to avoid kidnap or assassination. As a result of the leaked revelation that Gerry Adams's car had been bugged during the Northern Ireland peace talks, we now know that he changed his vehicle and his route to meetings at least once a day.

Even burglars appear to be creatures of habit! A recent report by Dr Mandy Shore, a criminologist at the University of Huddersfield, concluded that once a house had been broken into, there was a greater chance of burglars returning because they were familiar with the property and it seems to increase the probability of subsequent burglaries significantly. Thirty-seven per cent of the people experiencing one crime against their house went on to experience another and of those, 43% went on to experience yet another.

It is the same with management of corporations; it is so much less stressful to continue in the old ways, rather than to adapt to the new requirements of changing marketplaces. The same is true with customers' relationships with brands; so many frequent purchases are highly routinised, with the same limited roster of brands being chosen over a period of many years. New brands, offering product or service innovation, have to battle to achieve trial and repeat purchase. Once they succeed, they can look forward to a sustained period of loyalty, especially if the brand positioning, communications and behaviour are consistent and reinforcing of the habit.

Hence there is a paradox: on the one hand a powerful human desire for routine and a strong tendency to conservatism, on the other hand an attraction to new brands which offer interesting new features, often based on new technologies or reflecting important underlying social changes. This is why strong branding is so essential to defeating the product lifecycle of launch, maturity and decay; the power of a brand gives a product or service the 'benefit of the doubt' in the customer's mind and buys the manufacturer time to innovate using new ingredients, processes and techniques.

We are also creatures of habit in respect of our thoughts and beliefs. The learning process, in brain chemistry terms, seems to be one of establishing pathways that constitute 'trains of thought'. The more we think upon similar lines and use the same set of neural connections, the easier and quicker it is for a thought wave to travel. The brain is like the rest of the body – anything for an easy life!

Our speech patterns are also repetitive; we use a relatively limited vocabulary and the modulations of our voices fall within such a specific range, that voice recognition software is rapidly becoming a practical reality in everyday usage. Crucial to the accuracy of its usage is the enrolment process, in which the speaker has to read many passages of text in order for the machine to 'learn' the voice and establish a speech profile which can be recognised consistently and turned accurately into the written word. There is evidence that children 'enrol' in the language in a similar way through listening to and verbally interacting with their parents, school and environment. We all know how quickly a young child picks up 'bad words' from television, the playground and the careless adult!

It is obviously the case that industries, professions, close groups of friends and teams drawn together for a particular project very often develop a common set of nicknames, jargon, buzz-words and the other shared verbal property which are a key part of the creation of a peer group. Indeed in the book *The Wisdom of Teams* by Jon R. Katzenbach and Douglas K. Smith, the authors show that the power of the team is in many ways a function of the 'private language' that the group develops. To the outsider, the 'in jokes' hardly seem funny at all, not to say irritating because of their exclusive nature, but this is the very strength that insiders gain – a sense of belonging, of 'us' against 'them'.

In this context, the repetition of key words and phrases, often accompanied by particular gestures or facial expressions, acts as a powerful reinforcement to the group's self-esteem and its sense of being special. Acquiring these group 'habits' can often create the habit of success, but also the seeds of failure if left to stagnate and eventually ossify. From the corporate point of view, creating these habits should be a priority. A company with a common language, which is as particular as possible to their culture and which captures the essence of the brand, is a very powerful tool in building a set of behaviours which can truly deliver the product or service offer to the customer.

There is another sense in which people are creatures of habit. This is in terms of the 'story' they spend their lives creating for themselves. The 'when I' syndrome is typical of this, for example, the boy-made-good always referring to his past and regaling his audience with tales of 'when I lived with rotting walls and rats the size of rabbits' and anecdotes about the privation and squalor of his youth to show how far he has come and what he has achieved. This tendency affects all levels in society; the Ivy Leaguer who always manages to mention Harvard or Yale at some point during the evening, or the fan who never fails to name-drop famous connections. The vast majority of people arrive at their story relatively early in life – most by their early 20s. This is a personal story which has been originated, rehearsed, modified, read, drafted, and finalised during the maturing years of teenagerdom and young adulthood.

The adoption of particular fashions and styles may be transitory as a teenager, but once into the early 20s or 30s the main features of most people's physical presentation is pretty well set. Friends and associates would be deeply shocked if a woman, known to be a regular wearer of smart business suits and dresses at the office, suddenly appeared wearing jeans and a T-shirt. A man with a conventional haircut, who arrived one day with his head shaved, would be disconcerting to his colleagues, and probably taken to be ill. Very often these personal appearance characteristics are an integral part of the 'story' – the man with his luxuriant moustaches, the woman with her talon-like fingernails and the teenager with body tattoos and piercings. The same thing happens with brands and companies; customers will continue using the same one until it does something untoward, causing them to rethink their usage, as Coke and Persil found to their cost when they attempted to introduce new formulations in substitution for their 'originals'.

Individuals quite often move politically from the radical or left-wing in youth steadily towards the moderate or even right wing with age, but it seems relatively rare for people's views or tastes in many other areas to change significantly over a lifetime and certainly beyond their formative years. The lover of classical music at 25 is still likely to be one at 65. When people 'go off the rails', the very metaphor we use to describe this reminds us of what a single-minded track most pursue in life; we speak of a mid-life crisis or even a mental breakdown. We really do like regularity in the world that surrounds us, and in the behaviour of our family, friends and business associates such that we remark upon it when someone behaves 'out of character'.

The most important thing about a personal story is that the person is good at telling it, and that it gets a relatively predictable and satisfactory reaction from listeners. The fact that this makes for repetition is a benefit. The protagonist storyteller already knows the stock reactions to their tale and is unlikely to receive any surprisingly different reactions or indeed challenging or worrying lines of questioning. The storyteller literally knows all the answers and has defined the expectations of the listener. There is great security in this.

This concern with the development of the personal story is very deep in the human make-up. It relates directly to the enormously high degree of preoccupation with self, which is such a fundamental part of the social and physical survival process. Individuals can be seen to be constantly 'broadcasting' to those around them in a continuing effort to maintain their interest and attractiveness.

Again, people are creatures of habit; it is so much easier to talk about oneself than to make the greater effort to enquire about others. The 'good listener' is so prized in social circles because they are so rare. Great salespeople are almost always professional listeners – they all too easily elicit the prospective customer's needs and concerns, answering the former and allaying the latter. But how do companies convert their employees from 'broadcasters' of their 'story' to become 'listeners' to customers? Furthermore, if people spend their lives repeating their own story to anyone who will listen, how does a corporation or brand get its story to be told by its employees, with the same attention to detail and intensity of transmission? Clearly the goal must be to make the company story as compatible with and as integral to their personal story as possible. Further, the company's story must be as enhancing to as great a proportion of the personal narrative as possible. If this is not the case then there will inevitably be continuing tension between the goals and objectives of the company and individual.

Perhaps at the very heart of this habitual, self-interested behaviour is the desire for security and specifically self-confidence. It's the handsome self-confident boy who always gets the prettiest and most out-going girl in the movies (though the anti-hero has a confidence all his own and the Pygmalion story never fails to appeal). If unfamiliarity, surprises, and breaks in routine are all threatening because they undermine self-confidence, then companies wanting to create the most productive working environment must do everything in their power to avoid these shocks to their personnel.

It is hard to imagine a company which has no clear sense of direction, no defined set of values, and no consistent basis for its behaviour, being a self-confident one. By the same token, it is hard to imagine the employees of that company to be in themselves self-confident. It is a characteristic of self-confident people that unless they fall prey to arrogance, their relative lack of need for constant reassurance from others frees them to give that reassurance to others. Companies need to create an organisation in which employees are sufficiently confident in themselves that they can focus much more single-mindedly on their customer.

To a surprising degree we really don't like surprises! Isn't it extraordinary that Hollywood promotes its movies to us by showing us all the best bits in a trailer? Far from spoiling the story, familiarising us with it actually increases our sense of anticipation and our keenness to see it again in full.

One of the key factors that leads to a film becoming a true blockbuster is that it generates repeat visits amongst its audience. According to CAVIAR, the cinema research survey, *Titanic*, one of the biggest-grossing films in history, had a repeat visit of an astonishing 16%. From childhood we love the repetition of our favourite stories.

Many recipients of a surprise birthday or anniversary party would actually have enjoyed the occasion much more if they had had the chance to look forward to it and savour the event in advance. Whilst the time and effort that goes into producing such an event is in itself a great compliment to the recipient, actually it is the surprise element that often makes them very uncomfortable. This can prevent them enjoying the party as much as they might have done; names can't be put to faces; their dress code may not be quite right; unanticipated guests from their distant past may present challenges to their 'story'.

Companies and brands should therefore build on the innate desire for continuity and repetition in their employees. They should also do the same with their customers. Any executive decision, which on inspection looks likely to break an important habit, should be very carefully evaluated before it is taken. But how does this square with the need for change in a rapidly evolving business environment? Little and often is the mantra. Companies need to have their antennae quivering in the customer breeze, their fingers constantly touching their pulse. 'Relaunch', 'reposition', and 'restructure' are very often signs of failure, and evidence of being out of touch. Continuous evolution and constant nudging at the corporate tiller are essential to the seamless transition that preserves the sense of familiarity whilst achieving a new position, allowing people to 'keep the faith'.

Corporate identity specialists are often roundly criticised for spending huge sums of money researching a company and its markets with a view to developing an updated logo, which when it is unveiled has an uncanny similarity to the one that preceded it. The work by Addison for BP in the era before the 'flower' logo was a classic example. The new BP letters and colours were only marginally different from their predecessors to the layman's eye. However, the important lesson to be learned from the corporate identity specialist is that these very subtle evolutions of a logo style are an essential part of the process of maintaining the familiarity which consumers crave. They are also the mechanism for pushing it forward in the little details of typography and colour to ensure that it maintains a contemporary feel. Looking back over the history of the BP logo illustrates this gradual process (Figure 25).

The furore which greeted the painting of the British Airways tailfins with a whole variety of designs, often of foreign cultural or ethnic origin, was as much a result of the break with a tradition as it was of nationalist feeling injured by the removal of the Union Jack imagery. The recent

Figure 25 *BP logos.*

volte-face, some years after the initial decision was taken to change, and at enormous expense, is indicative of the continuing strength of feeling on this subject. The irony is that, had BA gradually introduced motifs from around the world, whilst maintaining traditional elements from the British flag, it is quite likely that by now everyone would have become used to the idea. It was the trumpeting of the redesign that caused most of the problem.

One of the most powerful manifestations of the human desire for continuity is the phenomenon of the soap opera, so-called because detergent manufacturers such as Procter & Gamble sponsored the original versions. The first soap opera was a radio programme called 'Ma Perkins' in 1933, created by a husband and wife advertising agency, Frank and Anne Hummert, and sponsored by Oxydol, a washing detergent. With the success of the show in selling Oxydol, P&G started to sponsor other shows. Then in 1937 Irna Philips, the queen of the soap opera, developed 'Guiding Light', which was later transferred to TV, and still runs on CBS to this day, the longest-running drama show in the world!

Soap operas are amongst the most popular and enduring of programmes, both on television and on radio. In the UK, 'Coronation Street', which started in December 1960 and its newer competitor 'EastEnders' launched on 19 April 1985, are required viewing for millions of people three or four times a week. On BBC Radio 4 'The Archers' has been running for 49 years and is the longest-running soap opera in the UK. In a survey by the NOP, carried out on behalf of *Marketing Week* on 2 July 1998, it was found that 72% of people in England watched a soap opera, and of these, 82% try to watch every episode.

It's clear that the actors and actresses who work in the soap operas effectively have dual identity, and their audience feels this too. It's uncanny how often the storylines, dramas and crises played out in the soaps become interwoven with the 'real' lives of both actors and viewers. Conversation at the coffee machine is fuelled by the latest developments in a favourite soap and becomes part of the social currency amongst groups of friends, or in an organisation.

A new sort of programme in a similar vein has emerged in recent years with the advent of the 'docusoap'. These are 'fly-on-the-wall' documentaries about real people, living their lives through a camera with 'Big Brother' in the summer of 2000 being the logical extreme. It is the realism of these programmes that draws in the viewers with their gritty reality and the Schadenfreude as the 'stars' expose their most embarrassing inner fears, foibles and character weaknesses in front of audiences of millions. To paraphrase Andy Warhol, they start with dreams of their fifteen minutes of fame, but repeatedly it's infamy they achieve.

There are some companies who have a storyline of their own every bit as powerful as that of a soap opera. Virgin and its new competitor in the David and Goliath stakes easyJet, are led by publicity-seeking entrepreneurs who write the script for the company on a daily basis. How powerful that is for the employees of those companies; their lives are intrinsically dramatic and exciting because of where they work, and this reinforces their self-confidence enormously. But not every company is led by a combination of visionary leader and astute businessperson. In the absence of that charismatic quality at the top, corporations need to create all the elements of their own soap opera, involving common language, common themes, continuity of purpose and astute communications to create a world in which the 'story' for the company and the individual are closely intertwined. This will then create a greater sense of inclusion and meaning for employees, making them motivated to truly engage and find out what's happening, to take greater responsibility for their work, to feel part *of* the company, and not just a part *in* the company.

Habits are the reason people ask: 'Why change?'. By providing a compelling, higher-order vision (or dream), and driving this through to reality by a series of single driving issue programmes, management can answer the question in three ways: firstly, in terms of the benefit to the customer; secondly, in terms of the improvements to working life in the company and thirdly, in terms of the financial benefits that flow through to shareholder value from the improved customer experience. This enables everyone to tackle the emotional, political and spiritual – as well as the traditionally rational – case for change. It then falls to the CEO and the management team to develop the sensitive hand on the tiller and create a culture with in-built forward momentum and the ability to evolve its habits over time and so stay on the crest of the business wave. Key to this is a corporate 'narrative drive' or storyline that includes everyone in the unfolding drama, and includes them in it.

12

Reducing Stress in the Organisation

Control is a paradox for the CEO. On the one hand it is in the nature of leaders to control the organisations they head, and, as we have seen, people are creatures of habit who thrive on a controlling environment, which defines the boundaries and parameters for their behaviour. On the other hand, if the working or social context is too controlling it becomes counterproductive as people lose their sense of individuality and self-determination, which can lead to stress and dysfunctional behaviour. Understanding the dynamics of control for the individual is key to creating an environment which can both constrain and liberate.

Human development can be characterised as the exertion of control over the self and the environment. There are few places in the world which do not bear the trace of human interference and few species which have not been killed, herded or cultivated. We like to be in charge, to have authority, to be self-determining. Although we resent and sometimes fear them, we acknowledge the driving energy of the 'control freaks', who so often lead the fast-growing entrepreneurial organisation.

The single-minded conviction of leaders like this, and the success they often bring, is very compelling and draws those with a weaker sense of direction and lack of such complete self-confidence towards them, like iron filings to a magnet. We find it easier to conform to what they believe because this is easier than developing our own direction and train of thought. We are reluctant as human beings to stray from the easiest route, which in this case is to follow the entrepreneur for whom we work.

Another aspect of our development is establishing control over our emotions. This is a self-protective measure. In England we don't like other people to see how we are feeling too easily because this obvious display makes us vulnerable to an attack by others. By contrast, in America people tend to be very overt in showing people how they are feeling, as is demonstrated by the openness in the use of therapy, and this opposite strategy effectively neutralises any criticism of it. Because we, in England, are very sensitive to this issue, we recognise in others the ability to mask or control their emotions under situations in which we ourselves would be more likely to show them.

The Victorian era generated the concept of sang-froid, and the Empire-building 'stiff upper lip' became the trademark of the Englishman abroad. Indeed, it is only relatively recently that this deep-seated characteristic has become displaced by a more open and emotional response to others and to events around us. The huge emotional outpouring at the time of the death of Diana Princess of Wales probably marked the turning point and since then there has been a rapidly accelerating process whereby it's no longer deemed unmanly to cry nor unwomanly to fight. The increased role of women in society and the widespread feminisation of the workplace may also explain this shift in attitude. Women are increasingly portrayed in the media taking the more aggressive roles and matching the men at all levels, whilst men are often depicted as passive, more emotional characters.

One aspect of the process of maturing from childhood into adulthood entails the establishment of control over one's own actions, and this means wresting control from others, such as parents, older siblings, relatives and teachers. Having established that position of strength, we are then grudging in our relinquishing of it. For example, we think long and hard before getting into long-term relationships with a partner; it takes time to build true intimacy and a situation in which we can abandon all self-control.

However, we also like the sensation of being out of control, as long as we're in charge of doing so. We deliberately abandon our inhibitions and innate need for security and self-possession through pleasurable intoxication, taking a white-knuckle ride at a theme park or seeing the latest horror movie. These experiences have a cathartic effect as we expose ourselves to overwhelming sensations beyond our control. The ultimate expression of this is when we fall head-over-heels in love; nature's trick is that we embark thinking we're in control, and then lose it to the benefit of the species!

Indeed, it could be argued that the institution of marriage evolved as a controlling social mechanism, designed to create an acceptable framework for human relationships. Within the protection of the marriage contract, people can evolve through the whole spectrum of emotions, ranging from initial infatuation, through genuine love and on to a mature and enduring relationship, for the protection of each other and the family. All the evidence suggests that this is in steep decline. The UK statistics are striking; the percentage of people getting married has fallen by 20% from 1986 to 1996 and this trend has continued into 1997. In this time the average age of marriage has increased from 26.3 to 29.3 and divorce had also risen. Over 45% of all children born in the UK are now born to single mothers. It would seem that the majority of people no longer want to live in the relatively controlling status of a marriage contract.

The same could be said to be true of relationships with employers. It used to be the case that 'jobs were for life', but nowadays we are in a situation where careers are perceived not in terms of longevity with a particular company, but more in terms of a series of short job hops from one to another. We seem to have lost the ability, or the inclination, to entrust our working lifetime into the hands of a single employer. Perhaps we should not be surprised at this. So many companies have restructured, reorganised, down-sized and de-layered that the concept of job security is meaningless for many people. *The Times* reports that the time spent by people in top jobs is very short, and is getting shorter. The CEOs of major companies are shown to have been in each company a shorter and shorter amount of time, some being in companies only for a few years before moving on.

Sometimes it's useful to look at the very extremes of a situation in order to understand what's really going on. For example, when considering how to improve a consumer brand, it's often more informative to ask its harshest critics why they dislike it so much, than to ask its most loyal users why they are such fans. This doesn't mean to say that a simplistic conclusion should be drawn and a decision taken simply to adjust the product or service to suit the disenchanted. It is more likely that the aspects that have been identified as polarising pro and con should be further enhanced and emphasised.

So, by extension, if life itself and the full enjoyment of it is one of the most fundamentally desirable things that each and every one of us has the opportunity and perhaps a right to achieve, then the loss of life is surely one of the greatest penalties. If we could even begin to understand the highly complex and particular circumstances under which an individual might voluntarily, albeit under the most enormous pressure, end their own life, then this might give us an insight into how to achieve the opposite effect – namely a full and enjoyable one.

In Japan, stress at work has fuelled the suicide rate to an alarming degree. The number of Japanese who committed suicide in 1999 may exceed 30,000 for the second year running. In 1991 16.1 out of 100,000 people committed suicide; by 1998 this number had risen to 25.4. Most commentators attribute this situation to the recession-induced ending of the powerful tradition of lifetime employment. The social stigma about unemployment has simply been unbearable for too many people, whose whole concept of their working life has been undermined so alarmingly quickly.

According to research by the Samaritans, the leading UK charity concerned with the issue, in the early 1990s it was estimated that there were 100,000 cases of attempted suicide per annum referred to hospital in the UK. This indicated that the UK has one of the highest rates of attempted suicide in Europe. Their research reveals that the parental relationship is a very important factor and that in general, adolescents who attempt suicide often grow up in families with more turmoil than other groups of adolescents. More of them come from broken homes (due to death or divorce), or homes where there is parental unemployment, mental illness, or addiction. Problems with employment (including unemployment) and studies are also very important and appear to affect young men more. In the case of attempted suicide, alcohol and drug abuse are problems, which are less frequently reported than the others, but significantly more often reported by young men than young women.

It would be facile to attempt a full explanation here of the very complex causes of suicide, but it would seem reasonable to suggest that there is a common strand which unites many of the factors identified by the Samaritans' research, the data from Japan and other studies. This is the lack of a stable or controlled familial, social or working environment. By extension, is it too far-fetched to suggest that a working environment, which is 'uncontrolled', is more likely to lead to an unhappy workforce, an increased incidence of stress-related illnesses, and ultimately the potential for suicide?

It is too early to say whether or not the trend against marriage and towards single parenthood will be a success in societal terms, but the Samaritans' research does not augur well. It will certainly be very interesting to see the long-term effects of the dismantling, in a matter of only two or three decades, of the social contract of marriage which had evolved successfully through over two millennia of social testing.

As a direct psychological counterpoint to the desire for self-control, we very much resent being under the control of others, especially involuntarily. One of society's main sanctions against those who offend against it is the removal of freedom through imprisonment. Because we fear such a sanction ourselves we naturally assume that it will act as a deterrent to others. Interestingly, though this may bring some protection from future harm and a sense of vengeance to the wronged, there seems little evidence of its effect as a deterrent to the hard-core criminal, or as a remedial therapy, much to the irritation of the 'hang 'em and flog 'em' brigade.

The Howard League for Penal Reform has published statistics showing the reconviction rate within two years for people discharged in 1994 from custody was 56% and for community service was 54%. It showed that there was a greater chance of reconviction in young males, 75%, and it was proportional to the number of prior convictions. For more than 11 prior convictions the reconviction rate was 78%. The type of offence also showed variance in the reconviction rate, with those committing burglary, theft and handling of stolen property more likely to re-offend, than those committing sexual offences, fraud and forgery and drug offences. This is of great concern as the prison population was at an all-time high in 1998 of 66,516, of which one in six were young people and 21% committing theft and handling. Here we see the irresistible force coming up against the immovable object with the issue of control by others and the preservation of self-control at the heart of it. Any culture based on involuntary control seems doomed to failure if it has any higher aspirations than mere containment.

The pace and pressure of modern life seems to have a strong tendency to undermine the individual sense of being in control. Crowded pavements, packed public transport and traffic jams are all a function of more people having more disposable income to go to more places more of the time. However, time is the one thing that we have less and less of. A significant proportion of people in Westernised economies can be described as 'money rich and time poor'.

Is it any wonder that we seem to be spawning new types of 'rage' everywhere we look? We have road rage, air rage, trolley rage, computer rage, portable stereo rage and ski-queue rage. These social explosions, born out of stress and frustration, while statistically small, make big headlines, and touch such a chord with their readership that newspapers are probably right in thinking that they represent the tip of a very large iceberg.

The Federal Aviation Authority reported that there were 178 instances of air rage in 1999, which is a tiny proportion of total passenger movements, but incidents on aeroplanes do seem to attract much of the attention. No doubt this is to do with the fact that air travel is intrinsically worrying to many people, and this seems to affect celebrities perhaps even more than ordinary people. The list of those who have been involved in air rage incidents, include numerous idols such as Oasis, Anna Kournikova, and Prince Naseem (who, ironically, was one of the stars featured in the latest BA advertising).

Passengers (and celebrities who are used to being totally in control) literally put their lives in the hands of the pilot and the airline. Very often business travellers are *en route* to an important meeting, which could make or break their bonus prospects, if not their career. The free availability of alcohol is very often a root cause of the problem. It is much more active in the onboard environment and the fact that a passenger might already be jet lagged and even hypoxic through lack of oxygen, leads to much quicker intoxication than usual.

If an individual is already feeling somewhat nervous about air travel *per se*, has had a stressful journey to the airport, is on a business mission with high stakes attached, hasn't eaten properly and then imbibes quantities of alcohol, they can easily become an air rage incident waiting to happen. A common thread in many of these cases is that the offender saw himself or herself as originally offended against by not being treated as an individual, but as just a passenger number. This lack of recognition under stress seems to be at the heart of the problem.

Again it is instructive to look at extreme cases such as the 'rage' phenomenon because they contain lessons for more normal situations. As the stressful globalisation of corporations gains increasing momentum, and as procedures and processes become unified, the potential for individual self-expression within an organisation becomes repressed. Is the company not analogous to the airline carrying passengers to a destination that they all desire, but on a journey and under conditions, which many feel are extremely stressful?

To pursue the analogy, many airlines are now taking much greater pains to screen passengers before they get on board. Should companies not take more trouble to check employees before they are taken on? Virgin Airways believe that a low-key approach is the best way of handling problem passengers and they have a policy of recruiting people who are good with people. Their strategy is to encourage a disruptive passenger to talk about whatever the problem is in an attempt to defuse the situation. BA takes a tougher line and in 1998 introduced a 'yellow card' scheme under which a passenger is formally instructed to desist from his or her bad behaviour.

Historically, corporations have been managed on very 'controlling' lines, with a highly centralised and pyramidal structure. Employees, particularly the mass of them involved in manufacturing or other repetitive tasks have been very much at the behest of remote decision takers and have had little or no control over their daily working lives. Increasingly, modern organisations are moving away from these 'command and control' management styles towards a more collaborative, egalitarian, empowered employee approach, or at least they say they are. But one wonders to what degree the 'dress down Friday', or the 'call me Bob' informality is merely paying lip service to the concept and that beneath the pleasantries lies the same old culture of constraint imposed by fear.

The crux of the matter is this: people have a fundamental need to exercise self-control over themselves and their environment, both social and physical. Companies, which try to remove this basic human need, are unlikely to win hearts and minds. On the other hand, humans need the security of a structured framework within which they can feel secure; a controlled context of someone else's making to which they voluntarily sign up. The challenge for the corporation is to strike the balance within which everyone can feel self-confident but not imposed upon nor left adrift.

It seems clear that we can achieve human individuality only if the following are present: recognition, self-expression and control. It follows that if an employee feels the lack of these then they will want to move on to a new and fresh environment with greater potential. Often high staff turnover cannot be attributed to the actual organisation, its physical setting, its location or personal remuneration, but instead to the lack of sufficient resources for self-development.

If employees cannot express themselves, are not recognised for their contribution and are not given control within their working life they simply blend into the rest of the organisation and just become an anonymous part of a complex machine. The result is the perception, and perhaps the reality, that their efforts are neither important nor noticed and that this lack of individuality is synonymous with little or no accountability. The consequences are that employees grow frustrated and hence strive for a different environment that can provide tasks which are meaningful and which provide a real purpose. The trick therefore for the modern-day employer, is to detect and correct such a feeling of frustration before it escalates into stress. Furthermore, it is crucial employees feel that their superiors are approachable, have the power to change their fate and genuinely care about each and every one of them as an individual.

The concepts of job enrichment and job rotation are not new phenomena yet they seem to be at the core of creating an environment that will allow employees to have greater control over their direction. There is a deep human need to be recognised for what we do and to express ourselves through the type of work that is chosen.

Control is complex and organisations have to embrace it in a way which provides the necessary psychological support for management and employees, whilst giving them the feeling that they are actually in the driving seat of their own career destiny. If the corporate culture has a clear set of values and a vision against which personal endeavour, behaviour and achievement can be assessed, then everyone involved will feel ownership of the collective mission; it will own them but they also own it. The security of embracing and being embraced by the vision is liberating.

Personal freedom of manoeuvre and the creative self-expressive act of interpreting it in daily working life give a greater sense of self-control, and simultaneously reinforce the controlling strength of the culture. The key to reducing stress lies in building self-confidence through clear boundaries, encouragement, nurturing trust and developing the potential of each individual. The notion of 'jobs for life' is rather dis-empowering, in a child-parent way and it should no longer exist. When people are continually developing and learning, the customer and employer benefit. They also have correspondingly more career options.

Section Two
Encounters

The second section concerns how we interact with one another and to illustrate it we have chosen four topics: defending the brand, minimising corporate distance, managing the irrational and how trust fits in.

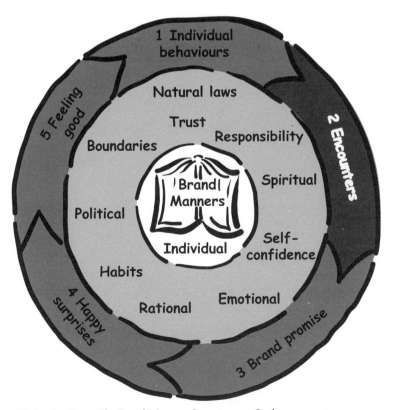

Figure 26 *Section Two: The Brand Manners Improvement Cycle – encounters.*

13

Being Ready to Defend the Brand

Corporate cultures and the brands they support are valuable assets, which need careful nurturing and investment if they are to survive and thrive in fiercely competitive and fast-moving markets. For the majority of management, employees, customers and other stakeholders this can be done in a spirit of positive co-operation and honest endeavour.

However, there is a potential enemy, both within and without the corporation, which does not respect conventional codes of behaviour. CEOs should not be lulled into a Barings-like false sense of security. They must retain an alertness, almost paranoid in its intensity, to the potential downside and be ready to treat threats to the culture with 'zero tolerance'.

Whilst it is clear that for the majority of people a combination of wide degrees of freedom and gentle constraint within defined and acceptable parameters is the ideal, there is a significant amount of evidence to support a contrary view to be applied when taking account of a certain segment of the population.

There is little doubt that there is a very substantial criminal underclass operating in most societies and it would be naive to believe that this group, which has developed its own very strong value system in opposition to 'straight' society, is susceptible to the same moral, ethical and social codes. Statistically, any cohort of employees will contain some people of this sort, and thus senior management needs to come to terms with this reality and be prepared to defend their culture, and their other employees, against them.

Many years of experience have led most people to believe, contrary to what the Howard League for Penal Reform would say, that there is a hard-core group whose world view means that they only understand, and react to, rule by force and fear of reprisal. However, ever since the late 1960s when the liberal *laissez-faire* movement really came to the fore and has its apotheosis in the current vogue for political correctness, it has been unfashionable, certainly amongst the 'talking classes' to countenance the idea of countering force with force.

The relevance of this for CEOs of major corporations is that there will always be some people and some issues within the organisation that will need to be dealt with strictly and even forcibly in order to preserve the integrity of their culture and the brand. They need to have the strength of purpose, the measured perspective and the evidence in support to do this convincingly. Prevention is better than cure and in future, screening of potential employees will become more exacting albeit within the constraints of the legislation which increasingly errs on the side of the individual against the corporation. Honest staff will not object to this and indeed will welcome the protection and security it will afford them and the brand they work for.

Indeed 'Big Brother' is already watching us. On an average day in London, an individual is filmed by more than 300 cameras from 30 different CCTV networks; in Soho alone there are 126 visible, and over 85% of councils have CCTV as part of their crime-prevention strategy. There are reports that the introduction of CCTV cameras has reduced the incidence of crime in the centre of Stirling, Scotland by 75%, at Gatwick Airport Car Parks by 70% and at Chesterfield Railway Station by a staggering 96%. The impact of CCTV in solving the tragic case of James Bulger, the young infant beaten to death by two young children, was clear to see. But for the role of the video in identifying the culprits the case might still be under investigation.

The interesting question is what ordinary citizens feel about this extraordinary level of surveillance. To discover the answer, research was conducted on behalf of the authors by Access, BMRB's telephone omnibus in September 1999 amongst a sample of 1,014 adults. This was very revealing in respect of what ordinary members of the UK public found acceptable, or not, regarding the sensitive issue of data protection and personal surveillance.

The first question put in the Access survey was simply: 'How much do you approve or disapprove of closed circuit TV surveillance in shopping centres?' The approval rate was overwhelming at 91%. It seems highly likely that people understand that criminals don't like being seen, are deterred by the fact that they are being filmed and that such evidence may be used later against them in the event of them committing a crime.

Cartoon 2 *'Cat and mouse'*.

In order to explore this a little further the second question was: 'Do you agree or disagree that increased surveillance, use of identity cards and other forms of personal data would help reduce Social Security fraud, street crime and other illegal activities?' Again, the level of agreement at 84% is striking. Law-abiding citizens clearly see the benefits of this surveillance to honest people, and in this context 'Big Brother' actually watches over you in a protective way.

But the respondents were not blindly in favour of giving away their secrets, for when asked a supplementary question namely: 'How much do you approve or disapprove of the amount of your personal information which is held by Government, credit-scoring agencies and other commercial organisations?' the level of approval was significantly lower at 28%, with 56% disapproving. Clearly, people suspect the motives of the many organisations that are traditionally involved in this area and quite rightly perceive that the benefits of data gathering are primarily for third parties, and not for the owners of the data themselves.

In order to confirm this, a final and much tougher question was asked: 'If an organisation that you trusted were to issue a national identity card containing all your personal data such as Passport, Social Security, National Health and National Insurance number in an attempt to reduce crime ...

would you approve or disapprove of this scheme?' Put in this way 71% of the sample gave their approval. The implications are clear: the trustworthiness of the sponsor and the benefits of such an identity scheme are absolutely crucial.

More and more companies nowadays have to implement increased levels of security to protect both their physical premises and their information-technology systems. We are on the edge of the era of the widespread use of biometrics in order to ascertain the correct identity of employees and customers alike. Very soon mobile telephones or personal digital assistants will have a combination of pin number, voice recognition and perhaps fingerprint readers designed to ensure absolute security, especially in financial transactions carried out by mobile or m-commerce. Many offices and retail premises will be using iris scanning and signature recognition systems to do the same in person.

This is very necessary as a set of precautions because the incidence of e-crime is already widespread. James Finn of Unisys forecasts that financial losses from computer crime will reach $10 billion by 2001. Sixty per cent of the Fortune 1,000 have already experienced security breaches and 51% of them reported financial losses.

In the rush to join the e-commerce world companies are forgetting that opening up an electronic gateway to markets creates a two-way street, along which criminals as well as honest people may travel. In these fraudulent attacks, 57% use the Internet as the way in. In the USA, whilst only 2% of all credit card transactions are on-line, over 90% of the credit card fraud is. Perhaps of even greater concern is the profile of the hacker. The evidence suggests that they resemble the perfect employee: young, aged between 19 and 30 years old, with no criminal record, and likely to be employed in data processing or accounting. The hacker is bright, creative, energetic, adventurous, highly motivated, outwardly self-confident and willing to accept a challenge. Someone who fulfilled this description almost precisely caused the catastrophic effect of the 'I love you' virus!

The potential problem that this increased level of security and surveillance could cause, unless handled sensitively, is that the large majority of the honest people in an organisation, or visitors to it, will be receiving daily doses of potentially negative signals from their employer. Swipe cards on entry, registration in a visitors' book, identity badges and password protocols on their PC, to give just a few examples.

As evidenced by the respondents to the Access survey, employees will want to be reassured about the motives of the employer. They in turn will have to have established a trust relationship with them in order to ensure their full co-operation in enrolling in security systems, thus marginalising the criminal element in their midst. There is a fine line to tread between watching out for the company and invading people's lives, if there is trust between employee and employer facilitated through communication, then this line will be easier to maintain.

The risk is that, unless done well, the 'distance' between employer and employee will be further increased. It's only within the last generation that the majority of workers have moved from clocking on and clocking off as they arrive and depart from work, and from receiving a weekly pay packet in their hand. Nowadays they receive their remuneration anonymously and directly to their bank account and as we evolve from a manufacturing to a service or knowledge economy, an increasing number simply log on and log off their PCs at the beginning and end of the working day.

In this context how does the employer maintain rapport with its people? How does it show that it cares on a regular basis? How does it avoid its employees feeling they're 'just a number'? There must be an opportunity in the remuneration process, and the behaviour that could surround it, to close the gap between management and employees and give the staff a greater sense of self-worth and thus self-confidence.

People are very sensitive to 'corporate body language'. That is to say, the way in which the corporation presents itself in all respects; how it looks, how it acts, how it talks to people, how it talks about itself, what it believes in, who its friends are, and who it regards as enemies, what it loves and what it hates. Very simply, corporations are like people and people react to them in human terms.

For example, corporations are expected to be proud of themselves and to have self-esteem. It is assumed that they will actively advertise and promote their products and services, and do so in a way that suggests that they are enthusiastic and fully supportive of them. Customers understand that advertising is expensive and that it will be undertaken only if the product that it is promoting will meet with sales success: 'no advertising' can be inferred to mean 'poor product'. This is also why strict attention to the details of corporate identity is so important. If a logo style appears consistently and is treated with some veneration, then the customer perceives that, and is likely to treat the brand accordingly. As Ludwig Mies van der Rohe said: 'God is in the details', and these details need to be policed.

As an example, companies, particularly those with large retail estates, are very often tempted to put off the costly business of painting buildings, renewing fascias, or refreshing interiors. It's so easy to say that 'it doesn't look too bad' or that 'it will last another year' and to put the saved expenditure straight to the bottom line. The years pass with nothing being done and apparently with no effect. The truth is that the older, more traditional customers may have grown used to the slightly down-at-heel look and feel of the organisation, or simply don't notice that much, but the younger customers, who will have no sense of what to expect inside, certainly will. First impressions matter so much that it is essential to maintain an up-to-date and desirable image. Customers may return to an old-fashioned shop if they know it gives a good deal, but few will enter it for the first time if it looks a bit drab and dreary.

In the UK, Marks & Spencer has found to its cost how quickly this can happen. This once proud doyenne of the retail scene has been humbled by the rapidity of its decline. It is suffering the consequences of a corporate body language whose signals effectively said for years 'we know we're right'. It manifested this by its policies not to advertise, not to accept credit cards, not to modernise shop-fittings, lighting and displays, not to buy more cheaply abroad, but to be very tough with its British suppliers, and not to stock merchandise according to local store catchment area demographics. In so doing, the distance between M&S and the rest of the High Street gradually widened whilst newer younger potential customers quietly voted with their feet, saying 'we know they're wrong', on their way to Matalan or H&M.

There are key lessons for corporations to be learned from this; the core culture of the enterprise must be protected and the majority of its people will welcome a strong response against those who threaten to undermine it. If there is a clear code of good brand manners, then it must not only be encouraged through positive reinforcement, it must also be policed against those who deliberately exhibit bad behaviour. If the company leadership fails to do this, then people will assume the top management 'don't care', and if the bosses don't care, why should they?

Management need to demonstrate on a daily basis that they really do care about their company and that there are no 'broken windows' left unrepaired. To do this they need to survey their 'property' constantly. How secure is it against the dishonest staff member? How hacker-proof is the e-commerce system? How does the brand look really look, to customers and staff? Does it really perform against its competitors? How well is the business really doing at its leading edges of customer acquisition, customer loyalty, employee recruitment and retention? The CEO, Board and management need a regular feed of these key market and employee metrics, which will give them the pulse of the culture and early warnings of any murmurings of dissent. Employees also need to feel valued as individuals – never to feel like 'just a number'. The corporation must show that it cares for customers and employees alike.

14

Minimising Corporate Distance

There is an intrinsic tendency for 'distance' to grow up between the CEO and other corporate leaders and their employees. This is a consequence of growth and the increasing complexity of business life, which means that the CEO's time is very scarce. In order to mitigate 'distancing', processes of creating 'closeness' are a fundamental part of brand manners.

Employees need continuous reinforcement in the values of their brand and the communication of this to them by the company leadership is one of the most powerful ways of doing this. However, if these preventative measures should fail and a crisis occurs, then the closeness that has been engendered will still be of enormous value in mounting a rapid and effective response. Employees at the sharp end of the problem will have greater confidence in revealing the full extent of it, leading to a quicker, more effective resolution.

As companies grow, by definition their founder management adds layers of people below them. In a very short time in a successful organisation, the CEO may not know the names of all the employees – this can easily happen when the numbers rise above fifty or so. According to Nigel Nicholson of the London Business School, 40% of the world-wide workforce is employed in companies of more than 150 people, whilst the major corporations, for example the Forbes 500, have an average of 373,000 employees. What this means is that a very substantial proportion of all enterprises, ranging from the medium to the mega, face the intrinsic problem of distancing between their top management and their employees. Business experience shows that work teams of up to twelve people are optimal and it's interesting to note in this context that team sports have evolved to contain remarkably similar numbers of players per team (Figure 27).

Cricket	11
Rugby	15
Soccer	11
Baseball	9
American football	11
Hockey	11
Water polo	7

Figure 27 *Table of team sports, with number of players.*

Compounding this problem is the globalisation of business. The big companies with very large numbers of employees also have very large numbers of sites. For example, GE works in 88 countries world wide, and General Motors has operations in 50 countries, with a global presence in 200. Hewlett-Packard has distributors in 120 countries, and Microsoft has subsidiary offices in 59 countries. In addition, organisations are usually divided into operating companies, within which there are functional groups or departments. This facilitates production or servicing, but inevitably creates vertical segments or 'silos' between which the contact and communication is often poor.

In the interests of cohesion and efficiency, many such companies have adopted a single business language and it's quite often English. This has resulted from the combined effects of the British Empire, the dominance of the USA in global commerce and information technology, plus their lead in key cultural areas such as popular music, TV and movies. Even a proudly German company such as Daimler, has English as its official language. According to the English Speaking Union, there are 377 million people who use English as their mother tongue, with 226 million of these in the USA, and 56 million in the UK, representing 6.2% of people in the world, second only to Chinese. In reality, and including usage as a second language, and as a business tool, over a billion people speak English, and it's estimated that over 80% of all information stored in computers world wide is in this key language. However, the downside of this is that very high proportions of the people in these companies will not be communicating with head office, or indeed their colleagues, in their mother tongue.

This means that quite apart from geographical distance, there's a major linguistic one, which increases the in-built potential for miscommunication and misunderstanding and poor or insufficient communication is nearly always at the root of major corporate problems and issues. The reverse is also true; great communicators build great companies. The best CEOs are the 'story tellers', and it's essential that the story is heard as often as can be by as many employees, stakeholders and customers as possible. However, some companies actually still believe it's important to maintain confidentiality about issues affecting the organisation which are not really that secret. Senior appointments, the implications of mergers or acquisitions, or even bad news on the sales front are often suppressed long after any competitive, legal or regulatory requirement to do so. Their caution in internal communications also extends to their external public relations.

However, these companies reckon without the increasing effectiveness of the office grapevine, fuelled by e-mail and pervasive telecommunications. In the absence of information and communication about an issue of interest or concern, employees will simply invent their own 'ghosted' version of it and nearly always their speculation on any given issue will paint a far more negative picture than the reality. Employees' water cooler or coffee machine gossip will soon build speculation into rumour, and rumour into unattributable fact. The same tends to be true of journalists. If they have no real relationship with a company or its senior officers, then it's much more likely that they will go into print with a negative story before bothering too hard to find out whether there's another more positive side to it. CEOs and top management should beware of allowing these 'ghost stories' to live on their corporate 'street' and should operate on the basis that there are no secrets and that it's hard to over-communicate with employees.

This need for communication doesn't just operate at the shop-floor level. Many global consulting firms hold annual 'retreats' for all the members of their industry groupings, in addition to other senior management meetings and conferences and for them it's the biggest investment made in the business apart from recruitment and remuneration. They have found that converting information into knowledge and experience into expertise can only be achieved in a multi-national consultancy by creating regular personal contact. If we acknowledge that this sort of communication can be so valuable, why do many CEOs and senior managers seem to avoid it? Why do many companies spend so little time talking with their employees on the shop floor? Perhaps in part it's due to the fact that when these visits are made, or conversations had, the customers or employees involved seize their chance with a senior person to off-load a whole series of problems and issues. This can be an uncomfortable, embarrassing or even threatening experience and naturally enough many senior managers tend to avoid it. The experienced client relationship manager knows that the longer the gap left between contacts, the harder it is to pick up the phone next time. If there's been a problem, the gaps can get longer, just at the time when contact needs to be closer and more frequent to put things right. The same is true with the internal relationships between managers and staff.

Another aspect of corporate distancing occurs between the company and its customers, for example, in the vital area of qualitative market research, where a number of normal practices conspire to create barriers between the top management and the reality of the customers in the focus groups. Typically, the marketing department will subcontract the job to an independent third-party research company. When the groups are being conducted, it's not at all unusual for no client personnel to be in attendance as observers. The locations for the discussions can be far from home and the focus groups very often happen in the evenings, so it takes a more than averagely committed brand manager, let alone marketing director, to take the time and make the effort to be there. When the debrief is presented to the marketing department it's typical for it to be done in the form of a verbal presentation accompanying bullet points on charts, and illustrated by selected quotes from customers. It's relatively rare for a full written report to be produced and it's almost unheard of for someone from the client company to actually listen to the tapes made of the focus groups, let alone tape record the debrief. When the findings are presented on up the management hierarchy, it's hardly surprising that they don't get anything like the richness of understanding and insight they should.

When quantitative research is being planned, it's rare that senior company executives outside the marketing department are included in questionnaire design and sign-off. This is a missed opportunity for them to get involved in customer issues and understanding how the brand is seeking to gain greater insight into them. These managers should also be required to pilot the questionnaire themselves as a part of this process of putting themselves in their customers' shoes. During the real fieldwork it's valuable if company representatives accompany interviewers to gain valuable flesh to add to the bones of the statistical analyses that will follow. At the coding and analysis stage they should look at random samples of questionnaires to get a feel for the open-ended responses and the real customer language used. The marketing team and other interested departments such as R&D should brainstorm the likely special analyses that may be required and these should be specified as part of the initial data preparation to save time and money. This process is also a useful discipline on questionnaire design.

It could be argued that it is the responsibility of the marketing department to gather this sort of customer information and to be the guardians of it on behalf of the brand. However, there is a high turnover of personnel in most marketing departments with a consequent loss of 'brand memory'. Worse, only about 20% of major UK companies have a marketing director on their main board. Given that their average tenure is only eighteen months, it's easy to see how the CEO and key decision-makers can become distanced from the reality of their customers and not receive the key marketing metrics on a regular basis.

This phenomenon of 'distancing' can be genuinely dangerous to the brand, as evidenced by what has happened to the giant Coca-Cola Company in recent times. Their full co-operation in preparing the following case history is in itself a reflection of the new approach they are taking to tackle the problem.

Case History: COCA-COLA

The Coca-Cola Company really began to pick up critical mass in the 1980s, and the company began centralising to capitalise on the new global economic dynamics. Suddenly, it seemed, Coca-Cola was available in 200 countries with a worldwide infrastructure that was truly global in scale and able to supply demand that exceeded a billion drinks a day. However, since 1998, Coca-Cola has dropped from eighth to twenty-eighth in the top 500 international companies based on stock market value, and this means that a lot of damage to their brand reputation has occurred, but how?

The 'Belgium Scare', which occurred in June 1999, saw nearly 200 school children in Belgium complaining of headaches, fatigue, nausea and sickness after drinking Coke (Coca-Cola). The result was the recall of 65 million bottles and cans of Coke across four European countries. Belgian psychiatrists diagnosed the problem as being caused by psychosomatic illnesses originating from unpleasant odours. Isy Pelc, Head of Psychiatry and Psychological Medical Services at the Brugmann Hospital in Belgium, said that the country's dioxin-in-food crisis and student nervousness during exams were key factors in the crisis and that a ratio of two to one of the sufferers were particularly suggestible children. Psychosomatic or not, this cost the Coca-Cola Company an estimated $200 million. But perhaps the greater damage to the brand's image was the sense that the company had been unconcerned and rather slow to react; it was almost as if the Belgian crisis was being treated as a little local difficulty in a very minor Nielsen region.

Similar scares occurred in France and the Netherlands with the effects spreading as far afield as Italy and Poland. The explanation was that substandard carbon dioxide had been used in the manufacture of Coca-

Cola in Belgium, whilst the outside of the cans originating from Dunkirk had been contaminated with a fungicide used to treat the pallets on which the cans were transported. Charles Frenette is Executive Vice-President of the Coca-Cola Company and President of Coca-Cola Europe and Eurasia. He summarised the severity of the situation when he said: 'I've been with Coca-Cola for 25 years, and I've never seen anything, including New Coke in the United States, have such a deep impact on our company. What happened was that the very forces that were making our planet more interconnected and homogeneous than ever before were suddenly enabling people in communities all over the world, and particularly in Europe, to defend their own right to control their local culture, politics and economies.'

Meanwhile, Coca-Cola had been subject to accusations from both Pepsi and Virgin. They had expressed concern that Coca-Cola had been taking advantage of its position within Europe by encouraging retailers to stop stocking other cola products by offering loyalty bonuses and exclusivity agreements. Such allegations carry a potential fine of 10% of turnover. This led to dawn raids in several bottling factories including UK and Belgium. Further commercial setbacks came in the form of anti-trust allegations surrounding Coca-Cola's attempted $1.85 billion take over of Cadbury Schweppes which was intercepted by European regulators. Similar problems beset their proposed acquisition of French soft drink firm Orangina in December 1999, which was turned down by the French competition authorities, despite an $840 million agreed bid.

The next blow to Coca-Cola's reputation was a lawsuit by black employees alleging racial discrimination. The first emergence of this sensitive issue was in 1995 and related to a memo, which detailed how black employees felt: 'Blacks were not going to move any higher than the lower-paying jobs'. The statistics seemed to support the complaint; at the time three-quarters of the administrative roles at Coca-Cola were held by blacks while all the managers were white. Although some of the suggestions which were made by Mr Ware, Coca-Cola's then highest-ranking black executive were implemented, it was generally thought that Coca-Cola did not go far enough. Moreover the US Department of Labor found in 1997 that Coca-Cola had violated several rules regarding labour and racial diversity. In frustration, black employees formed 'networking groups' to compare discriminatory occurrences and in December 1999 all 2000 of Coca-Cola's black employees joined an action to put a stop to the alleged practices such as being passed over for promotions and being paid less than their white counterparts. It was settled in November 2000 at the record cost of $192.5 million.

Whilst these problems – health scares, anti-trust and allegations of racism – were unrelated, there was a strong inference drawn by commentators, and widely reported in the press, that the Coca-Cola company, the epitome of the open, relaxed, youthful fun lifestyle had become distant and insensitive. In the face of all this controversy Coca-Cola were losing customers and market value, and the brand, which had taken so long to be built, was being damaged rather quickly. It became clear that something had to happen, and fast. Decisive action was taken with the appointment of Douglas Daft as the new CEO and he in turn acted fast to impose his authority. In his view Coca-Cola went astray by becoming over-centralised, slow and insensitive and he described the series of unfortunate events as being 'Just what we needed. For a couple of years, the world was moving in one direction, and we were moving in another'.

Within 6 months Daft had replaced practically all of Coca-Cola's senior management in Europe with local executives, and there is only one in ten American managers who remain as Divisional Presidents in Europe. The reason for such rapid change can be seen in the explanation for these moves given by Daft:

> Every problem we've had can be traced to a singular cause: we neglected our relationships. You need a network to prevent the danger that people will stop telling you things and a company that is today centralising it's decision-making power has not understood anything about the way in which the world is currently evolving. In our recent past, we succeeded because we understood and appealed to global commonalties. In our future, we'll succeed; we will also understand and appeal to local differences. The 21st century demands nothing less.

This swing to putting local nationals in senior positions is a key part of the strategy and the new approach adopted by Coca-Cola through Daft is guided by three principles. These are firstly by expanding from global to local through thinking and acting locally, and will be achieved by placing responsibility and accountability in the hands of colleagues who are closest to those billions of individual sales. Secondly, by leading as model citizens in every community served, and by believing passionately Daft's concept that 'We do not do business in markets; we do business in societies'. This builds on the long-standing belief held at Coca-Cola that

'Coca-Cola always flourishes when our people are allowed to use their insight to build the business in ways best suited to their local culture and business conditions'. With respect to the question of alleged racial discrimination Daft has installed a series of measures that reflect a real commitment to managing diversity and has been tying his own remuneration to achievement of his diversity goals. Daft's ambition is to make Coca-Cola 'The most advanced and truly diverse corporate culture in the world'.

Thirdly, Daft has reaffirmed that it is essential to build the core of the business on the strength of the brand: 'All our success flows from the strength of our brands, and our ability to relate to people. That's why we have to be the world's best marketers and any diversion from that mission will inhibit our success.' Though this is the long-term strategy for Coca-Cola it was crucial to take immediate actions which would help them to pull back some of the customers that were lost through the disasters in Europe. According to Charles Frenette, 'Corporate apologies and clever television advertising alone would not get the job done. We had to get out into the streets and personally put an ice-cold contour bottle of perfect tasting Coca-Cola into the hands of the people in the places where they were having fun and enjoying life and enjoying each other.' An example of this new system in place and these new values in practice can be summarised by a comment made by the marketing director for Coca-Cola in Brussels and Luxembourg: 'We can do things now that would be have been unthinkable a year ago because Atlanta wouldn't have approved it. Now I am told to go until I'm told to stop.' In Brussels, hostesses go to discos and hand out free Coke to teenagers who have been drinking alcohol to demonstrate the pleasure of a Coke break. 'Belgians are party animals, we knew that, but Atlanta would never have known it.'

Whilst essential for the internal recovery of the company, and vital in terms of customer relationships, it was also crucial that the new 'closer' management style be extended to external relationships with governments and regulators too. The approach being adopted by Coca-Cola was described by Daft to Karel Van Miert, a European anti-trust chief who was seen as one of Coca-Cola's leading enemies through the crisis. He said that although known for aggression and perhaps even arrogance it was time for Coca-Cola to become conciliatory and to create good relations with governments around the globe. Twelve days after Daft was appointed as chairman, Italy's anti-trust agency headed by Guiseppe Tesauro fined the company the equivalent of US $16.1 million for anti-competitive sales and marketing behaviour. In a 'defining gesture' exemplifying the new attitude, Daft went to meet with Guiseppe without lawyers, much to the Italian's surprise. He did this because he believed that Coca-Cola's Atlanta-based lawyers had played too large a role in the corporation's mis-steps in Europe and that their voice was too loud within the organisation.

Past experience has shown that when things go wrong, for example in instances of product tampering or contamination, such as Tylenol and Perrier, a rapid and public action is the best approach. This is more likely to be achieved by a culture of closeness wherein there is a high degree of trust between the leadership and operational management and employees. In these rare instances the brand has to be ready to say 'sorry' loudly and clearly, and act accordingly. Coca-Cola were slow in doing so to begin with, and have reaped the consequences, but now that they have made fundamental changes to their management, culture and structure it seems very likely Coca-Cola will reassume its mantle as undisputedly the world's greatest soft drink brand.

Actions to minimise 'corporate distancing' should include:

1. Keep close to customers – do not subcontract out all your market and competitor research. Encourage people to 'go the extra mile' for customers – to act until told to stop.

   (a) Whenever qualitative market research is conducted, there must be a company observer present at every group. The CEO or Country Manager should attend at least two customer focus groups per year. The verbal debrief should be tape recorded and transcribed for distribution and the record. The tapes of the research groups should be listened to and transcribed.

   (b) When quantitative research is being planned, senior company executives outside the marketing department ought to be included in the processes of questionnaire design and the marketing people should get more involved in fieldwork, and analysis.

   (c) The company or brand website should include a market research facility and there should be a director responsible for marketing on the main and executive boards.

2. Recognise that the corporation is a business in society, not just in markets. Forge close relationships with local market regulators, government authorities, opinion formers and journalists.

3. Create and implement a mandatory cycle of value chain tours which enable top management to experience annually every stage in the product or service delivery system in their own company, and how this can affect the customer.

   (a) Manufacturers should implement a mandatory cycle of annual factory work experience for senior managers and retailers should create and implement a mandatory cycle of in-store working.

   (b) Retailers should create and implement a mandatory cycle of store visits, which include meetings with store staff as well as the manager. The CEO should visit every property with a regularity which reflects the frequency of staff/manager turnover, and at least every two years.

   (c) Service companies should create and implement a mandatory cycle of senior management work placements at each point in the service delivery process.

4. Establish objective measures of the level of communication between the key constituents of the business. This could be between head office and branches, divisions, regions or geographies. All channels should be covered, including letters, memos, e-mails, phone calls and face-to-face meetings. Trends in the comparative frequencies of communication can be used as a key barometer of the relationship between the parties. Recognise the challenge of multi-lingual environments.

   (a) Invest in and exploit telephone and video conferencing facilities. The company should create a webcasting and chat facility on its intranet to enable much more frequent communication between the CEO, managers and employees.

   (b) Depending on the size of the company or division or department, the relevant team unit should get together informally once a month. There should be an annual all-company meeting per geography or region, depending on numbers/cost.

15

Managing the Irrational

Many CEOs get to their positions having had a financial training and career progression. Law is also a frequent background, but at some distance behind finance and accounting. Both these areas of professional discipline are largely rational in their content and suit people who have more aptitude for 'left-hand brain' thinking. What this means in practice is that the valuable areas of the emotional and irrational do not get the attention they truly deserve. As a result companies are under-using hidden motivational and performance assets in their businesses; employees are far more disengaged than they need be. Utilising the irrational in interpersonal encounters, both internally and externally is a powerful aspect of a complete set of brand manners.

Corporations tend to be political organisations, with the focus on the rational. Even companies, which are overtly creative in their business activities such as advertising, design and architecture, employ only a minority of their people in what could be termed right-hand brainwork. Roughly three-quarters of the people are involved in left-hand brain activities with a strong emphasis on the rational and the functional. For example, the copywriters and art directors in the creative departments of UK agencies who actually produce the advertising and marketing communications account for only 14.6% of the total numbers of people employed, according to the IPA (Institute of Practitioners in Advertising). Even adding in the staff involved in creative production at 13.3%, and assuming that a proportion of the rest of the employees are 'creative', this only amounts to perhaps half the people involved.

In general, there has been a strong tendency to suppress the emotional and the irrational in the interests of promoting certainty and precision in the corporate process. Indeed, the very language we use to describe office or working life emphasises this. We talk approvingly of companies being 'professional', 'organised' and 'efficient', and are much less likely to use adjectives such as 'funky', 'free-wheeling' or 'fun'. Conversations between management and employees are typically purposeful and professional, as opposed to discursive and personal. The spectacular demise in mid-2000 of boo.com, the European on-line sportswear retailer, has no doubt reinforced the stereotype of the 'fun' organisation being flaky.

This means that very few corporate cultures are overtly enjoyable, and the rewards that people get from working there are typically described in terms of job satisfaction, career achievement and remuneration. Words such as enjoyable, relaxing, stimulating or exciting are not usually in common parlance in the corridors or around the coffee machine. The idea that 'We're pretty good at the "hardware", not so good on the "software" of business,' is frequently expressed.

Some companies, sensing this weakness, work hard to engender these attributes, but usually have to resort to off-site team-building and bonding exercises to achieve them. Sadly, the numbers of employees for whom these approaches are affordable are relatively low. Frequently the adrenalin 'high' and heightened sense of comradeship that can result from successful 'awaydays' rarely persists for more than a couple of weeks. Once the participants are back amongst their peers and no longer have the daily reinforcement of the charismatic trainer, who apparently achieved so much with them whilst they were away, they tend to backslide into their old habits and ways of doing things.

Surely there must be ways of creating more integrated and continuous reinforcement of the good feelings and improved relationships? How can management create an environment and work culture, which of itself suggests better methods of doing things? One simple answer is to bring the motivational techniques of the charismatic training gurus into the organisation on a permanent basis. This may imply giving human resource development more budget than it conventionally has in so many organisations. It puts a premium on charismatic leadership. It also means that CEOs and senior management must spend a much greater proportion of their time simply talking to their people. Indeed, as electronic communication increases, the premium on interpersonal contact grows disproportionately in value. The problem is that the available time is simply not there, particularly at the very top of the corporation; management are too busy managing the business to manage the people, let alone talk to them about it.

This raises the possibility of a new role within organisations, or at least a much-enhanced one if it is already there vestigially. This is the role of internal communications, allied to line management and spiced with brand guardianship. There needs to be someone at the most senior level of the corporation, probably reporting to the Board at the same level as the CEO, who is the keeper of the corporate vision and whose primary responsibility is to manage the irrational assets within the organisation. This person must care deeply for the culture and be a touchstone for its values. In the heyday of the Hard Rock Café the company had a 'Director of Attitude'. She was a woman and one of the burger chain's longest serving waitresses. Her role was invaluable in training new employees and in representing the brand at new restaurant openings.

Perhaps there is an analogy between the 'Director of Attitude' and the 'Fool' in the mediaeval Court. The Fool had no authority beyond the patronage of the King, but was engaged to ensure that he kept the monarch in touch with reality and the complex currents of emotion and politics in the Court. The Fool would achieve this by telling stories, humorous and often at the King's expense, to the point of disrespect. There was many a word of truth spoken in jest and the Fool would act as a lightning rod for tensions between ruler, Court and subjects. The Fool would also be the repository of the folk memory of the history and traditions of the Court, acting as a sounding board for new trends and ideas.

Watts Wacker, futurist and co-author of *The 500 Year Delta*, describes himself as a contemporary version of the classical Fool. He travels the world 'collecting stories to tell his clients', and is able to give the CEOs of major corporations a combination of reality check and policy critique which company Executive Vice-Presidents usually do not have the vision or political courage to deliver. How inspiring it could be for so many companies if they had their own Fool, or Director of Attitude instead of just a Director of Corporate Communications.

The majority of people see their working hours as the necessary dues they must pay in order to do what they really want to do, which is to enjoy their non-working hours in leisure pursuits, financed by their earnings from the less pleasant part of their day. It is rather unlikely that the workplace can ever be as rewarding as private life, but perhaps the over emphasis on the rational, and in effect the suppression of the irrational is one of the factors that leads to the imbalance. If employers do not acknowledge and then address this issue, then their organisations are going to be based on a conflict model by definition, and this negative cultural effect will inevitably translate itself to customers and third parties.

In their private lives very large numbers of people seem to believe in the irrational to some degree or other. For example, virtually every daily newspaper, from tabloid to broadsheet, publishes horoscopes, and so do virtually all women's magazines. Even if the owners of these publications do not believe in the horoscopes that they print, they no doubt accept their readership statistics, which show that many millions of people read them daily. The degree of seriousness with which these horoscopes are read varies enormously from the extreme 'dicemanlike' addiction of those who won't make a serious decision without an astrological consultation, to the vast majority who just enjoy their 'reading' in the paper and comparing notes with friends. Reportedly, even the US Government employs an astrologist.

The authors of these horoscopes become minor celebrities and clearly have substantial followings amongst their readers. In 1999, the *Daily Mail* reputedly offered £1m. to Jonathan Cainer in order to retain his services, and stop him going to the *Express*, a rival UK newspaper. The reason was that he already earned in excess of £1 million from his 50/50 split on premium rate horoscope phone lines with the paper, and often brought in over 100,000 extra readers per day.

Scientists have been working for some time on trying to identify personal characteristics linked to date of birth. Recently a study was published suggesting that those born in the winter months were more likely to be above average weight due to their greater propensity to store fat in the colder weather, than babies born in the warmer summer months. This in turn may have implications for their relative susceptibility to coronary heart disease in later life.

It seems quite likely that over the coming years more and more will be discovered about the linkages between the date of birth and all sorts of other physical, emotional and psychological characteristics. What this means is that science and scientific endeavour will have put a rational explanation for something that many people, drawing on centuries of evolving folklore and no little astrological expertise, have always known. Indeed, hardly a day goes by without a report of a scientific discovery that merely confirms a long-held belief, even if that belief may be regarded as uncomfortable or politically incorrect. Perhaps we should be more trusting of the folklore in society and build upon generations of experience, rather than dismissing it out of hand?

During the last decade of the 20th century the more enlightened doctors became more tolerant of alternative medicines and were prepared to recommend them informally to patients for whom their own conventional solutions appeared to have done relatively little.

The placebo effect has been well known in medicine since Hippocrates' time, but has always been rather swept under the carpet as a slightly embarrassing thing the professionals in the world of medicine are slightly uncomfortable about. For example in the UK neither the General Medical Council nor the Royal College of General Practitioners nor the National Health Service itself has any formal guidelines on the use of placebos as a medicine.

This is interesting given that many experts agree that up to 30% or even 40% of any drug's effectiveness is attributable to the placebo effect as opposed to the result of chemical interaction. In fact it is used as a benchmark for new drugs: if they cannot beat the placebo effect then they are not introduced. In a way it's quite extraordinary that an effect which is as significant as that which some of the best known drugs can achieve has not been documented, codified, and prescribed in a more structured way than it has been. But then again, given the reaction of the medical establishment to alternative medicines, perhaps it's not that surprising.

Something that is often said in companies, although not always acted on, is that in personal presentations, the audience makes up its mind about the speaker and the content, within the first two or three minutes of their beginning. Further, a study carried out in 1971 by Albert Mehrabian of UCLA called 'Silent Messages', proved that the following is how people interpret a speech: visual/body language 55%, voice/tone/inflection 38%, content/words 7% (Figure 28). The uncomfortable fact is that there is always a victory of form over content.

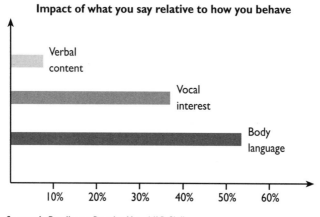

Impact of what you say relative to how you behave

Verbal content

Vocal interest

Body language

10%   20%   30%   40%   50%   60%

Source: A. Bradbury, *Develop Your NLP Skills.*

Figure 28 *Chart of body language, tone and content effect.*

In the same vein, sales people and other professional communicators concentrate as much, if not more, on body language, than on verbal content in a dialogue with a prospect or customer. Mimicking body position, facial expressions and hand gestures are more important and subtler means of building rapport quickly than just reflecting tonal pitch and pace whilst playing back the other party's name, words and phrases. Human beings seem to have an extraordinary capacity for recognising this mimicking behaviour and clearly it makes them comfortable when it happens to them. This is probably a result of simple egocentricity; we love ourselves and we love other people looking and behaving like us – imitation really is the sincerest form of flattery. But if the power of this process is so well known in the selling situation, i.e., when a company representative is dealing with their customer, then why is it that so little attention seems to be paid to deploying the same thing internally amongst employees?

Do dinners in more expensive restaurants actually taste any better? Perhaps we just expect them to do so because of the environment around the product. The designer decor, the exquisite attention to detail, the knowing waiter and the almost psychic service heavily influence us. Even the difficulty of getting a table and the personal recognition that success implies and confers all lead to superior value in the experience, despite, or probably because of, its exorbitant price. The placebo effect works its magic.

This sort of information is rather challenging to the rational, a school which would much rather believe that content is all important and would err on the side of precision in that department as opposed to concerning themselves with what they might see as the superficialities of presentation. For them 'smoke and mirrors' smacks of the fairground huckster or the street-market charlatan. As we have seen, very large numbers of people believe in the irrational and partake of it as an enjoyable part of everyday life. Even if it's not taken that seriously, it doesn't matter if it brings nevertheless the benefits of social interaction as well as personal exploration, often with a strong element of wish-fulfilment or fantasy.

In most major economies nowadays there are lotteries which engage quite remarkable proportions of the populace. In the UK for example, the National Lottery achieves a weekly number of players representing over 68% of the eligible population, with an awareness figure of 90% of the adult population. And yet the odds of winning are less than one in 13,983,816, that is to say, it is less likely that someone will win the jackpot than be run down in their street by a car. In the USA 68% of the population participate and the odds against winning are similarly infinitesimal.

The pundits who spend acres of newsprint pointing out the futility of buying lottery tickets and puzzling over why so many people continue to do so, don't seem to take into account the enormous pleasure and social mileage that a £1 purchase of a lottery ticket can deliver. The *post mortem* after the lottery draw with friends, the bemoaning of their fate for not having quite got the three additional numbers that they really needed and the anticipation of next week's draw are all very much a part of an enjoyable ritual. So also is the discussion about whether or not to stay with their special numbers, and the repeated debate on whether these special numbers are actually a trap. How awful it would be if one weekend those numbers weren't booked and then they came up! Plus of course the fantasy of 'what I would do if I suddenly became a lottery millionaire'. The sheer enjoyment of speculating about which house, which car, which holiday or which piece of cosmetic surgery would be made possible with the new-found fortune is such inexpensive fun and does a lot to divert attention away from humdrum everyday life.

Whether employers like it or not, virtually everyone in their organisation is spending a significant portion of their time actively involved in the irrational, and getting a great deal out of it. Beyond the impact of personal presentation and body language in communication and the rich fantasy life that people are able to get out of the purchase of something as mundane as a lottery ticket, there is considerable evidence to show that human suggestibility is extremely powerful.

On the London Underground, there is often severe overcrowding which results in many people being pushed dangerously near the edge of the platform, regardless of whether they have a suicidal inclination to be there. In experiments to find ways to reduce the risk of accident, it has been discovered that painting a yellow line about 1 ft in from the edge of the platform has a significant effect on where passengers will stand. Nearly everybody resists crossing the yellow line. There may be an explanation in the conditioning that people receive at passport checkpoints or in other official queuing situations.

This example of the irrational in action reminds us again of the potential effect of the environment on our frame of mind, and how much we interact with and are influenced by our surroundings. The point of all this for the senior management of corporations is that they should embrace the reality of so-called 'alternative' approaches and put them to work in their own organisations, and by extension in their relationships with all their stakeholders.

The rational actions or transactions within a company could be enhanced by 30% or more by adding emotional and psychological values through appropriate surrounding behaviours and rituals. By combining the spiritual, political and emotional elements with the rational, organisations can create a life of their own which energises all who work for them, to the corresponding benefit of the customers. A large part of this concerns 'how' things should be done, as well as what should be done. This is best achieved through horizontal working, across the organisation, using natural work teams to drive improvements in the customer experience.

16

How Trust Fits In

We are growing increasingly doubtful about the so-called 'pillars of society', as examples abound of behaviour in high places that is leading to our loss of trust in these institutions. Meanwhile people are becoming relatively more trusting of corporations and brands. As we go further into the digital era, and remote communications between companies and customers increase, trust will become one of the most important brand values in underpinning their encounters. In addition, as corporations attempt to become better managed in the best sense of the word, and as they implement their systems of brand manners, they will have to ensure they achieve a position of mutual trust with their employees and key stakeholders.

It's hard to imagine the placebo effect operating in environments where there is no trust. People need to believe in the doctor and to be persuaded by the sincerity of the behaviour surrounding the diagnostic and medicinal procedures in order for it to work. In the same way, employees of organisations need to be able to trust them and their management. Customers too need to trust the organisations or manufacturers that they're buying from.

Accepting a job with a company and deciding to adhere to its specific code of behaviour and brand manners is in part an act of faith in the employer, taken in the trust that the corporation will keep its side of the employment bargain. When we buy a brand we trust its reputation and believe that it will deliver the product or service benefits we expect. We like to be confident that the after-sales service will be efficient and effective. We want to believe that our statutory rights will be protected and that guarantee schemes will be honoured. However, hardly a day goes by without some strong reminders that we live in increasingly turbulent times in terms of trust. The most powerful nation on earth endured an almost 5-year long spectacle of its President offering a succession of specious, mealy-mouthed excuses and mendacious statements in his craven attempt to avoid impeachment. Astonishingly, through his semantic gymnastics, he escaped his threatened removal from high office, a position from which many people would have expected an honourable man to resign under the circumstances.

The collapse of the centuries-old Barings Bank as a result of the actions of a rogue trader, was simply one of the more spectacular manifestations of dishonest dealings by untrustworthy people in the financial services industry. Virtually every formal stock exchange announcement of mergers or acquisitions activity is preceded by a ramp up in the share prices of companies involved, some of which may only be attributable to insider trading.

Our world of sports has also been very seriously tainted by untrustworthy behaviour. The questionable actions of many International Olympic Committee members in accepting over-elaborate hospitality and lavish gifts, tantamount to bribes, from competing national organisations, have all but snuffed out the idealistic flame of the Olympic Games, which used to be such an aspirational symbol of sportsmanship. This scandalous behaviour by competing national organisations in the increasingly cut-throat process of winning the right to stage the games has underlined the degree to which commercial considerations have overtaken the original Olympic ideals. The tainting of the event continues with the running sore of illegal drug usage by the top athletes, apparently connived in and covered up by senior coaches. The Millennium Games in Sydney Australia have caused additional clouds to form through the massive allocation of the best seats for the main events to corporate hospitality packages, thus marginalising the ordinary sports fan.

Perhaps most depressing of all the game of cricket, which used to be perceived as the apotheosis of fair play, has been shown to have fallen prey to match fixing which has been particularly prevalent in India and Pakistan. This has been brought about by financial inducements to key players proffered by agents of the billion-pound illegal betting industry, centred in the Far East and which surrounds Test matches and other significant games. Even the avowedly religious captain of South Africa, Hansie Cronje has admitted to 'throwing' games for money, and persuading his team mates to co-conspire, in a series of revelations that have shocked his nation to the core, and cast doubt on the results of many significant matches over previous years. No more can the expression 'that's not quite cricket' be so easily used as a standard for fair behaviour.

More evidence of the very widespread nature of dishonest behaviour and therefore untrustworthiness can be seen in the sheer size of the black economy. Informed estimates suggest that in most Western European countries it ranges from 8% to 15% of GNP, and up to 25% in several cases. In 1999 the Audit Commission reported that 230,000 bogus applications had been made to local councils involving benefits worth £104,000,000 in England and Wales in the previous year. The Department of Social Security has suggested that approximately £600 million a year may have been paid out in bogus housing benefit claims, i.e., about 5% of the £11 billion total paid out annually. Overall the UK black economy may be worth as much as £50 billion a year. With this all in mind, it is not unsurprising to see that research carried out by the Henley Centre (Figure 29) shows that once trusted institutions are falling behind High Street brands in terms of public confidence.

Given that so many key institutions and leading individuals in society seem to be untrustworthy, is it surprising that, when asked in market research surveys such as those conducted by the Future Foundation, people in the UK express a strong desire for exactly the reverse? The vast majority of citizens want companies and people to be trustworthy (Figure 30).

In this context, faced with the situation in which there is endemic untrustworthiness, any organisation that can convince its employees, its stakeholders, and its customers that it stands for the opposite, can create a very significant competitive advantage. One way of getting a perspective on how this situation has arisen and how it now might resolve itself in future is to consider the following model of the social evolution of trust.

Institution	Level of trust/%
Local doctor 'GP'	85
Kelloggs	84
Cadbury	83
Heinz	81
Our bank	72
Coca-Cola	65
Our church	64
The Police	62
Parliament	16
The Press	7

Source: The Henley Centre, 1998

Figure 29 *Levels of trust.*

Requirement	Mentioned by %
Honesty	88
Fairness	78
Trustworthiness	70
Helpfulness	66
Innovation	60
Friendliness	37

Source: Future Foundation/Consumers'
Association/Richmond Events, 1999.

Figure 30 *What people want from their ideal company.*

Not very long ago people would be born, live their lives and die in tiny communities, numbering perhaps no more than 100 people, and in dwelling places from which they might never have strayed more than eight or ten miles in a lifetime. In this village life, there was inevitably great intimacy – everybody knew of everybody's business. People's characters, their honesty, or lack of it, and their trustworthiness would have been apparent to all. It was hard to behave badly with impunity (Figure 31).

As small hamlets turned into villages, and then into towns, this direct personal measure of trust was no longer possible, so reputation became more essential as business and commerce developed. The growth of rules and regulations surrounding markets and the early stock exchanges were designed to prevent criminal activities such as cartels, and bidding rings. But, ironically, insider trading created one of the most powerful concepts in

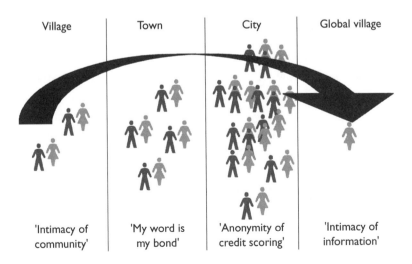

Figure 31 *Village, town, city, global village.*

trust we have yet seen. The idea that an Englishman's word is his bond began as a way round these regulations because verbal agreements left no trace for regulators to find and thus inside information could continue to be exploited for illegal personal gain. Up until quite recently in the City of London, multi-million pound trades would be carried out purely on these verbal contracts between gentlemen.

The growth of towns into great cities meant that reputation could be less and less relied upon as a measure of trustworthiness. Financial institutions, in particular, had to resort to increasingly sophisticated systems of credit scoring in order to establish whether or not a person should be deemed credit-worthy or bankable. Much of the customer distrust of financial institutions can be attributed to the problems caused by people being rejected for loans or having overdraft facilities withdrawn due to adverse credit-scoring judgements. Customers strongly resented being treated as a number, or as an actuarial likelihood and not a human being. Perhaps this sense of being treated merely as a statistic has had a direct influence on people's tolerant attitude towards tax evasion, the black economy and a fall in ethical standards in general. They may well have felt that if 'the system' exploits them, then why should they not exploit the system back?

Now we're in a new era of intimacy, the intimacy born of information. The arrival of the era of digital media and the Internet, with its one-to-one interactivity, means that companies will gather increasing amounts of detailed information on their customers. Through the same and technological means, individuals will also know very much more about companies. Recently in the UK, there was an outcry because an Internet company released a CD, costing £299, which contained all the names and home addresses of all the Company Directors in the country. This information has always been available, but only accessible with considerable effort. Now this data has been made widely available and many Company Directors don't like it, especially the ones that have a poor record in terms of previous bankruptcies or legal judgements against them. Most major corporations have websites and the level of transparency and accessibility of data about them grows daily. The notion of hiding information or keeping corporate secrets as a long-term strategy is becoming increasingly untenable.

The future is going to go full circle and with the increasing use of alliances within the business world, create an intimacy of information community. This means companies with similar ideals will share ideas and information, and work together with a high degree of trust as their bond. The Internet is facilitating these alliances, particularly in the area of procurement, and already major deals have been done in the automotive, steel and food service industries. But the key to realising and creating these enormously powerful trading relationships, often between companies that previously would have seen each other as arch rivals, is the degree of personal trust that exists between the CEOs involved. If the corporate leaders have mutual credibility and trust then deals, which would normally founder in legal negotiation, can be concluded much more easily, but only between principled principals.

As we have seen earlier, the honest majority has no problem with the idea of their personal data being held by a third party, as long as that third party is trustworthy and their motives are clear. Thus for companies and brands who will increasingly do business over the Internet with customers with whom they have had no physical contact, and perhaps not even any spoken dialogue, trustworthiness becomes a fundamental need. The word 'trust' is rapidly becoming one of the most used in advertisements for companies seeking to do business on the Internet. They all realise that in order to be successful in remote transactions brands have to give their customers the confidence to purchase. Research from the leading companies in the field such as Forrester, confirms that the very significant numbers of abandoned shopping carts or aborted purchases are attributable to the lack of human intervention and personal contact via a helpline.

In the USA, the Internet companies and the banks are beginning to open retail branches because they have been unable to achieve the necessary customer trust which might enable people to carry out higher value and higher margin transactions over the Internet. They see that physical presence in the High Street is an essential component in achieving the necessary credibility and reassurance, whereas in the UK banks are closing down their High Street branches. This could be premature considering what the ROAR data below has to say. In the ROAR (Right of Admission Reserved) survey amongst young people aged 15–24 (Figure 32), there would seem to be support for this thesis; brands with a strong physical presence do well, remote institutions do far worse.

Boots is in nearly every town in the UK as the High Street's historical dispensing pharmacy, providing medicines and personal care products; it has acquired an outstanding reputation and the trust of the people. It's nicknamed 'Mother Boots' and in conceptual terms it's literally the matron for the nation. Hardly surprisingly, at the other end of the spectrum we have the European Parliament, a remote organisation, invisibly located in the obscurity of Brussels, whose self-serving bureaucratic motives even the most pro-European of voters suspect and distrust.

Trust a little/a lot

Organisation	Percentage trust
Boots	87
BBC	81
British Airways	74
UN	64
Police	59
Microsoft	52
UK Labour Government	40
European Parliament	28

Source: ROAR 15–24 age group, 1999.

Figure 32 *Trust in companies.*

It seems entirely plausible that the swing towards 'clicks and mortar' deals in the emerging dotcom industry is not just based on the need to get some real assets and some profitability into these loss-making businesses. Many retailers have gone into catalogue marketing and many mail-order companies have opened shops. Companies dealing through intermediaries have opened up direct telephone sales operations. Wholesale warehouses have opened their doors to non-company, ordinary members of the shopping public. In doing the reverse of each other, or in augmenting their traditional trading patterns, these companies have simply opened up extra channels of distribution and means of contact with their customers. Perhaps in future there will be relatively few 'pure' Internet companies because of the basic human need for the trust engendered by personal or physical contact in so many purchasing situations.

One of the more popular exercises in team-building programmes is the 'trust fall'. In essence, an individual allows himself or herself to fall backwards off a vaulting horse, or elevated structure of similar height, into the arms of colleagues. The collective physical act of catching the falling person does two things. Firstly it demonstrates what a team can do which an individual couldn't possibly, i.e., prevent a heavy adult from hitting the ground. Secondly it demonstrates that an individual can safely put their trust in their colleagues. This physical demonstration of trust is a powerful way of engendering that feeling in a group, and is much more effective than simply talking about it.

Over the years the research company, MORI, has tracked corporate reputation and the degree to which members of the public feel favourably or unfavourably disposed towards major companies (Figure 33). One basic finding that has emerged consistently is that, in general, the better known a company, the more favourably it is regarded. Sheer brand awareness or brand

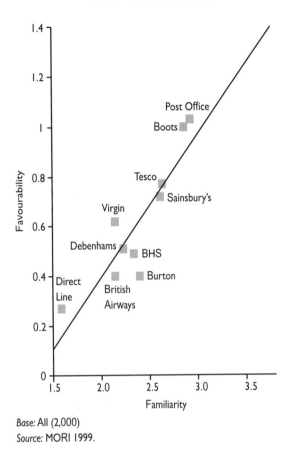

Base: All (2,000)
Source: MORI 1999.

Figure 33 *Company familiarity and favourability among the general public.*

fame is a fundamental building block in the establishment of trust. But in order to convert familiarity and favourability into trust itself, it is clear that corporate actions are going to be far more influential than words alone.

The task for the CEO both internally in the organisation and externally for the market is essentially the same. The words used to describe the dream and codify the brand manners need to be precisely and absolutely mirrored by actions. If the words with which the brand promise is made are supported by its manner, then both employee and customer expectations will be managed perfectly and trust will result. Hans Snook, of the hugely successful Orange mobile phone brand, described it as follows: 'We were never just another mobile-phone company. The way you define a brand is as a promise deliverer. And we've always delivered – to our staff, our customers and our shareholders.' Note how, in the case of Orange, that 'staff' comes first in Snook's list.

97% satisfied with Bank's decision on ethical policies
97% believe stance has a direct effect on customer recruitment
89% believe it has a direct effect on customer retention
89% feel proud to be an employee of the Co-operative Bank
88% perceive the company to be a responsible member of society
87% feel business is mindful of its impact on the environment
82% believe stance has a positive effect on customer service

Source: Co-operative Bank Employee Survey, March 1998.

Figure 34 *The impact of ethics on Co-operative Bank employees.*

As another example of the impact a code of behaviour can have on staff, look at how the Co-op Bank's employees have been galvanised by the adoption of an ethical investment policy by their employer in a fundamental re-positioning exercise which took the Bank right back to its roots (Figure 34).

How many other organisations have achieved this level of support and buy-in to a corporate vision? The ethical 'glue', which the Co-operative Bank applied to itself in terms of an investment strategy, has become a motivating force for employees and an attractive brand proposition to customers through agency partners BDDH. The key was the work the Bank did in order to take the ethical high ground and make their claim. It took several years to disengage from investments in questionable companies and wipe the slate clean. Had they not done so with such rigour they would have been open to attack by journalists, regulators and competitors alike, thus undermining their trust position with staff and customers who needed to be convinced the stance was genuine.

As the Co-op Bank case demonstrates, the staff has to trust that the managers will look after them, and the managers must trust the staff will do a good job. The customers have to trust the staff that they are not being misleading about a product or service – they need to know the 'why' as well as the 'what', and the customers have to trust that the managers are not exploiting or ripping anyone off to deliver the product. Then the managers have to trust the customers so they can inform them about why they are changing things, and where the company is going. Finally, the staff has to trust the customers and try and build a rapport that will last.

The end point is a three-way triangle of trust (Figure 35). With the managers, staff and customers at each corner. Trust is built on the personal interactions that each person has and is the fundamental building block for good relationships. At its core is the set of distinctive brand manners that binds the company together and projects its collective vision through words and deeds, both internally and externally.

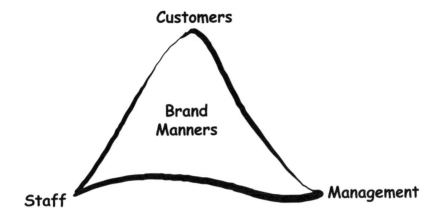

Figure 35 *The trust triangle.*

For the CEO, establishing the reputation for trust in the minds of customers and indeed in employees and other stakeholders is increasingly important. If everyone has a clear idea of what is expected from them, from the management to the staff to the customer, then it is easy for people to measure how well they are doing, and therefore how trustworthy they are. For the way to build trust is simply to be seen to be doing the thing you said you were going to do. If an inspiring goal and brand dream can be clearly set out and articulated by top management, and then be followed successfully by everyone, this increases the bond of mutual trust. As the old saying goes: 'practise what you preach'!

Trust is key to building self-confident organisations. At the individual level, trust can be developed by managing the three components – credibility (what value the individual can add), intimacy (the opportunity to share personal as well as business agendas), and risk (professional and personal aspects need to be identified and managed).

Trust is the 'glue' which binds relationships between individuals – as employees and also between the employee and the customer. It gives people the confidence to go beyond standard practice and can enable the employee to 'take a risk' to help the customer and deliver outstanding service. With the emergence of the 'global village' and the intimacy of information, trust is one of the most important natural laws to be understood and nurtured.

Understanding, accepting and embracing the notion that service can be freely given as well as 'bought' is fundamental both to Brand Manners and to the capacity for each of us to fulfil our potential and lead more worthwhile lives. Similarly, for corporations, when people recognise that authority actually flows upwards as much as downwards, there is a tremendous release of latent energy and enthusiasm. The employee moves from a 'Child' (them) to a 'Parent' (corporation) relationship to an 'Adult' one, with both being partners in the service of the customer.

Section Three
The Brand Promise

The third section deals with key issues surrounding the brand promise. We look at four aspects: the impact of high-tech communications technologies, the rise of the New Consumerism, how problem identification can be part of the solution and how to protect the brand.

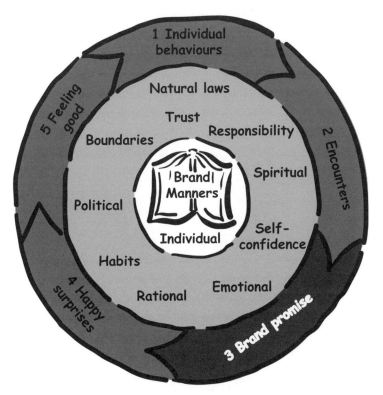

Figure 36 *Section Three: The Brand Manners Improvement Cycle – brand promise.*

17

High Tech, High Touch in Branding

Because CEOs and top management are rarely customers of their own companies in the conventional sense – they get special terms or other forms of preferential treatment – they are often in blissful ignorance of the problems that confront their actual customers when they try to make contact. For most companies, the opportunity to reduce the costs of customer interaction by routing it through telephone or e-mail systems has been seized upon with alacrity.

In the process, they have distanced the company or brand from the customer and usually erected barriers which frustrate communication. Superficially, expenses may have been saved, but at what cost to the customer relationship? The problem arises because these new information-handling systems are typically seen as a replacement for personal intervention. They are designed to remove the expensive human element rather than integrate it and enhance it in a total customer service interface.

Most companies are in the process of embracing automated, digital communications with customers in order to drive down the cost per interaction and improve profitability. Very rarely are these systems designed to improve customer service. The first wave of this process was in the creation of call centres within the organisation. But quite often this was found to be an unsatisfactory solution for all but the largest organisations because they did not have the volumes to achieve cost-effective utilisation of the resource and justify an in-house set-up. Hence many individual operating units within an overall business have been amalgamated, or often managements have resorted to the more cost-effective option of outsourcing these services to call centre operators.

"Hello... This is the Police.
If you are being attacked from
behind by a mad axe-murderer,
press 'One'..."

Cartoon 3 *'Phone therapy'.*

According to Datamonitor, the UK is now Europe's biggest market for call centres, with 5,050 in 2000 compared to the next biggest country, France, at 2,800.

From the customer's perspective, there are a number of problems with this approach. Firstly it is very difficult to forecast call volumes, and therefore operator resource allocation, especially at the outset of a sales or product recall campaign with enquiries being triggered by advertising, direct mail, sales promotion or public relations activity. Because it is costly to set up the call handling for a new campaign – questionnaire design, software programming, operator training, etc. – companies tend to err on the side of caution. Hence the typically long wait to be answered, aggravated by annoying automated messages informing the caller that, 'your call is waiting in a queue' (as if you didn't know) and 'will be answered shortly' (unlikely).

Some call-centre operators claim to be able to add extra resource at short notice, either by bringing in more staff to their own premises, or by cascading calls out to other call centres. However this doesn't avoid the set-up costs and usually such contingency plans are never made, the client perspective being 'too many calls is a problem we'd like to have' and essentially embarking on their programme fully prepared to alienate potential customers. It is more expensive to employ operators at the weekends or outside normal working hours, so the chances of getting through to an operator when the customer has free time to do so, i.e. outside their own hours of work, is slim.

The most likely result is either no response at all or just an answer-phone message with an instruction to call back during the day, Monday to Friday, and usually with no facility to leave a message – transcribing them costs money! It also means that one of the peak days for telephone response is Monday, when everyone is back at work and busy on the company phones responding to advertisements, following up product faults or booking service calls the needs for which have arisen over the weekend.

Secondly, and most obviously, the call-centre telephonists often do not work for the company they are temporarily paid to represent. However, they purport to do so by answering calls in the company or brand name. The problem occurs because, with the best will in the world, training cannot prepare them for much beyond the content of their on-screen questionnaire. Thus whenever the customer dialogue strays off the predetermined script, even in the context of the defined subject area (e.g. does this model use the same parts as the previous one I've got and wish to replace?) they are incapable of dealing with it.

In addition, the call-centre employees are rewarded on a piecework basis; the more calls handled per hour, the more they get paid. Thus there is an inbuilt disincentive to pursue any customer calls, which are 'off piste' as far as the defined programme is concerned. If a customer does not get satisfaction at the first, operator level, then with persistence they can get a supervisor on the line. However, this rarely results in a much more productive dialogue, with the outcome at best being a message left for a real client representative to call back later to resolve the enquiry or issue. Even assuming this message is passed efficiently and the baton is successfully taken up by the company, the whole process is frustrating and time wasting for the customer.

The second wave in the outsourcing and automation of customer telephone calls, is the adoption of multiple-choice call-handling systems which work with touchtone handsets and operate on menus designed to route traffic to operators or fully automated answering systems. Even using the best of these is a time-consuming process, which is barely user friendly, let alone a brand-enhancing experience. Similar problems occur; it is hard to anticipate all the types of customer enquiry and thus provide menu options to cover them. If a customer wishes to pursue more than one issue per call, there is rarely a way of transferring across to the appropriate channel. If difficulties are encountered, there is no way to 'cry for help' and gain access to a real live human voice. In the rare cases when there is human operator intervention, all the same limitations described earlier still apply.

We're now in the third wave of this distancing process and this is being brought about by the advent of e-mail availability on a mass scale. It is being pioneered by Internet companies, but given the very low cost per interaction and the electronic record of each one, it seems highly likely that most corporations will adopt it as their preferred means of communication with customers. E-mails are expensive to handle by a keyboard operator on an individual basis, but very cheap if processed and replied to by robots. This inevitably means predetermined answers to predetermined questions, which will not cover the numerous eventualities that customers will present.

Forrester Research has shown that the conversion rate of Internet shoppers is very low, and the level of abandoned shopping carts is very high (Figure 37). The main reason cited was that customers had to fill in lots of details and this gave them time to change their mind. They also blamed the difficulty of the buying process coupled with the fear of giving out personal information. Lack of personal assistance was also key.

It may well be that in the future, increasingly intelligent expert systems will be able to minimise or solve many of these common problems encountered with semi- or fully-automated call handling or e-mail systems. However, this is likely to take a few years and in the meantime, what can

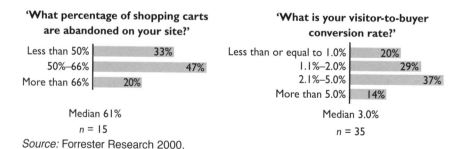

Figure 37 *Internet shopping statistics.*

Figure 38 *A call centre.*

companies do to mitigate the problems and instead of doing untold damage to their brands, find ways and means of enhancing them through technology?

The first point for CEOs and top management to take on board is that the era of increasing high tech in communications is creating extra value in quality personal interaction with customers; using technology to create 'high touch', i.e. powerful interpersonal contacts is the goal. But before addressing the end game, we need to start with the basics and at the call centre. Consider Figure 38. It shows a typical call centre, which would probably look little different whether it was in-house and dedicated to an individual company, or an independent outsourcer.

Notice the serried ranks of Dilbert-style cubicles and absence of any signs of personal touches. No wonder that employees of these call centres are complaining of stress-related illnesses! A recent survey by CBE training consultancy on call centres showed that 6% of people suffered from serious psychiatric problems, double the rate for a normal work force. They claimed that the reason for the stress is to do with the production-line style of work with the inability of staff to switch off mentally. Working in such an environment where they have no control leads to stress and lower motivation. But herein lies the opportunity for the willing client company. If the business is subcontracting a vital part of its customer relationship handling to a third-party organisation, then it is incumbent on the owners of the brand to do everything in their power to co-opt its employees by proxy into their family.

How much more rewarding a working experience will it be if the call-centre operators are imbued with the brand's manners? What if they are given visual cues as to its identity and character or fully briefed on its heritage and language? Or if they're provided with a simple means of pushing calls up to well-informed supervisors, who themselves can route calls direct to actual client representatives if need be.

A model for this process is provided by HARMONI, the acronym for Harrow Medics Out of hours Network Inc., which pioneered the concept of 'telephone triage' and thus changed the general practitioner out-of-hours service. Before HARMONI, GPs in the Harrow area north of London, often worked a 'one in three' shift, that is one night on duty for every three days worked. After the introduction of this radical new co-operative service, the on-call requirement fell to one six-hour shift every two months! There has been a consequent improvement in the lifestyle of National Health Service (NHS) general practitioners. Indeed HARMONI has gone on to be the only GP Co-operative winner of an NHS Direct franchise (West London) and Dr David Lloyd, one of its founders, is a member of the NHS Modernisation Action Team, charged with spending the extra £13 billion pounds granted by the UK Government in mid-2000.

One of the secrets of HARMONI's success was the development of a computerised decision support software package (CDSS) within an industry standard call-centre to help nurses to decide on the best health management for callers. The software helps the nurse to make a comprehensive assessment of the problem and decide what sort of care is needed.

The second success factor was having trained nurses as the telephone operators, so that the greatest possible sensitivity to patient enquiries could be delivered as cost-effectively as possible without tying up the more expensive and scarce resource of doctors themselves. HARMONI started, and now NHS Direct has continued, the practice of using community nurses, accident & emergency nurses and health visitors as triage nurses, enabling them to maintain a clinical commitment as well as delivering NHS Direct. This has refuted one of the criticisms of NHS Direct that it would destabilise the recruitment of nurses in hospitals and the community.

The third factor was the triage philosophy, which underlies the operating software. The triage nurses do not make a diagnosis but make a decision about what sort of care a caller needs, the motto is that a West London caller with a health care need will receive:

- the right care
- by the right person
- at the right place
- at the right time
- with the right information.

About one-third of callers are diverted to less intensive care than they imagined they would need and about one-third are told they need more intensive care than they thought.

The fourth success factor was having fully trained doctors on hand. Doctors work in a different way from nurses and are trained to deal with problems that do not fit their protocols and guidelines, but much research has shown that most callers prefer speaking to a nurse! Thus the whole strategy was in effect an implementation of the 'high tech, high touch' philosophy, using modern information technology to leverage the skills of doctors and deliver their expertise to the patients that really needed them in a timely and cost-effective manner.

Case History: THE NEW ZEALAND HERALD CALL CENTRE

Another example of how a call centre can be galvanised is the case of *The New Zealand Herald*, a Division of W&H Newspapers, one of the two largest media companies in New Zealand and as of 1998, a part of the Irish Independent Group, led by Tony O'Reilly. *The Herald*, their flagship daily paper, based in Auckland, had been under-performing on a number of dimensions when John Sanders, one of the rising stars in Rupert Murdoch's News Organisation in Australia, was recruited to turn things around.

Sanders had been the youngest Managing Director of a News title at the age of 27, and had a reputation for grasping nettles and resolving issues. He in turn recruited another News colleague, Darryl Olson, as Advertising Sales Director, to join the relaunch team in October 1998. Olson had particular expertise in classified advertising sales, the lifeblood of a paper such as the *Herald*, and he was clearly very much needed as at the time of joining, the business was under-performing its 'par' share of the classified market, based on circulation, by some 60%.

One problem that was quickly identified was their in-house call centre: call waiting times were as long as twenty minutes in the worst instances.

Another symptom of malaise was the abandoned call rate, which ranged between 15% and 20% as compared to the call centre average of 3% to 5%. Angry advertisers, kept waiting too long were more difficult to deal with and text errors were running at high levels, as were mistakes in terms of wrong day and wrong classification. In this environment it was hardly surprising that *Herald* customers were defecting to other papers.

It also soon emerged that the incentive scheme then in place was actually conspiring to drive down classified ad revenues and produce less effective copy for advertisers at the same time! The reason for this was born out of a crazy logic which said that if an advertiser booked a big ad, defined for the purpose as anything above five lines, then 'they were going to take it anyway' and thus should not qualify for the incentive scheme, which would therefore apply only to small ads of less than five lines, which could have been 'sold' by the individual phone room operator.

The net result of this was that the operators worked pretty hard to get marginal advertisements reduced in length to below the five-line threshold by the device of increasingly abstruse abbreviations. Clients perceived this as 'good service', because they believed the operators were saving them money, but ended up with ads which were often only comprehended by the regular *aficionado* of classified copy and pretty impenetrable to the ordinary browsing reader.

The diagnostic approach involved interviews with managers, operators, customers and other people within the *Herald*. In all a list of sixty problem areas were identified for rectification. In order to tackle these areas and implement the change programme Olson recruited Rachel Osborn in May 1999, initially as a consultant with particular expertise in call-centre management drawn from the telecomms and banking industries, but then subsequently as full-time Advertising Customer Contact Centre Manager, as the old 'phone room' was now re-named.

Key amongst them was making the call centre feel a part of the business again; they had become isolated from the rest of the organisation and resented the fact. Another negative factor was that the team managers had emerged from the general operator pool as a result of length of tenure, rather than because of their managerial skills, and were not accountable for the performance of their teams.

So whilst there was a feedback process in place (the meetings were scheduled during normal working hours with no cover on the phones, hence the twenty-minute call waiting time when they were in progress!)

it did not operate in reality and the operators themselves felt that none of their issues ever got beyond their immediate manager layer to a level where they could be addressed effectively. The operators felt a de-motivating lack of control over their working situation and this contributed to their under-performance.

Another important issue was that of environment: the call centre room was badly decorated, poorly furnished and badly lit. This was in stark contrast to other areas within the *Herald* and the operators were made to feel like second-class citizens – galling considering they knew they were the key point of contact with the customers who generated 60% of the advertising revenues.

Olson and Osborn set about tackling the sixty-point hit list and all the key actions were taken within twelve months. Several manager positions were made redundant, recalcitrant teams were broken up and new smaller teams formed, a new Customer Care team was recruited, targets and review processes were restructured, an A\$ 200,000 investment was made in up-grading the telephony and software system, and in refurbishing the centre, with employees being involved in decisions over décor. But perhaps the single most important factor in the re-launch was the intensive period of consultation involving senior management and the operators at the sharp end of the business designed to redefine the customer service standards and unblock the barriers to delivering them.

This culminated in a major presentation and dinner for 170 call-centre employees at which Sanders and Olson laid out their vision for the business. They even arranged a special follow-up session for the thirty people unable to make the first one to make absolutely sure everyone was included. One of the key communications at the call centre re-launch events was designed to manage the expectations and aspirations of these key staff. Sanders and Olson shared with them the parallel process of reorganising and re-motivating other key elements of the business, as they had done with the call centre. They also described the ongoing process of redefining what the *Herald* really stood for as a brand.

Despite its 170-year history, the paper, like most others of its type in the world, did not have a clearly stated vision. As with its peers it had been led in content terms by the editor of the day and promoted with advertising and sales campaigns of an essentially tactical nature. There was nothing to glue the organisation together in terms of common values, language or manners, nor was there a core idea, which would orient the brand in the emerging world of the Internet and digital distribution of news and other content.

Sanders and his management team had defined the mission for the *Herald* in the following terms:

- Mission
  'What we are building: the most valued multimedia database on New Zealand'.
  In this context the task was described as:
  Our job
  'To connect people throughout the world with the most valued and professionally packaged information on New Zealand which drives profitable transactional traffic.'

The guiding principles for everyone involved were uncompromising in their clarity of presentation in similarly down-to-earth language, which anyone in the organisation could understand and relate to:

- Guiding principles
  - people passionate about making a difference
  - team-based solutions
  - a performance culture which rewards measurable improvements
  - everyone does what they say they'll do
  - no surprises
  - maximum efficiencies with exceptional service levels.

For the Customer Contact Area this was translated into Key Result Areas for every member of the newly reformed teams in two areas.

- Customer Service
  - to achieve a customer service score of 70% or better within the very good and excellent ratings on the annual Customer Service Survey
  - to achieve an ad entry accuracy rate of 99%
  - to achieve a Grade of Service of 80% of calls offered to be answered within 20 seconds.
- Market share
  In conjunction with the Display Classified team to achieve by December 31 2000:
  - 87.6% share of the employment-market
  - 58.3% share of the automotive market
  - 44.9% share of the real-estate market
  - 59.0% share of the general classified market

The revelation to the call centre staff that there was a new brand vision in the creation, and that their feedback from their own process of reorganisation was a key input to it was one of the most motivating elements of the re-launch. Further they could see very clearly how their specific Key Result Areas would contribute to the achievement of the overall corporate goal. The new TCS software designed to forecast call levels and schedule staff rostering was installed in March 2000 and fully operational by May, but things had already begun to improve as a result of new management, better internal communications, the reformed incentive scheme and tighter recruitment criteria.

Clearly, the calibre of the Sales & Service representatives is paramount in an operation of this sort, but it is hard to recruit the right sort of people for what is a relatively repetitive job. The *Herald* sought people who exhibited signs of being team players and wanting to help others as evidenced by being involved in sports teams or in caring activities. However, the role is not simply that of 'order taker'; it's important that these employees are keen to be motivated to achieve more and have a genuine interest in making the ads work for customers. Specialist recruitment agencies were used to find suitable candidates and the *Herald* has now embarked on developing more specific aptitude tests to refine the process and improve success rates and employee stability. *Esprit de corps* has been fostered by the encouragement of the individual teams to give themselves names and identities – now the brightly painted Customer Contact Area is also decorated with the colours of the 'SWAT', 'WWW' and 'Commonwealth' teams.

Increasing team numbers, reducing team sizes, but still having a team leader for each has given extra support. There are also two Quality Analysts to coach the Sales & Service representatives and eight Customer Care managers whose role is to liaise directly with advertisers and ensure they are getting best value out of their classified advertising which, in the case of car retailers and estate agents, is a vital part of their businesses.

The improved telephony system also enables the occasional difficult calls to be easily routed to team leaders, on to the manager and then to the director, who receives on average about one a month. However, the facility with which awkward or genuinely upset clients are disarmed by this escalation process, and in particular when they reach the ultimate decision-maker has taken a good deal of pressure out of the total system.

As a key part of the new approach, in addition to the total company annual customer satisfaction survey by Foresyte Research, the Customer

Contact Centre embarked on the process of administering its own bi-monthly Communications Questionnaire. This survey was designed to help achieve the objective of improving internal communications, one of the lowest-scoring areas in the August 1999 customer satisfaction study. It was also intended to fulfil one of the guiding principles – 'no surprises' – by providing interim measures before the annual results!

This simple Communications Questionnaire is completed by each individual within the Customer Contact Centre, with respect to the person to whom they directly report. It's structured on a six-point scale ranging from 'Strongly Agree' to 'Strongly Disagree' and covers the following questions:

1. My manager/team leader provides me with the support I need to do my job well.
2. My manager/team leader provides me with clear guidance and direction.
3. My manager/team leader demonstrates openness and integrity.
4. I am kept well informed about matters that may affect my job.
5. Important information reaches me in a timely way.
6. I receive regular feedback from my manager/team leader about my performance.
7. Ideas and suggestions are listened to and consulted on.

There is also an area in the questionnaire for open-ended response under the heading: 'What can my manager/team leader do better to improve their communication?' To round out the research programme, advertiser satisfaction is measured via a monthly survey drawn from a random sample of *Herald* customers.

The new incentive scheme completes the circle of targets, communication and research. The telephone operators, now re-christened Sales & Service representatives, were given a new programme based on performance across a mix of key factors:

- availability = presence at their desk ready to accept calls offered
- quality = service as judged by two quality analysts during call observations
- accuracy = text errors %
- sales value = number of lines sold per hour.

The low ebb in terms of Grade of Service was reached in January 2000 with only 44% of inbound calls being answered by an operator within twenty seconds. By May GOS was running at 60%, in June it was 70% and by July it was running at the declared target level of 80%. From this secure platform the business was well positioned to move to the next stage of providing multiple access channels for advertisers, i.e. enabling them to book advertisements via letter, fax, phone, internet or direct input. In all these channels the GOS will be defined, as will the key results areas.

Far too many corporations are relying on 'high tech' alone and leaving millions of customers in the limbo of an automated call-answering system which is not only intensely frustrating, but seriously undermines the brand values that have been established through good product or service experiences and marketing communications.

CEOs must make it their business to be customers of their own business and to experience regularly the interfaces that it creates in order to be sure that there is enough 'high touch' to ensure added brand values are being delivered.

In the Internet era there are very few companies which are not going to have to grapple with the task of communicating directly and much more often with their customers. For the CEO and the top management team this has to be an absolute priority area in which to establish the necessary technologies and the appropriate brand manners in order to deliver the best possible impression and service standards to customers.

18

Dealing with the New Consumerism

Consumerism is not a new phenomenon, indeed its origins in modern times can be dated back to Ralph Nader's campaigning in the 1960s and whose name became synonymous with the consumer movement, 'Naderism'. He started out with cars, publishing *Unsafe at Any Speed: The Designed-in Dangers of the American Automobile* (Grossman) in November 1965. Perhaps the fact that he's a political candidate in the year 2000 is testimony to the long-term strength of his appeal.

The Consumers' Association was founded as long ago as 1957 and its highly influential publication, *Which?* is still making waves in boardrooms, most recently with its attack on new car prices in the UK in a report titled 'The Great British rip-off!', in late 1999. This showed that new car prices in the UK were on average 11% more expensive than in the EU. This resulted in a Government enquiry, which in turn has made sweeping recommendations, and led to changes in the Fair Trading Act, which could have far-reaching effects on the motor trade.

But there seems to be a new energy in consumerism, which is of a different level of intensity, and seems to have been created by three main factors: firstly the maturing of the Westernised economies, secondly the increase in popular shareholding, and thirdly the commercialisation of political issues. The maturing of Westernised economies has led to quite unprecedented levels of material wealth, not just amongst the middle and upper classes, but right the way through the demographics. For example, the penetration of mobile telephones is already above 40% of all adults in the UK and much higher in several Scandinavian countries. Many homes have two or three TV sets and video recorders are commonplace. Watts Wacker, futurist, puts it simply: 'We've all got enough stuff'. In this context people are naturally turning to other, less materialistic concerns.

As argued in *Brand Spirit*, this has led many people to raise the horizons of their purchase criteria to issues beyond the traditional brand values relating to rational or functional product features, or emotional and psychological attributes. Encouraged by conservationists, environmentalists, consumerists, and lobbyists, customers have become much more concerned about the role of corporations in society and are questioning what they're putting back into the communities in which they operate, beyond their taxes and the employment they provide.

The second key factor has been the massive increase in popular shareholding. Traditionally buoyant in the USA, the recent opening up of stock market trading via the Internet has pushed ownership of shares by private individuals to unprecedented levels – 40% by the end of 1999 according to the NYSE. Charles Schwab, one of the pioneers of on-line trading reported that over 79% of all their trades in 1999 were conducted on line.

The same recent pattern has occurred in the UK with a plethora of on-line stock-broking companies launching in the wake of Schwab. This new channel to market has opened up popular share dealing. This in a country where a series of privatisations of major utilities, such as British Gas and British Telecom, and the de-mutualisation of major building societies, such as the Halifax and the Abbey National, had already put shares in the hands of millions who previously had no interest in the Stock Exchange. This trend has been further encouraged in the mass market by the flotation of leading Premier League football clubs such as Manchester United and Chelsea. The penetration of share ownership by private individuals in the UK stood at 55.7% at the end of 1999 and looks set to continue to grow.

The result of this is that very large numbers of people are now both customers of, and investors in, many major corporations. This means that boardroom events and financial announcements involving these companies now have an interest for a mass audience that they did not previously have. It used to be the case not so long ago that 'City' news could be disseminated through the narrow channels of the specialist financial press and the business sections of the quality dailies, in such a way that the general public would never see it. Nowadays even the mass-market tabloids cover the main points of company news because their readers are shareholders.

What this means is that companies have to be fully aware that news of any aspect of their activities, especially including their financial transactions, will be picked up, and if it has a sensationalist angle, such as top executives share option schemes, 'golden hellos', or more commonly 'golden goodbyes' (the eight retiring board members of troubled M&S shared £1.38m between them), make it into the general news pages and often the front page. A classic example of poor public relations management occurred when Sainsbury, already in trouble on a number of fronts, allowed its then Chief Executive, Dino Adriano, to appear in the 'Back to the Floor' TV programme in the hope that he would be seen to be taking a real interest in the grass roots of store operations as a part of his recovery strategy. Unfortunately, he looked like a fish out of water in his own company and was seen by many of the UK viewing audience to be an incompetent on a checkout cash till. His pay-off when he left Sainsbury was £1.2 million. The need for co-ordinated news management and communications has never been higher in order to protect the brand.

The third key issue facing corporations is the commercialisation of political issues. As many product and service fields have tended to commodity status, and it has become harder and harder to sustain competitive advantage on the basis of rational and functional benefits, companies have relied increasingly on emotional and psychological aspects of brand differentiation. But, as noted earlier, even these values have been losing sway with customers who are rather more motivated by ethical or even spiritual attributes of brands.

Green environmentalism was the first of the major 'political' issues to be exploited commercially, and in particular retailers such as Tesco in the UK made it a key plank in their product and positioning strategy during the late 1980s and early 1990s. Then came the focus on country of origin and the labour used in production. Marks & Spencer were attacked on this ground in the documentary 'World In Action', by Granada. They berated M&S for their alleged exploitation of cheap labour at a North African clothes factory, and for passing off clothes as made in England when they were not. Marks & Spencer took the television company to court in protest and eventually won their case, but in the meantime a lot of the mud had stuck due to the enormous media coverage the allegations had generated compared to the minimal reporting of their legal victory. Nike, too, famously suffered from damaging allegations of using 'sweatshop' labour in the Far East to manufacture trainers, each pair of which would sell in the USA for reportedly many times the weekly wage of the factory workers paid to produce them.

Most recently, there has been the complex issue of GM or genetically modified foods. Monsanto has been at the forefront of promoting the potential benefits of these new biotechnological advances. However, things did not go well from quite early on. Monsanto's problems were exacerbated

Cartoon 4 'GM *maize*'.

by the Government's less than decisive lead on the subject and their key spokesman at the time, Lord Sainsbury, Minister for Science, quickly became vulnerable when it emerged that he had personally invested in companies closely involved in biotechnology. His familial links to the grocery superstore of the same name also presented competitor retailers with a golden opportunity to exploit a political issue.

The main protagonist in this was Iceland, a hitherto relatively low-profile specialist frozen food retailer which had begun to make some waves with its full-scale launch into home delivery through its purchase of a fleet of Mercedes vehicles. However, it was the outright ban on any GM foods that really grabbed the headlines for Iceland, capitalising as it did on the emotions of a naturally apprehensive population and adding fuel to what was already becoming a sensationalised issue.

In this new era, corporations need to adapt their management behaviour to anticipate events and reactions much further than before in acknowledging a much more interested, media literate, shareholding customer base. The potential strategic downsides need to be explored much more fully to anticipate and prevent the possible chinks in the brand armour or the hostages to fortune that may be created by a new marketing or communications initiative. The total brand behaviour needs to hang together in a cohesive set of manners, which all parts of the organisation can understand and abide by.

Perhaps the most salutary example of how the new consumerism can bring even the mightiest low is that of Barclays Bank and their 'big' positioning strategy launched in the UK in early 2000.

Case History: BARCLAYS BANK

A recent example of how badly things can go wrong if there hasn't been adequate anticipation and if there isn't an agreed set of 'manners' is the case of Barclays Bank in the UK. Early in 1999 Barclays appointed a new advertising agency, Leagas Delaney to its account with a brief to develop a corporate positioning for the bank. Whilst there had been a number of successful campaigns for Barclay's individual products and services, most notably for Barclaycard, the bank had struggled, like many large, long-established financial institutions, to achieve a convincing and distinctive brand positioning.

The problem for Barclays was that in the customers' mind, banks were surrounded by negative associations, with the words 'big bank' having become synonymous with exploitative, non-customer friendly behaviour. No matter how many advertisements had tried to persuade people of the friendly caring nature of their local bank manager, the cold, aloof, even intimidating imagery remained. Banks are perceived as a necessary evil and all as bad as each other. This plus the inertia created by standing orders and direct debits explains the paradox of an industry where such negative imagery doesn't lead to brand switching on any great scale and where it's notoriously difficult to build new financial service brands without literally buying customers with loss-leading interest rates.

Barclays, like its competitors, had tried all the conventional routes to creating a positive brand positioning and always ended up to a greater or lesser degree with approaches which denied the essential truth of what it was as a business. Perceiving this, Leagas Delaney, proposed to Barclays that they should embark on a radical campaign. Radical because for once it would tell the truth; it is only as a big bank that Barclays was able to offer the reassurance born of sheer size, plus the expanding range of specialised financial services only really made possible through scale and strength in depth. Barclays was to be unashamedly positioned as 'big' and the campaign would demonstrate over time the customer benefits that bigness conferred.

The board of Barclays, encouraged by positive consumer research on the proposed 'big' positioning, committed to the campaign and the filming of the first set of commercials commenced in the autumn of 1999.

A great coup was scored in securing the agreement of Sir Anthony Hopkins, of *Silence of the Lambs* fame, to star in the 60-second launch film.

It was to be a multi-media campaign and included in the package were some spectacularly 'big' double-page colour press advertisements in all the major broadsheet newspapers, a size which few advertisers can dare to afford, but which in Barclays case would be a classic example illustrating the truth of McLuhan's famous saying: 'the medium is the message'.

Plans were well laid for the campaign launch in the spring of 2000, with media booked, commercials filmed and press ads produced. There was also a full programme of internal communications designed to brief the whole of the bank on the new 'big' positioning and preview the advertising to them. The reactions were generally very positive; the work made employees and managers proud to be in Barclays and the campaign gave them permission to be true to what they were, namely employees of one of the biggest banks in the world and not have to apologise for it. Sadly apologies were to be the order of the day only too soon.

There had been a long-term trend towards the reduction in branch networks; by any standards the UK was 'over shopped' in the financial services sector. Just taking banks and building societies in 1999, there was still a total of 2,400 building societies and 13,500 banks despite the fact that in the last 5 years alone there had been 2,700 bank branch closures. This trend had been accelerated by the advent of telephone and Internet banking and encouraged by the widespread use of credit, and debit cards, which could be used to withdraw money from the ATM network, the 'hole in the wall' money dispensers of which there were 28,435 in 1999 in the UK.

There had been a steady trickle of branch closure announcements from the various banks and building societies, which had not attracted much attention apart from within the particular localities concerned, but when Barclays declared its programme it decided to do so in one national announcement. Though the absolute numbers of branches involved was relatively small, 171, in some cases the closures would leave a small village or town without a bank at all. The storm that broke was intense with newspaper headlines galore and questions in the Houses of Parliament.

Meanwhile, a separate issue was rapidly bubbling up to the surface, that of customer charges for the use of the national network of ATMs. The basic problem was that the major banks, whose infrastructure it was, resented the fact that smaller financial institutions had the use of them on behalf of their customers and therefore gained a *de facto* national presence that they could otherwise not have afforded. The big players,

"Apparently, on a clear day you can see both Barclays Banks!"

Cartoon 5 'Barclays!'.

such as Barclays, felt it not unreasonable to charge such customers for the privilege of using their machines, and were locked in negotiations with the other members of the so-called LINK network of ATMs. Progress was slow, and perhaps in an attempt to break the deadlock, Barclays broke cover and declared that it would impose a £1.50 transaction charge on any non-Barclays customers using its ATMs, describing it as a 'disloyalty fee'. Again the furore this caused was intense with politicians, consumer groups and the press having a field day.

In this climate of branch closures, and ATM 'taxes', the last thing Barclays needed was another controversy, but sure enough it was lurking there waiting to be discovered. This additional issue concerned the remuneration of the new CEO, who had been recruited after a number of false starts following the departure, in less than happy circumstances, of Martin Taylor in 1998. It had taken time, and money, to lure a candidate of suitable calibre to what had become seen as a high-risk appointment. Pending the recruitment, at an annual salary cost of over £1m., of Canadian Matthew Barrett as CEO, Sir Peter Middleton took on the role of Chairman and Chief Executive, and he was rewarded with a pay packet and bonus of £1.76m. This was announced at the same time as the branch closure programme.

The press, already lining up against Barclays, soon picked up on what in other circumstances would have hardly merited more than a couple of sentences, and blew this new example of 'fat cat' salary levels into another big story. Then the 'big' campaign broke onto the nation's TV screens with Sir Anthony Hopkins playing himself immaculately as a big movie star talking about his 'big day', 'big car', 'big bucks', 'big deal', 'big hitter', 'big movie' and 'my fee which should be big', and all hell broke loose.

It's hard to imagine how Barclays top management, aware of this major long-researched new corporate brand positioning, which had been agreed and communicated within the bank, had allowed the branch closure programme to be announced in the manner and with the timing it had been, and for their aggressive ATM policy to be declared in the same timeframe as the new campaign launch, let alone be drawn into a public debate over top executive remuneration.

Now the press really did go to town. Not only were Barclays criticised for their insensitivity in airing commercials glorifying 'bigness' at the time they were leaving small rural communities without a bank branch and proposing to penalise people for using their ATMs, they were also attacked at a product level. Journalists, scenting blood, started comparing interest rates and charges to show what poor value Barclays was offering compared to the best available. The headline in the *Sunday Times* on 30 April 2000 read 'For big savings steer clear of Barclays'. Such price comparisons are commonplace in any financial section of any newspaper any day, but spiced with pictures of Sir Anthony Hopkins and in the context of major television and press advertising, they became big stories.

To cap it all, the Barclays Annual General Meeting fell right in the middle of all this. In a scene reminiscent of the Marks & Spencer AGM at which an irate shareholder, Teresa Vanneck Surplice, got up, modelled her stockings and told the Board their underwear was dull and boring (she got her way as *Agent Provocateur*, Soho designers and retailers of sexy bras, panties and other garments were subsequently hired by M&S to revitalise their range with great sales success), the Barclays meeting was high-jacked by pensioner Jessie Bonner-Thomas.

She attacked the bank for its recent misdemeanours and was especially withering in her condemnation of the CEO's £1m+ salary in the context of the increase of £1 in the current year in her own tiny pension as a Barclay's widow. She was particularly scathing about the £15,000 being paid by shareholders to help look after Barrett's tax. The Chairman, Sir Peter Middleton was forced to make a public apology, which made all the papers. The headline 'Barclays says sorry for its handling of bank closures' appeared in the *Financial Times* on 27 April 2000.

At this point things really could have unravelled for Barclays, but fortunately they didn't. Perhaps a significant element in the recovery was the grace under pressure of Sir Anthony Hopkins. To the great credit of their star, the use of a celebrity in advertising did not backfire on Barclays as it had done for Pepsi with Michael Jackson. Hopkins refused to be drawn into the controversy and his dignified, disarming stance was worth his appearance fee all over again, as he made it clear that it was just an ad and that he had no personal axe to grind. 'Sir Anthony sidesteps "big" row' was the headline in the *Financial Times* on 28 April 2000.

To the credit too of Barclays top management, who must have been under enormous pressure to stop the campaign, they held their line and continued with it. To have buckled under would have compounded the public-relations disaster, but sticking to their guns sent a powerful signal to their employees and their customers. The bank really did believe that 'big' was best and that its customers would benefit as a result. They were also encouraged by early results from the campaign tracking study, which seemed to vindicate their bold new strategy and revealed no significant customer negatives, despite the massive amounts of negative p.r. the bank had experienced during the fieldwork period.

The Barclays experience is that nowadays the total behaviour of the corporation as a brand must hang together in a co-ordinated and holistic way. Clearly the stance that Barclays took with its 'big' positioning had in-built risks, given the historical customer perceptions of the major clearing banks, and it was essential that the positive benefits be conveyed rather than the negative ones. Unfortunately the company behaviour regarding the ATM and branch closure issues came across as high-handed rather than highly principled, alienating people and giving a hostage to fortune to the likes of the Halifax and NatWest who subsequently announced they would waive the ATM charge. When embarking on a new communications campaign it's crucial that the CEO and the top management run through the total behaviour that it implies, and then ensure that all relevant policies fall in line.

With customers increasingly being shareholders, the political stakes are raised. Combined with an increased emphasis on the role of corporations in society, management needs to pay more attention to the political and spiritual dimensions.

19

How Brand Problems can be Part of the Solution

Problems create opportunities. In identifying problems the pre-condition of a solution is created. In acknowledging customer problems fully, the brand can actually strengthen its relationship. An important dimension of a brand's manners is this capability of owning problems rather than allowing them to own the brand. Companies need to create a culture wherein the whole organisation embraces this idea and acts upon it.

Man is a problem-solving animal and many of the greatest inventions have come from tackling the difficulties encountered in a manufacturing process or a scientific exploration. In a very real sense problems are the stimulus for creativity and therefore a key task is to identify them in order to trigger a positive response and deal with them. Thus the brand manners of the culture need to be such that people who bring problems to the fore are seen as contributors not destroyers; 'bad' news now needs to be seen as the potential for 'good' news later.

This is not the prevailing climate in the traditional 'command and control' organisation where problematic issues are much more likely to be swept under the nearest available carpet or passed on to an unsuspecting colleague. Clearly the political aspects of the organisation need to be addressed if there is a need to move from a 'blame' to a 'claim' culture, i.e. one in which people are rewarded for identifying, owning, and solving problems. Employees need to see themselves as critics in the best sense of the word, discovering the good and the bad things, and then bringing them to management, ideally with a proposed solution. Individuals need to feel free to share solutions they have found to their problems with the rest of the team so that a thousand other people can avoid the mistake that one person has made.

The company's cynics are the great enemies of this sort of constructive thinking and the brand manners need to be defended against them. The word 'cynic' comes from the Greek word for 'dog like'. This was because there was a group of people in ancient Greece who gave up all of society's offerings, and went to live more naturally in caves, wearing natural fabric, and with the freedom to urinate wherever they happened to be, much like dogs. However, despite their 'back to nature' lifestyle they did not stop criticising modern literature, and the arts. Thus Diogenes of Sinope their founder was likened to a dog, 'kynikos' in ancient Greek, and hence the cynics were born. Taken literally in a contemporary context, cynics are people who piss all over other people's ideas!

Cynics are a favourite topic for Frank Dick, OBE. He is one of the world's leading conditioning coaches, who has advised such stars as Daley Thompson, Boris Becker and Katarina Witt. He has a very clear picture of the key types in an organisation facing change and these are set out in the following graphics.

Figure 39 shows the typical hierarchy from the top level of the Board all the way down to work teams. Across the organisation will be a spectrum of dispositions, ranging from the 'enthusiasts' to the 'cynics'.

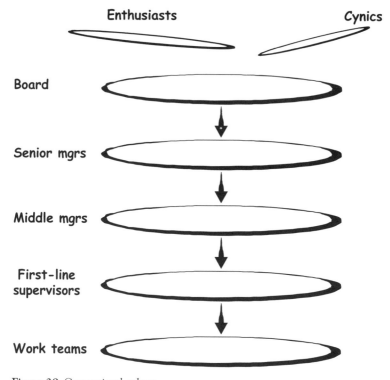

Figure 39 *Conventional culture.*

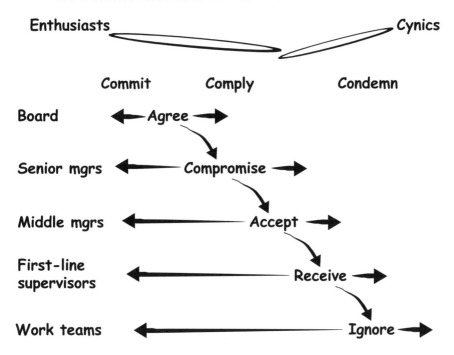

Figure 40 *Conventional culture change.*

Imagine that the Board decides upon a new initiative, which entails change. In order to achieve this they must communicate effectively both down the hierarchy and across the personal typologies in the company. Frank Dick uses a very clear graphic sequence (Figure 40) to show the wrong and right ways of enlisting support for a new direction.

This is where the problems start. Typically each level of management will communicate the new strategy, plan or programme to the level below it, but each level will itself contain a spectrum of people ranging from those who commit, comply with, or condemn the new idea. Thus as the communication cascades downwards it is diluted at each level. Whilst the Board may all agree, senior managers will often compromise the idea, based on their previous experience. Middle managers may be more accepting, but in a compliant manner, whilst first-line supervisors will simply receive instructions. It's hardly surprising then, that work teams, the people who will most likely have to bear the brunt of most of the real change and effort, are more inclined to ignore what they may see and receive as yet another half-hearted management scheme.

In Figure 41 the solution to this syndrome is proposed: the key is for the communication of the new initiative to be effected amongst all the company's enthusiasts to get them enlisted and committed, before rolling out the programme horizontally to the rest of the company. As Dick points

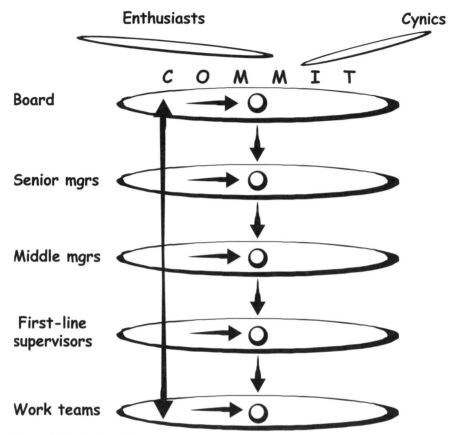

Figure 41 *Real culture change.*

out, cynics are useful at one level – they can see and articulate the problems in any given situation, but do so in a negative manner. Within companies at least the position of the cynics is clear, as is that of the committed enthusiasts. It is the 'collaborators' who are dangerous because they are compliant, tend not to declare their true position and are quite likely to ignore a problem with a new approach and wait for an accident to happen, rather than be constructive and bring it to anyone's attention.

Perhaps every company should have a 'problem box' as well as an 'opportunities box', not just a single 'suggestions box', in order to remind people of both dimensions which surround an issue. This should be made visible both in reality and on the intranet. Julian Richer describes in his book *The Richer Way* how he has built his business, Richer Sounds, using an incentivised staff suggestions scheme as a key element in his highly successful brand manners. Many of his innovative ideas were put into action by Archie Norman and Allan Leighton in their celebrated relaunch of UK supermarket chain Asda, now owned by US giant Wal-Mart.

To build on this approach, the team on a particular product or service brand needs to spend time on negative scenario planning as well as the more enjoyable positive blue sky thinking and dreaming. Another way of systematically breaking down defensive barriers is to set up a programme of regular mutual review boards. Teams within the company critique each other's strategy/production/process/packaging/positioning/communication and in so doing pre-empt competitive moves or avert potential difficulties. External consultancies can be used to great effect in this process, as long as there is a trust relationship between client and advisor; third parties need to have the confidence to report that 'the Emperor has no clothes' without the fear of being fired. In producing the strategic positioning for the brand, considerable time and energy should be deployed on competitive analysis, benchmarking and critiquing the brand, as well as on the more overtly positive aspects of creative development, production and implementation.

Test marketing of products and services has always been a key part of the new product development (NPD) process, as indeed have exploratory qualitative research via individual interviews, focus groups, quantitative hall tests, and in home trials. All these techniques can help in identifying problem areas and therefore providing the springboard to solutions, or the justification for aborting a project with no viable prospects before too much more capital is expended. One useful variation in the NPD process is to recruit a panel of product or service rejecters, in addition to the acceptors, and get them to critique your brand. Their articulation of the negatives can lead to modifications, which could widen the product or service appeal and very often sheds valuable light on the brand's strengths too.

When customers complain, especially by phone, letter or e-mail, it's very important to acknowledge fully their problem. This requires an important piece of brand manners, because it's often very difficult to do this when the customer is being very aggressive or rude. In fact, the quickest way to defuse an angry customer call is to repeat back to the customer exactly what they have said to the employee, as in: 'So your problem is that …' then repeat their precise description of it. In behaving in this manner, the brand representative literally takes the problem from the customer and in playing it back so accurately demonstrates to the customer that their problem or complaint really has been fully understood. The other effect is that very often, in hearing back their own language, denuded of its angry or aggressive tone and stripped back to its verbal content, they realise how unpleasant they're being and the embarrassment calms them. The brand also needs to know how to say 'sorry' when the situation requires it; rarely is there anything more disarming than a sincere apology.

When customers write in to the company with complaints, these can be very useful guides to issues in the product or service – how often do these letters get beyond the customer service desk and on to the brand managers, let alone the CEOs? When customers write to publications complaining about poor service or product performance this can generate negative p.r. How many companies stay really close to the key journalists and broadcasters in their market sector in order to get first notice of potentially damaging stories? The Internet, with its news groups, chat rooms and citizen sites is a rich new source of risk for brands. In this context disaffected customers may not bother e-mailing the company that has aggrieved them, they simply tell other people about their problem. This presents a very significant logistical task for brand managers wishing to ensure their brand promise remains intact. A possible solution could come in the form of new types of software from companies such as vigiltech.com, which can search the Internet looking for any new occurrences of company or brand names, immediate competitors or other relevant key words. This automatic robot surveillance of the net is likely to become a standard tool for protecting the reputation of brands. There are consultancies such as myreputation.com springing up which seek to do just this for corporations and famous stars who may have literally thousands of fan and fanatic sites in their name or variations of it, and many of these will be defamatory or pornographic.

When customers send back products it's a great opportunity to diagnose the reasons for rejection. Too few companies do what successful direct marketer Lands End do which is to include a simple questionnaire to be completed as a part of their returns policy. Given that in mail order clothing up to 30% of a particular garment may be returned, this represents a major low-cost data-gathering exercise and it makes the customer feel it's a responsive, professional organisation.

A mandatory product recall, for example in the case of a model-wide fault in a motor vehicle, can present manufacturer and dealer with an expensive logistical exercise, and one which can seriously inconvenience customers. However, if handled well, and with the driver's interests at the forefront of considerations, it is possible to turn this potentially negative situation into one which actually reinforces the relationship. In another key consumer durables sector a recent survey by DMIS showed that 8.2% of people thought the most important factor in customer loyalty in the telecoms, satellite and TV sector was that companies sort out problems quickly. People are realists – they appreciate that things can and do go wrong – what they look for are brand manners which are equally realistic in their respect for the rights and convenience of the customer.

Case History: GATEWAY 2000

An excellent example of a corporation which has taken the idea that problems are part of the solution to the very heart of its operations is Gateway, the direct-sell personal computer company. Ted Waitt, the founder of Gateway, started the business from the family cattle farm in Iowa in 1985, the year after the celebrated TV commercial from Apple was aired in a break in the Superbowl and crystallised the idea that 'Big Blue', as IBM was referred to, was the enemy of personal freedom of thinking in computing. The Gateway enterprise was one of the earliest in the newly emerging world of personal computers to embrace the idea of selling direct to customers as opposed to through a distribution network of re-sellers. Almost by definition, this business process creates a problem in the context of personal computer systems. Not only is this because each individual may have slightly differing needs and thus require a variation on the personal computer specification, but also because the Holy Grail of 'plug and play' still eludes significant numbers of people whose technical knowledge may be challenged by the simplest of instructions. Thus the selling and specifying processes and the after-sales care, which are crucial for any PC company, become a matter of commercial life or death in the case of a remote direct-sell operation where physical personal contact is designed out of the distribution system.

Gateway is now a Fortune 250 company. It was ranked number one in USA consumer PC revenue in 1999 and was rated among the top ten best corporate reputations in America according to a survey conducted in August of 1999 by Harris Interactive and the Reputation Institute and published in *The Wall Street Journal*. In 1999, Gateway was seventh in total return to shareholders among Fortune 500 companies and tenth in total shareholder returns over the past five years. Gateway had total global revenue of $8.65 billion in 1999 and shipped 4.68 million systems. Gateway began its European operations in 1993 when it opened its manufacturing plant and European, Middle East and Africa headquarters in Dublin, Ireland. Today, the company is firmly established throughout Europe and sells into Austria, Belgium, France, Germany, Luxembourg, Ireland, the Netherlands, Sweden, Switzerland, Spain, the UK, Middle East and Africa.

Part and parcel of their success has been their visual identity and their marketing communications programme. Gateway's first national magazine advertisement in 1988 was based on the farm and its Holstein dairy cows, which are common in the Midwest. The cow mascot led to the creation of the distinctive black-and-white spot corporate identity and product packaging design, which became imprinted on the boxes in 1991. These cows have remained central to the Gateway advertising campaigns ever since. Clearly, for a provider that never meets its customers and sends its products by courier, the computer boxes themselves have become powerful visible ambassadors for the brand. The cow imagery carries with it something of the freedom of the prairies and the romance of the cattle drive immortalised in so many Hollywood movies.

Gateway's original mission was, and still stands as: 'To humanise the digital revolution' and the cow spots identity serves as a reminder of the company's roots and values of hard work, honesty, friendliness and quality (Figure 42). On a farm, every animal must be looked after, assessed and treated according to its own needs and criteria, as does every client at Gateway; they are all treated according to their specific characteristics, not collectively. One can imagine the chaos that would break out on a farm if all animals were fed the same food and exercised in the same manner. Perhaps there is an analogy with Gateway's clients; if they are all assumed to have the same technical know-how and their systems to

Figure 42 *The Gateway box.*

all have the same specification needs, then the majority of clients would rapidly become disillusioned with the service.

Gateway has three chains of distribution: telephone, stores, Internet; they started with telephone sales, and then branched out into retail and the web. From a very early stage they have been client focused (their buyers are not referred to as customers) and the company continues to emphasise the importance of long-term relationships with clients. Alec Maycock, Vice-President of Client Care for Gateway has observed, 'We feel that the word client emphasises our commitment to a long-term relationship, whereas customer implies a one-off purchase'.

The maintenance of this long-term relationship involves ensuring that clients and employees understand the needs, capabilities and upgrade opportunities of each and every system as a personal and highly client-specific project. As a result the Gateway client feels very much in control of their system, irrespective of their level of technical know-how. Gateway place heavy emphasis on their client understanding what they need from their system and indeed, what the system has to offer them. This is achieved through personalising systems to exact client needs and avoiding all categorisation and stereotyping, e.g. 'students only use word processors'.

It is true that until something goes wrong, Gateway have limited contact with their clients, though it should be noted that all contact that does occur is proactive and to a degree unexpected compared with other companies. After a system has been ordered and delivered from the Internet or any other source, a proactive welcome call is made to ensure that the client is happy with the system and it is this attention to client care and welfare alongside Gateway's excellent problem-solving systems that is the driving force behind this leading PC company's success.

Gateway believe that value can be really added to their brand through their client interactions when things go wrong with a system or with their processes. This is achieved by the ethos and environment, which is so heavily embedded within the culture of the organisation. Staff are motivated and encouraged to deliver a warm and friendly service, by several means. Firstly, although the call centres do not differ from many others in terms of their utilitarian ' cubicle layout (Gateway believe that this has little bearing on employee performance), the staff are monitored in a different manner. The absolute number of calls is not important. Instead customer satisfaction and first-time resolution of problems are considered to be the crucial determinants of success. If call-centre productivity were measured in terms of numbers of calls then staff would be less concerned about client welfare and more conscious of time spent per call. Staff are constantly reminded and encouraged to 'treat the client as they themselves would wish to be treated'.

Alec Maycock's view is that 'Gateway techies don't feel that they are fixing the system, but that they are helping the client' and that this is a critical mindset, which stems from the client-focused philosophy within the company. Often in personal computer companies it is the technical staff that creates the alienation and distance between the company and the client because they become stereotyped as 'weird, with no human skills'. At Gateway constant client contact between the 'techies' and the client reinforces their approachable and friendly nature.

According to Maycock, Gateway have no mission statements or management tools to achieve these results, 'it is simply a case of walking the talk'. So staff take their management seriously and develop close and genuine relationships. People really do interact on the same level, and there is no sense that the manager is more important as a person than a client-care assistant. Living the brand manners of the organisation is a relatively simple task as the core values of Gateway are all human qualities, which are easy to reinforce providing everybody is committed to them (Figure 43). 'If there is a piece of rubbish on the floor, whether

Figure 43 *The Gateway exploded box.*

the manager or a customer-service assistant walks past it, they will pick it up.' There are no bureaucratic policies, which prevent employees doing what is best for the client.

It is the client care, not the routine ordering system which provides the real added value to the relationships which form at Gateway, especially when things do not necessarily go to plan and there is a problem with a system or another issue. Like FedEx, Gateway believe that they should routinise and automate the simple and straightforward processes and devote their energies into personally solving and correcting the client's system when things go wrong. This is how they are able to develop strong relationships when situations are less favourable, and as a result clients feel confident to use the Internet or other technical means with more routine issues as they have faith that the system works. This creates a win-win situation: Gateway employees are aware that in fact providing an outstanding service when things go wrong is likely to cause fewer calls and complaints in the future.

So how does Gateway really make the best of their problems? If a client detects an error on their system they will call a member of the client-care team. Often the problem can be diagnosed over the phone and so the solution can start to be devised immediately. The client will be offered the chance to start the repair process or the system can be picked up and repaired at a Gateway site. If the client wishes to have a go at fixing it, they can be e-mailed, faxed or posted the solutions. Alternatively, they can follow step-by-step phone instructions while the client-care team are live on the line. There is also the chance to take part in Gateway's prepared on-line tutorials or to go into a Gateway chat room to talk to other customers who may have the same problem or issue.

This strategy is in place to ensure that every type of client is catered for. Some will want to at least start the fixing process themselves; others will want nothing to do with the technical side. From this early stage the customer is treated as a complete individual, no assumptions about technical expertise or preference are made hence ensuring the client has complete control. This puts them at ease and enables them to interact more efficiently with the Gateway team. The personalisation of Gateway's high-tech database enables employees to view all previous client interactions with the Gateway team and so assess their level of technical knowledge. Clients do not need to regurgitate their past experiences and process preferences. This can be embarrassing if, for example, the client has very limited knowledge. Using their database the

Gateway team can immediately see this and automatically arrange a pick-up of the system without having to go through the motions of how the client wishes their system to be fixed.

After the client has made this initial call a 'proactive client care call' is made usually about three days afterwards. This is to see whether the problem has been resolved, how well it was resolved and whether any further action needs to be taken to better the situation. This enables peers to assess each other's performance and also the client is reassured that their welfare is important to Gateway. Quite often questions will arise in the client's mind after the repair is complete, and this call therefore gives them an opportunity to sort out any outstanding issues when they are less stressed and without having had to make another 'problem' call themselves.

Key to this powerful culture, in which problems are genuinely welcomed as an opportunity to bond better with clients, is the calibre of personnel employed. Staff at Gateway go through rigorous training and assessment to ensure that they are the right type of person for the brand. These assessments include psychometric testing, which is entirely client focused and a great deal of attention is paid to the cultures, values and origins of potential team members. There's not much room for the cynic at Gateway.

The key lesson from this chapter is to make problem identification a positive element within corporate brand manners. Train everybody in the technique of 'problem acknowledgement' and profile the company's personnel to establish who are the 'committed', the 'co-operators' and the 'cynics'. Re-train or re-recruit to mitigate the second and third groups. Develop a clear set of behaviours for the way in which internal and external problems will be dealt with, including areas for discretion and upward referral. Create the concept of 'problem detection' and build a programme to collect systematically data on problems through the following techniques and channels:

- negative scenario planning
- internal mutual team review boards
- external consultancy audits
- competitor analysis and benchmarking
- customer correspondence

- customer complaints
- pro-active p.r. programme
- customer returns and product recalls
- customer database 'flags' to indicate problem history
- internet searches to capture brand references
- two suggestion boxes: 'problems' and 'opportunities'

The trick is always to view issues or problems as opportunities for improvement!

20

Protecting the Brand

If a brand is to protect its reputation effectively it has to acknowledge that the general trading environment has become much more hostile. Customers are much more likely to take legal action against companies. Some extremists will go much further and take direct action against corporations they detest. Thus an important dimension of a brand's manners is its attitude and behaviour with respect to risk assessment and self-protection. These increasingly essential precautions need to be taken to ensure that all the expense and commitment in communicating and delivering the brand promise to customers is not undermined or even sabotaged by a relatively small minority.

There has been a massive increase in legal actions against companies by private individuals. For example, firms of lawyers are now advertising on BSkyB offering to take on personal injury claims on a no-win, no-fee basis, thus encouraging plaintiffs to come forward! The UK Government and the EC have passed a series of employment laws which significantly increase the strength of the employee's position and make it essential that employers are much more careful about the ways in which they treat their staff. Nowadays in the UK, there is no financial limit for claims for wrongful dismissal at an industrial tribunal if it finds that someone has been unfairly sacked.

On the other hand, in the Internet and e-mail age, companies are having to become much tougher in protecting themselves: some reports suggest that 40% of employees' time spent on line at the office is for personal as opposed to professional reasons. Recently there was a case of a woman being fired for searching and booking a holiday, after doing 150 searches and then booking on line. Lois Franxhi, 29, lost her claim for unfair dismissal reported the *Daily Mail* on 15 June 2000. In a landmark out-of-court settlement, UK insurance giant Norwich Union (now CGNU) paid £450,000, after a staff member's e-mail was found to be libellous to a competitor. As a result of these sorts of incidents and the very real damage caused by computer viruses, perhaps it's not surprising that reportedly up to 55% of UK companies monitor staff Internet access. The Government has tried hard, but unsuccessfully to introduce legislation to enable widespread monitoring of e-mail traffic in the interests of national security.

In responding to these new problems companies need to be increasingly thorough in their human resources processes and policies. Senior managers have to be regularly appraised of the latest developments in the legislation, as they can no longer leave this sensitive area entirely to the specialists. Sadly, in this increasingly litigious environment a wrong word, ambiguous gesture or loosely worded e-mail can set off a potentially damaging train of events. With the publicity that so often accompanies cases between employer and employee, it is rare that the company, and therefore the brand, emerges unscathed.

Perhaps an equally, if not more threatening development, especially for the CEO and Board Directors of companies, has been the move by the UK Labour Government to introduce much tougher penalties for corporate misdemeanours. Frustrated by the apparent personal immunity to disasters caused by their company's errors of omission or commission, in May 2000 the Government announced its intention to introduce new categories of corporate crime to ensure that companies are far more strongly discouraged from carrying on their business in any ways which might endanger the public.

In 1996 the Law Commission published a report into changing the laws on manslaughter replacing it by reckless killing, and killing by gross carelessness. Home Secretary, Jack Straw's latest shake up proposes that there be a third category of unintentional killing. The proposal also goes on to say that Company Directors and employees can be charged with these crimes if direct responsibility can be proved. As this is often difficult to show, then companies themselves can be prosecuted, and since they cannot be sent to jail, then an unlimited fine can be imposed. Jack Straw wants to go further and try to get powers to disqualify directors, and charge individuals with corporate killing. Thus there may well soon be the crimes of 'corporate murder' and 'corporate manslaughter' for companies, and brands, to contend with.

Whilst this attempt to hold irresponsible individuals to account is laudable, this new legislation nevertheless presents litigious customers with a very threatening new legal means of attacking companies. As with so many things the Internet has accelerated the process of making transparent and available, information that has been legally accessible in the past but very difficult to find. The UK Company, 192, already mentioned, has opened up the private addresses and telephone numbers of all the company directors in the UK. Armed with such powerful sources of information and with the legal means at their disposal the 'consumer anarchists' are a real threat to brands.

Perhaps a lesson in how to handle this new threat more effectively can be taken from one of the world's foremost brand marketers, McDonald's. During the 1990s this leading company was involved in a two and a half year legal action, the longest libel trial in English history, after it tried to stop two activists in London from handing out leaflets detailing alleged crimes McDonald's were supposed to have been committing. The defendants, Helen Steel and David Morris, suffered from surveillance by private eyes, were denied legal aid, and had to wade through some 40,000 pages of background reading in order to mount their defence in the long trial. Whilst the judge ruled in favour of most of the points the couple were pursuing, they failed to have all their points vindicated, and were ordered to pay £60,000 damages. As they were broke they were unable to pay, but they did create enough media attention for McDonald's not to pursue the money. In the process of all this they created the anti-McDonald's website, Mcspotlight.org, which details the case in depth and has over 21,000 pages of information.

The problem for McDonald's was that despite their best intentions, they came across in the media as Goliath to the defendants' David and public sympathies seem to lie with the supposed underdog in these situations. They may have won the legal battle, but they lost the PR war. In a new, more proactive departure, McDonald's have now embarked on a programme of consultation with these activists in an attempt to come to terms with them. Their hope is that by being seen to be engaging in debate with these groups, they will win back public sympathy and in the process they will also gain valuable insights into the activists' agendas, which in turn may lead to corrective action. They have also begun communicating much more effectively what they bring to the local economy in order to counteract the caricature that is so often drawn of them by anti-capitalist dissidents in so many markets. McDonald's are stressing their role as local employer and their contribution in the community through social or cause-related marketing programmes that have become an important part of their brand promise.

Wal-Mart is another great USA brand to have suffered at the hands of the disaffected. A disgruntled shopper, Richard Harris, who was asked to leave after a manager thought he heard him mutter a racial slur, started up wal-martsucks.com. Richard vowed to cause a scene and certainly did with his web site. It is a forum for disgruntled employees and shoppers alike to share stories and rate stores on their effectiveness. Wal-Mart is aware of the site, but say that it does not affect their bottom line, and they remain proud of their customer and employee record. However, nearly a million people have perused the site since its creation on 31 August 1997 and this must create a pressure on the company that could not have existed before the advent of the web.

It's not just the huge corporations who are under increasing scrutiny, facilitated by the Internet. Nor is it just the role of disaffected customers or the more politically motivated consumer anarchists to expose malfeasance – it is a public service duty too. In the USA the New York Police Department puts up regularly on its website restaurant inspection data provided by the New York Health Department. Every legally registered eatery in the district of New York is there, with all the details about their last food inspection, including reports of all restaurants, which have given rise to complaints about hygiene standards. Some exclusive haunts of the rich and famous have been rather embarrassed to be revealed to be home to the same cockroaches, mice and flies that inhabit the neighbourhood café!

Problems of hygiene pale into insignificance when compared to the assault on Planet Hollywood. Perhaps already fading as a restaurant brand as the box office drawing power of its star backers such as Sylvester Stallone and Arnold Schwarzenegger declined, Planet Hollywood was dealt a body blow by a series of anti-American bomb attacks (ironic if it were not so tragic, in the context of the sort of movies which made their fortunes) such as the one with customer fatalities in Cape Town, which hit their South African business badly.

In this climate of transparency, affluence and freedom to act, which favours the individual to a high degree, there does seem to be a newly emerging group of consumerists who have taken a much more aggressive stance on the issues they feel strongly about. Often very well educated and well off, they commit themselves to the pursuit of companies and causes with the full array of communications channels at their disposal and a degree of sophistication which can defeat all but the most well-prepared. Again the Internet and e-mail allow people to spread their views much more easily, and this allows them to join forces with others of like mind from around the world: the chat rooms are rife with disgruntled people attacking things.

An example of this new sophistication is Huntingdon Life Sciences, a company which has been under sustained attack from animal rights activists. Such has been the ferocity of the onslaught and the threats to personal safety that this UK business is seriously contemplating moving its financial backing to the USA, so as to stop the risk of these activists acting against its present sponsors the NatWest through attacks on its high-street branches. The activists have already made provision for this move, joining up with activists in America in order to exert pressure on potential alternative suppliers of finance. No doubt this will make Huntingdon's cost of money higher, if it can obtain it at all under the circumstances. This financially driven strategy is a long way advanced from the placard protest. By the same token it's almost certainly required Huntingdon and the bank to look long and hard at their ethical stances in an area fraught with difficult issues.

Measures you may wish to consider in protecting your brand include the following:

- Assign the responsibility for crisis management and the development of a comprehensive prevention and containment strategy to a top executive.
- Commission a 360-degree risk assessment audit on an annual basis. This should cover everything from operational, to financial and contractual, to information technology and security through to the political. (See mmcenterpriserisk.com for more detail on what can be done.) Require key suppliers to do the same.
- Hire some 'white knight' hackers to attempt to break into the company's telephony and computer systems.
- Register the obvious 'negative' domain names around your own company or brand names. For example 'companynamesucks.com' or any obvious negative puns e.g. Ronald McDeath.
- Identify and open up dialogue with any activist or pressure groups that operate in your business sector.
- Build closer relationships with law enforcement agencies.
- Maintain an active marketing communications campaign for the company or brand that has as a significant component the efforts being made in the community or towards good causes. If none exists, create a Social or Cause Related Marketing programme.
- Agree standard levels of brand response to the main predictable threats – the manners in a crisis.

Adopting these measures will lower the probability of potentially serious damage.

Section Four
'Happy Surprises'

Having created the Brand Promise, we move to the direct customer interface, which should result in 'Happy surprises'. Here, we have chosen four topics: defining gestures, listening, customer pledges and moments of truth.

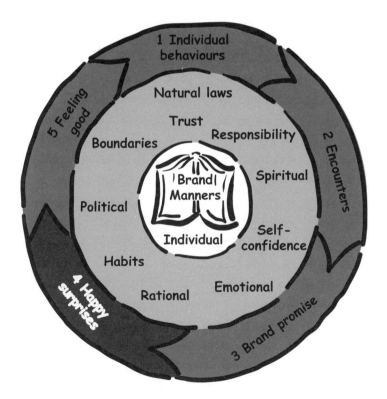

Figure 44 *Section Four: The Brand Manners Improvement Cycle – happy surprises.*

21

How Defining Gestures Build Brands

Certain 'defining gestures' or behaviours can crystallise in the customer's mind what the brand is all about. These are the key characteristics of an individual – the verbal ticks, hand gestures or mannerisms which make them instantly recognisable and distinctive. As such, these defining gestures are an important element in a brand's system of manners. Some can be deliberately created and even included formally in the brand identity or its advertising in the shape of a logo or a slogan, but others emerge out of a culture conducive to great customer service.

The defining gesture contained in a brand idea can become an internal as well as an external fount of brand identity and behaviour. The skills of marketing departments and their marketing communications agencies are such that powerful statements of the brand promise can be produced and placed in the media with dramatic effect. In making a public promise to the customer, a corporation is also making a promise to itself.

Thus the public promise becomes a 'flag in the ground', an inspirational distance ahead, and becomes a goal for the company to march towards. The fact that the 'flag' is repeatedly planted in public by advertising and other communications gives it a powerful reinforcing effect on employees and therefore makes it more likely that the goal will be achieved. By the same token, it is very dangerous to 'write cheques which the company can't cash' and it is essential that these public promises can be delivered on, thus making them come true.

Because of the complexity of everyday life and the sheer quantity of information that we are required to process on a daily basis, the 'defining gesture' fulfils a very useful function. The best of them are powerful visual or verbal summations of personality and policy, a shorthand for the brand promise and an easy reminder of it. They are often at their most effective when they are a counterpoint to the received view of a situation, or are a direct challenge to the key problem a nation, a corporation or a customer faces. For example, in the political world, they can take the form of distinctive personal accessories or gestures such as the self-confident wartime ones of Churchill's ubiquitous cigar and 'V-sign' made all the more powerful in a time of severe rationing and military pressure. Recently one of Margaret Thatcher's trademark handbags was auctioned on Ebay.com and made £100,000 because it had become such a potent symbol of her directness in pursuing her political beliefs. Marilyn Monroe's singing of 'Happy Birthday' defined as much of one American Presidency as did the lifting up of a dog by its ears did another.

In their clarity and graphic simplicity, defining gestures 'shorthand' for the mass of people what the leadership wishes to convey and become memorable, repeatable elements of the corporate story. They are particularly effective at the beginning of a new regime or period in office. They are also very effective at the point of customer contact, especially on first meeting. An early example of a defining gesture was when President Kennedy said he was going to use his 'First Hundred Days' to put together his programme for the country. Whilst people had always understood that there would be a honeymoon period with any new President, Chief Executive, or Prime Minister, John Kennedy was the first to 'package' this into a marketable concept.

Advertising campaigns are still one of the most powerful ways of sending controlled communications to customers and articulating the brand promise for them. They are also one of the brand's key 'defining gestures', which can set the preconditions for customer satisfaction through exceeding managed expectations. Perhaps one of the earliest brand positioning and advertising campaigns to achieve this objective was the famous one for Avis. The story of the 'We're number two we try harder' campaign is compellingly told in Robert Townsend's book *Up The Organisation*. The key point of the story is that it crystallised and codified the idea of the challenger to the brand leader and gave employees of the company very clear and motivating reasons. This technique of defining the enemy as a way of defining oneself is still valid today. Avis are still trying harder than Hertz, Pepsi is still waging war against Coke, and Procter & Gamble is still slugging it out with Unilever. Other good examples of these challenging copy platforms are Nationwide's copy line, designed to summarise its combative attitude, 'We never forget whose money it is',

Compaq's 'We never give a rival time' and Subaru's 'We have got the brains and the beauty too'.

Astute media usage can also create a powerful defining gesture for a brand. In a celebrated instance, Apple established itself in the mass consciousness as a major player through its extraordinary '1984' TV commercial, which positioned the company as the nemesis of IBM, the 'Big Blue' that was then enveloping the computer world. This spot was designed to run only once during the Superbowl, but due to its impact has received thousands of free airings since at awards festivals and in documentaries. The Superbowl remains perhaps the key annual showcase for brands, which aspire to greatness, but there has to be depth in the communication in terms of real brand promise, a quality that many of the recent dotcom pretenders have lacked. The key point about the Apple commercial was that it defined a complete attitude of mind towards the emerging world of personal computing. Apple positioned itself as the alternative to the boring, regimented world of corporate structures typified by IBM, and appealed strongly to the free-thinking creative entrepreneurial type. Despite the ups and downs that the company has experienced over the last 30 years, it has survived in the face of intense competition and its latest range of i-Mac computers are yet again making a powerful impact as an intelligent alternative.

However, there are dangers in producing superficially powerful campaigns, which turn out to be empty ones. Encouraged by slickly produced and often highly entertaining advertising, customer disappointment at the point of interaction with the brand can be exacerbated by the stark contrast of the media fantasy with reality. If, however, the brand can be one of the relatively few that actually deliver as promised, then 'happy surprises' will inevitably result. British Airways made a much more successful defining gesture in advertising terms with the famous 'Manhattan' TV commercial which launched the 'World's Favourite Airline' positioning and campaign. The key factor was that this campaign was supported by a radical re-training of thousands of staff to deliver on an advertising claim based on a true statistic in terms of passenger numbers carried and turn it into a reality in terms of genuinely positive customer feeling. So many things have contributed to the astonishing global success of Microsoft and it might be argued that its visionary leadership, aggressive innovation and outstanding product range were sufficient to achieve the dominance that it has. Nevertheless, their advertising campaign 'Where do you want to go today?' has been an excellent encapsulation of the 'anything is possible' attitude that the company has and which it conveys to its customers as the ultimate benefit of using Microsoft.

Another example where the company really made sure the product and service basis for a powerful claim was in position is provided by Tesco. The famous 'Chickens' commercial, featuring Dudley Moore, was the launch film in the 'Quest for Quality' campaign created by UK agency Lowe Lintas, which ran from 1990 to 1992 and adopted a deliberately (and at the time, unusually) light-hearted approach. Moore starred as a Tesco buyer who scoured the world in pursuit of an elusive flock of French free-range chickens, *en route* discovering other surprisingly high-quality products to add to Tesco's range. Products were chosen to demonstrate Tesco's new-found quality; the idea that they would stock free-range chickens was astonishing at the time. Most importantly this was the first time that Tesco had felt able to compete on the same quality ground as arch-rival Sainsbury. Building on its original print advertising with it's high profile 'Recipes' TV campaign, which featured famous celebrities favourite dishes, Sainsbury had 'owned' and indeed invented the higher-quality ground in mass-market supermarket retailing. Now there was a real pretender to their throne.

But the real impetus for the Tesco brand came from its significant improvements to product and store quality. The company understood that shopping is so much more than just the products that people buy and realised that none of their competitors were making serious attempts to improve the whole experience of shopping. Tesco capitalised on this by launching over 100 new initiatives which included mother and baby-changing facilities, the 'One in Front' checkout system, a new Value Line range and Clubcard. It was this series of improvements that inspired Lowe Lintas to create the advertising campaign idea that has run ever since and which has encapsulated Tesco's corporate vision so effectively. The advertising idea was that whilst not everything in life goes perfectly, Tesco were doing their best to make at least one aspect – doing the shopping – a little easier, hence the strap line 'Every Little Helps'. Whilst based on rational product and service benefits, the executional tone and style, even when dealing with price offers, has had charm and thus emotional appeal. Although each commercial has focused on one particular initiative, a single copy line has always been used across them, and also in press and point-of-sale applications to capture Tesco's new consumer-oriented philosophy of always 'doing right by the customer'. The introduction in 1995 of 'Dotty Turnbull', the 'mother of all shoppers' character played by Prunella Scales, and her long-suffering daughter Kate, played by Jane Horrocks, has increased the impact and involvement of the campaign. It has achieved this whilst continuing to communicate each of the Tesco initiatives, which Dotty puts to the test in store.

The Lowe campaign has been extremely successful and has contributed substantially to the overall growth and profitability of the brand. Their Grand Prix winning entry to the IPA Advertising Effectiveness Awards 2000, authored by Ashleye Sharpe and Joanna Bamford, gives detailed evidence for this and makes an excellent companion piece to the business-oriented 'Tesco Story', earlier on. Since 1993 'Every Little Helps' has moved from being 'just the line at the end of the commercials' to become the mantra for Tesco, and all the more powerful for its simplicity and applicability to every aspect of the company's operations.

Case History: DISNEY

Perhaps one of the best examples of a great American brand gone global through assiduous management of its defining gestures is that of Disney. They believe that 'Building a strong brand = building a strong brand experience' and that this goes beyond personal interactions. Disney strongly believe that they have built a strong brand by living the brand experience in all parts of their business. Of course the foundation of the brand experience comes from the philosophy and the beliefs of Walt Disney himself. Walt envisaged Disneyland as if it were a successful animated film; he wanted to create a three-dimensional version of Mickey Mouse and for it to be as powerful a live experience as it was a cinematic one. Walt, who did not believe that it made for a positive family experience, hated the traditional carnival or circus style entertainment of the time. Disneyland was created therefore, on the basis of being fundamentally different from them. This was ingrained firmly in the training procedures, which were different from anything ever created before: 'I only hope that we never lose sight of one thing, that it was all started by a mouse,' vowed Walt Disney.

Perhaps one of the quickest ways to understand the Disney ethos is to list some of their key definitions, as these give an insight into the complete world that has been created, including its own language, to enable employees to deliver to customers what we experience at Disney, both in terms of theme parks and in their retail outlets:

- Attractions: theme park rides and shows
- Backstage: areas behind the scenes not seen by Guests
- Cast members: all employees of Walt Disney World Co.
- Guests: visitors to any part of the Disney World Resort

- Host or hostess: a frontline Cast Member who supports Guests' experiences through contact in the show
- On stage: all areas visited by Guests
- The property: the entire Walt Disney World resort
- The show: everything and everyone that interfaces with Guests including entertainment, the property and the Cast Members.

'Performance excellence' is an initiative which has enhanced and evolved the philosophy within Walt Disney attractions. Its launch and implementation took place in 1993 and was conducted by Judson Green. He believed that in order for Disney to maintain its success in the future, it was crucial that every Cast Member became an active partner in the company's success, and this initiative is dependent upon passion and involvement. Since its initiation, the Guest return rate has risen by 10% and Cast turnover rate has dropped. Key elements of the initiative include the idea that leaders do not view their Cast Members as part of a team executing management orders, instead they are seen as centres of creative solutions; all Cast Members are viewed as if they possess the capability to implement creative ideas and solutions to problems.

How does this 'inclusive leadership' actually work in Disney? Firstly, weekly board meetings replace executive committee meetings, Leaders work frontline shifts and Cast Members have the authority to refund Guests. Through enabling the Cast, they have become relatively self-sufficient in the day-to-day operations of the company, and this acts as a powerful source of motivation. Cast Members reward each other for exemplary behaviour by exchanging cards, which say 'Guest Service Fanatic'. Disney are adamant that there is a definite relationship between how the Cast feel about their work and how this translates into the Guest experience.

The Disney orientation program, 'Disney Traditions' teaches the Cast about the heritage, the history and the quality standards of the organisation, but most importantly they learn that their job is to 'create happiness'. This ethos has a massive impact on how the Cast perform in the Show. The connection to a larger purpose is central to Disney's ability to motivate Cast Members across the Property to maximise their performance and create what they call 'magic moments' for their Guests and for fellow Cast Members. Disney's goal during this training is to 'ensure we win your heart and mind as a Cast Member'.

An example of such a 'magic moment' (or 'defining gesture'), is when on Main St. a Guest asked a Cast Member who was cleaning the street where he could get a cup of ice. He was then directed to a street vendor and in the short walk to the vendor the street cleaner radioed the Guest's request to the vendor who then, when the Guest arrived at the stall remarked 'I believe you're looking for a cup of ice', the Guest was stunned. 'That extra three seconds of the custodial host's time created a magical service snapshot that the Guest can share with family and friends many times.'

Magic moments are created all the time at Disney. It is estimated that there are a possible sixty interactions with a Guest on any typical day at the park. Each is an opportunity to create a magic, not a tragic moment, and to exercise what Disney call 'aggressive happiness': this is a proactive as opposed to reactive approach to service. The success of these interactions through Disney's Cast behaviour and distinctive style has its foundations within Walt's dedication to 'walking the front'. He was a fanatic about providing a consistent, quality show and would visit the park every weekend and ride every ride. Today Leaders are still encouraged to be partners and not police in the operations of a Property.

Disney's success is grounded on two basic principles, attention to detail and exceeding expectations. These two things permeate everything that they do. For instance, a Manager at one of Disney's expensive restaurants trains new dishwashers in the following manner. They arrive on their first day at the restaurant and are sat down at a table, which is fully set up with fine china and perfect linen, as it would be for a paying Guest. As the Manager and Cast Member are talking about the operations of the restaurant, the Cast Member notices that there are lipstick stains on the glasses, crusts of food on the rims of dishes and that the silverware is spotted. The Manager notices that the Cast Member is distracted and asks her why, to which she replies, 'The dishes haven't been cleaned thoroughly'. The Manager then says 'Imagine, how you would feel if you were a Guest who spent $100 for that meal'.

This highlights several signature features of Disney leadership, firstly, the idea that Cast Members must connect emotionally with their Guests. As Michael Eisner said when he was Disney CEO, the company is driven by an 'emotional engine', not an 'economic one'. It is also crucial that the Cast Members are immersed in the Guest experience, before they are trained in their specific tasks. In the restaurant example, the Manager allowed the Cast Member to 'own the Guest experience' by soliciting her feedback; this leadership style encourages and rewards employee involvement. Another Disney belief is that 'Marketing creates the brand, but training brings it to life and keeps it refreshed for customers and employees alike'.

Disney is often criticised for the level of scripted responses used within the resorts and across the company as a whole and it is often assumed that Disney require their Cast Members to smile all of the time. To the latter accusation, Disney respond: 'Of course we don't. Our training does focus on behaviours, but facilitating a sense of ownership also breeds motivation and excellent performance.' However Disney do not deny that they use scripted responses: 'Of course we do – we are an entertainment company performing a Show. For instance the Haunted Mansion is an entirely scripted role. The Cast are on stage and they are acting in character as any Cast Member in a play would do.' Disney World employs more than 55,000 Cast Members over its four parks, which are set over 47 sq. miles. A degree of scripting is inevitable, especially when people are doing the same thing over and over again.

Disney's attention to detail is impressive. They have recommended ways of dealing with certain groups of Guests. For example, Cast Members are encouraged, when talking to children, to get down on one knee so that they are on the same level. Good parents know this is a better way to establish rapport with their children than talking down to them from a great height, and Disney have carried this lesson from normal human behaviour into their code of brand manners. They also ensure that Cast Members can speak as many languages as possible so that all Guests can be addressed in their native tongues.

Another justification for these suggested Disney responses lies in the repetitive nature of so many of the questions asked by Guests. The second most common question at Disneyland after 'where are the nearest toilets' is 'what time does the three o'clock show start?' Obviously the question is really 'at what time is the parade likely to pass this spot', so instead of correcting the Guest the Cast Member will tell them where they should stand and at what time. This is simply a system of anticipating and understanding the Guest and turning every interaction into a positive moment with them.

Though the setting, the facilities and the quality of the grounds and location at Disney contribute to the Guest experience, it is the interaction with the Cast Members, which really separates the experience from any other. This is because of their rigorous hiring and casting scheme; nobody is simply 'employed' at Disney, people are 'Cast for a role in the Show'. This is based on the fundamental belief and understanding that everybody contributes to the customer experience. When potential Cast Members apply to Disney, firstly their paper application is screened and then if suitable, they are invited to watch a video. This is designed to give the Cast Members an opportunity to self-select out before the main interviews are conducted. It demonstrates the strict appearance code, the average day at Disney and the behavioural expectations and guidelines of all the staff. This process increases the likelihood of appropriate personality types putting themselves forward, thus achieving a natural 'fit' with the Disney brand and enhancing their potential to deliver the brand promise through appropriate behaviours. Then a series of interviews are conducted. These include spending time with other Cast Members. Throughout this whole process, even if the individual isn't hired, they are treated as if they were a Guest – after all everyone is a potential customer!

Once the Cast have been trained and have adopted the Disney Way, there are certain maintenance schemes, which strive to keep the Cast well motivated and enthused. This consists of a complex and rigorous system of taking care of the Cast Members and ensuring that their needs are attended to. Support systems, which are in place, include all Cast Members having walkie-talkies so that they all have a means of immediate communication. Back-stage support includes the availability of rest areas, which are not Disney-focused. 'We don't play "It's a Small World" in the background, we play music that the Cast want to listen to'. This provides a definite form of escapism for them. The working day is designed to be as convenient as possible through the provision of a barber, and even a place to renew one's driving licence! It is these little touches that keep the Cast energised and happy.

The core of Disney's successful brand manners therefore lies in the maintenance of two factors, firstly the fact that all Cast Members are emotionally involved in the Guest experience and secondly the commitment to the belief that everybody's role is to 'create happiness', a higher-order benefit that has enormous motivating power.

Defining gestures provide powerful 'stakes in the ground' to guide employees regarding good behaviours and to manage the expectations of customers around the brand promise, we suggest five areas which can be instrumental.

1. As in the case of Disney's 'create happiness', refine the key business issues facing the company into the single most crucial one.
2. Create corporate 'defining gestures' for the CEO, management and staff to project via personal usage, and reinforce this through marketing communications.
3. Ensure that there is a rigorous recruitment and training programme to underpin the brand's gestures and language and make them a reality for the business and the customer; don't write cheques in communication that the service experience can't cash.
4. Reappraise the 'defining gestures' on a regular basis and assess their continuing relevance versus wear out.
5. Ensure the defining gestures use a skilful mix of the rational, emotional, political and spiritual dimensions.

22

Really Listening Adds Real Value

The key point of this chapter is to reinforce the importance of really listening to members of staff, particularly those who are customer facing. Every day, there are thousands of interactions between members of staff and members of the public and each one of these is at least a piece of market research, and very often an opportunity to really delight the customer. If senior management taps into this resource regularly, it can be a very powerful way of keeping a finger on the pulse of the relationship between the corporation and its customer base whilst delivering 'happy surprises' with a high level of frequency.

One of the core skills of diagnosing the problems within an organisation is simply being a good listener to the people within the company, who very likely know better than anyone else, what the problems are and indeed what the solutions might be. So often the company itself is very bad at doing this and has to resort to outsiders to do the listening for it. When customers are in purchasing or complaining modes, they are united in the desire to have a brand representative listen to them properly in order either to assess their product or service needs, or to understand and then rectify their problem. However, daily experience in a multitude of different retailing or service situations shows that very few brands have achieved this basic level of ability when dealing with customers.

Creating a genuinely skilled 'listening culture' is one of the most cost-effective ways of motivating staff and making customers feel valued. By ensuring the corporate ear remains close to the ground, problems can be avoided before they happen and solved quickly when they do.

The key skills in listening are those of ego suppression and curiosity. We have a natural tendency to want to talk, either about ourselves or about a topic of our choosing. It's quite easy in a social interaction for one party, 'the good listener', to say very little and elicit masses of information from the speaker, who, after the interaction is completed, will report what a good conversation they've had, despite its one-sidedness. Unfortunately in life there seem to be naturally many more speakers than listeners and many conversations resemble alternating monologues than true dialogues. We are so preoccupied with ourselves that we, and those issues of close personal interest, naturally override those of others. This fundamental human trait presents a real problem for any CEO or the top management team, not only amongst themselves, but also in respect of their employees, if the organisation they lead has any ambitions to be excellent at customer service.

Interestingly, there seems to be a relationship between the volume of 'broadcast' and success in society; great leaders are great storytellers, who keep on telling their story with conviction and passion. If it's a great story, it will capture the imagination of millions and lead them to do extraordinary things, whether it be in warfare or commerce. It's as if we are prepared to subjugate our own narrative for another's if it is compelling enough, and taps into deep-seated needs and beliefs we hold dear. In our hearts, we know how hard it is to maintain convictions and passions over a long period of time and we acknowledge those who have the charisma and skill to do so with our listening. Great business leaders tell the brand story in this way and the companies that have such people at their head have a significant competitive advantage. However, in the day-to-day world of managers and employees, or employees and customers, 'broadcasting' the brand story (or more likely the personal agenda) rather than 'receiving' input from colleagues or clients can not only lead to missed opportunities, but can also be positively demotivating internally, or result in poor service externally.

Dr Bartholomew Sayle, CEO of The Breakthrough Group, has some excellent insights into the psychology of listening. He believes that the vast majority of people regard listening as 'the time they have to wait before they can speak again'. This manifests itself in several common tactics on the part of listeners who really want to speak. There is the 'but in' questioner who is not really asking a question to enable the speaker to elucidate their point of view, but is actually posing a 'leading' question to take the other party off in their preferred direction. There is guerrilla warfare in the 'multiple nodder' who appears to be agreeing violently with the speaker, but is in reality luring them into a false sense of security, which allows them an entry point as they pick up the rhythm and then take over.

Then there is the 'pause poacher' who, poised like a cobra ready to strike, watches intently for the speaker to take breath and then jumps in as soon as they do so.

There's an Eastern expression, which Sayle quotes which says: 'You can't fill a glass that is already full'. We have to make space to listen if we wish to discover things. Philosophically, the leadership of an organisation needs to believe that even the most junior person in the organisation may have something to teach them. Given that in most organisations it is these people who have most of the initial customer contact, this is very likely to be true. The successful corporation needs to be curious, to learn real listening skills and to give people the space to express themselves. Being expert or 'already knowing something' is a barrier to listening. Children or novices are more open. Diagrammatically this can be illustrated as shown in Figure 45.

There is a strong tendency, as we gain expertise to move from the 'discovery' mode to one of 'complacency'. This gravitation through the levels of complete ignorance, beginning at the position where 'we don't know we don't know', all the way up to the arrogant status of 'we know', is accompanied by an increased disposition to talk as opposed to listen. Picasso was famous for saying that it had taken him a lifetime to learn how

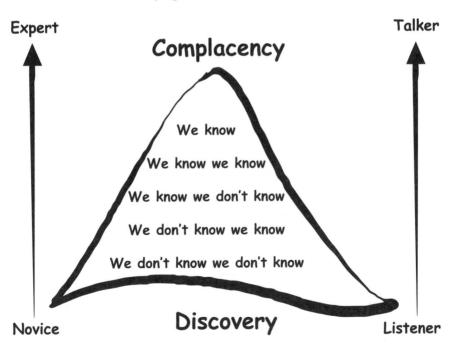

Figure 45 *Complacency–discovery chart.*

to see like a child, and the same is true of listening; it's a childhood gift that needs to be re-learned in adulthood. We need to learn how to put ourselves back into the innocent mode of discovery.

A very effective method to teach people quickly how to listen powerfully was devised by Bart Sayle, which he calls 'listening tubes'. Doing this simple exercise in concentrated listening reveals how incredibly easy it is to be distracted from what the person we are listening to is saying. Very quickly the listener's 'inner voice' will start up raising questions, hypotheses, personal memories, or simply conducting a running commentary on what the other party looks like as they are talking. The 'listening tubes' demonstrate how bad we all are at listening – and how easily we can transform this into more powerful listening if we firstly become aware of the problem of our 'inner voice', and then train to overcome it.

In really hearing the suggestions of colleagues or the complaints of customers, we genuinely take on board what they have to say. In paying undivided attention to them we give their views respect and we glean the maximum amount of information from them. It may be that having captured this data we subsequently choose to endorse, discount or ignore it, but at least we have it in our possession. This is the personal reward and ego satisfaction for the self-suppression that is entailed in positive listening; the power over the information that the speaker has imparted. Listening carefully can reveal great insights into the speaker's concerns and motivations. For example, every salesperson knows that if a prospect repeats certain words or phrases, these represent that person's preoccupations of the time. We are all flattered subconsciously when our language is played back to us in the vocabulary used and in the tone of voice or accent used. The skilled brand ambassador will pick up on these verbal clues (and no doubt non-verbal body language too) and play them back to their customer as a powerful way of establishing rapport. These key words or phrases, whose repetition indicates the prospect's concerns in the product or service area in which they are shopping, need to be matched to the brand's offer in order to facilitate a sale.

Advertising and marketing communications can do the same thing. Qualitative market research can discern the key linguistics of a market category and the distinctive variations attributable to a particular brand. These verbal descriptors become the building blocks for the brand's copy platform. In a very real sense the on-pack copy for a label, or the forty words in a TV script are the distillation of hundreds of thousands of pound's worth of market research and perhaps millions in business experience. This is why competitive analysis is so important – most of a brand's secrets are on display, either in packaging, advertising or retail presentation and it's puzzling why so little attention is paid to this area. 'Listening' to what the competition is doing can speak volumes about their strategy.

When senior management make store visits or walk the shop floor, they have all these personal listening issues to attend to. But they also have to find ways to overcome the barriers that occur simply because of their status. CEOs really do have to revert to the novice mode in this context. A good example is provided by the experience of David Williams when he took over the role as Burger King's President of Europe, Middle East and Africa at a time when the fast food retailer was having a tough time in the UK market. He spent the first few months in a classic exercise in MBWA (Tom Peter's Management By Walking About) and discovered quite quickly what the fundamental problem with the business was: the staff believed firmly that the management had stopped listening to them. Key issues that employees noticed and reported to their managers remained mysteriously unattended to. Often they were reiterated, but with no effect. Morale dropped to disastrous levels and eventually employees assumed that the company no longer cared.

Williams listened hard to what his people were telling him, and that was the first victory; word quickly went round through the company grapevine and more and more key individuals opened up to the first senior person in years to take them seriously. As a result he was soon to learn that the basic product quality and service standards were not being adhered to. He spent many hours counting the number and measuring the length of the Burger King French fries and found that there was unacceptable variation from the company ideal. The quality of buns was below standard and was rectified quickly. Now these may sound obvious points to identify and tackle, but suffice it to say they hadn't been for some time, and when faced with a competitor of the calibre of McDonald's, these failings become serous chinks in the brand's armour.

Williams also listened to customers, and in particular to what they had to say about Burger King's advertising. He learned that the key competitive differential and product benefit, namely 'flame grilled' was no longer the focus of the brand's communications. Again this was soon attended to with a series of TV commercials, which brought 'flame grilled' back into prominence through the use of famous pop songs such as 'Fire' by The Crazy World of Arthur Brown. Williams took a similarly successful tack in the key German market and Burger King's revitalisation as a brand was typified by its self-confident staging of a mock election campaign where the Whopper 'stood' as a candidate in the real German elections, generating massive media coverage. All this sprang from the simple expedient of listening hard to employees and customers.

Another listening problem that has to be overcome is the natural human reaction when hearing the presentation of a new idea, which is to see it as a potential problem, not a solution. F. Scott Fitzgerald defined true intelligence as the ability to hold two opposing ideas in the mind at the same time, and to still be able to function. People do find this very difficult to do. As David Bernstein, expert on creativity and author has said: 'Ideas are subversive, ideas are a criticism – they question the status quo.' For the CEO therefore, every foray into the realm of employees and customers represents a challenge to his or her view of the world. The skill according to Bernstein is for the CEO to be neither puppet master nor ventriloquist if he or she really desires to get the maximum creativity out of the organisation; they just need to listen with an open mind. It's also essential to create a culture where new ideas are welcomed as positive contributions to business progress, rather than inconveniences that are likely to lead to unsettling change. Achieving this will mean that creativity becomes part and parcel of the everyday life of the corporation, rather than an elitist activity reserved for small minorities in marketing or R&D, or something that only happens once a year at a 'Blue Sky' awayday.

One way of dealing with ideas as they emerge in management/staff interactions, which works as well with a formal business presentation as it does with proposals made in an individual conversation, is to use another technique developed by Bart Sayle. This is to 'frame' the response to any given proposition, whether given or received, according to the following criteria:

- What inspires you?
- What works for you?
- What's missing for you?
- How could we make this better?

Starting with the positive aspects of the response is key to preventing the internal voice doing its usual thing and immediately jumping to the potential negatives. Answering the question 'What inspires you?' forces the listener (and of course the speaker once they get into this habit of 'framing') to aim high and concentrate on communicating something of compelling value that works at an emotional or even spiritual level. Secondly, responding in terms of 'What works for you?' requires a more analytical approach, which helps the two parties to understand the rational underpinnings of what's been presented. Detailing, 'What's missing for you?' is the third part of the response but the first in which the audience is allowed to make any negative comments, but even these must be couched in the subjective sense for the listener, rather than as a critical attack on the speaker. The spirit of the process is to maintain a working assumption that what's being proposed is a good idea and it's just that the listener isn't fully grasping all the elements that make it so. The process returns to an overtly positive note with the final question: 'How could we make this better?' which leads into a collaborative discussion on ways and means of building on the idea and improving it.

Many businesses have status report meetings as a regular internal discipline, but they can easily become rather boring and sterile affairs. A simple technique, which can be used to structure such meetings is represented by the acronym ABCD. This stands for Achievements, Benefits, Concerns and Directions. At each status meeting, attendees with reports to make should be encouraged to present them in this format. 'Achievements' is the list of things that have been done since last time and this gives the manager an early opportunity to appraise and praise the performance of the individual doing the report. 'Benefits' are the positive aspects of those Achievements and the ways in which they have moved the company agenda forward. This in effect gives the reporter a chance to 'blow their own trumpet' a little and to claim due credit for their work. Note that as with the 'framing' technique the positives come first in the process. Then 'Concerns' are the issues that trouble the individual reporting; these might be areas that have not been achieved or problems that have emerged in the course of completing others. 'Concerns' can be a two-way street with the managers being able to voice any worries they may have about the progress of projects. Finally 'Directions' is a useful way of wrapping up the status report meeting and agreeing the next steps for the period ahead before the next review. ABCD is another way of structuring interpersonal relationships in business to ensure that the maximum opportunity is created for managers and staff to really listen to each other and ensure that the focus on delivering all aspects of the brand promise remains as clear as possible.

Case History: IPA (INSTITUTE OF PRACTITIONERS IN ADVERTISING)

The skill of listening carefully is not just one that very large companies have to learn. Smaller organisations have to do it too, and perhaps there's a sense in which they have to try harder at it, because there is a temptation to assume that because of the relatively small numbers of people involved, that communication is good by definition. Powerful listening is especially important in times of change and reappraisal.

An interesting example of how one small organisation has gone about this is the UK Institute of Practitioners in Advertising or, IPA. Much information about this professional trade body for the UK advertising, media and marketing communications agencies industry can be gleaned from the website at www.ipa.co.uk but suffice it to say here that the IPA has 200 corporate members who account for over 80% of all UK advertising, and who are regarded as world leaders in their field.

Like any trade body, the IPA must reflect the evolving needs of its membership and in the UK things are moving pretty fast. The media environment is rapidly changing with a continuing consolidation of traditional terrestrial TV stations at the same time as increasing numbers of digital and Internet channels are appearing. This is but one example of shifts in fundamental market factors that are affecting the ability of IPA agencies to serve their clients and operate profitably. These and several other key themes were articulated in the inaugural speech of incoming IPA president, Rupert Howell, in the spring of 1999, thus setting the agenda for his two-year term.

The plethora of media channels to market means that the traditional advertising agency, focused only on the 30-second TV commercial, is a thing of the past. Most IPA agencies nowadays are involved in the production of integrated multimedia campaigns, which are as likely to use a website or a petrol pump poster, as a direct mail shot or a print ad, in communicating a brand's promise. As a result, the membership of the organisation is gradually changing. Digital marketing and new media, sales promotion and direct marketing agencies are all joining the IPA.

Meanwhile, in the era of mass personalisation, the IPA has embraced the power of the Internet to transform itself from the relatively blunt instrument of a paper-based communications process to an electronic one based on the website and an increasingly sophisticated system of e-mail alerts. The goal is to deliver every single individual employee within a member agency 'their IPA', and in so doing enhance significantly the value for money delivered in return for their corporate subscriptions.

Given that the IPA secretariat comprises roughly 30 people, it is obvious that this changing environment and the new needs required by both it and the new type of member, present a challenge not only in resource management but also in retraining and re-focusing on new objectives and goals. Under the leadership of Director General Nick Phillips, the IPA has become an excellent example of an organisation committed to the ideals of the Investors in People programme and indeed the trade body has received the highest accolades in its most recent inspection. Phillips is also committed to a policy of openness and transparency. All employees of the IPA have access to the computer database with the result that there is no reason for anyone not to know what is going on. In Phillips' words: 'We have moved away from a "need to know" to a "right to be informed" culture.'

In this spirit, and fully aware that the Millennium year, would be his last full one in office (he retires in July 2001) and mindful of the President's aggressive agenda as set out in his inaugural speech, Phillips embarked on a major reassessment of the IPA's role during 1999. Given the industry environment described earlier, it was clear to him that the organisation needed to examine its performance in the light of the changing needs of its members and to realign itself to take advantage of the rapidly emerging digital communications era. True to his philosophy, he determined that there should be both a bottom-up and top-down process in order to achieve this. The goal was to ensure that all employees of the IPA, whether full-time staff or part-time consultant, whether director, manager or assistant, had a genuine sense of ownership of the new vision.

It would have been hard to do more in terms of consultative processes, workshops, brain storms, awaydays, individual interviews and departmental team meetings in ensuring that everybody was fully involved. Most of this work was done internally by IPA people, but there were two opportunities to use external agencies -- one in the context of the corporate identity project which was going on in parallel, and the other in facilitating a Directors' awayday. The result of all this was a new IPA focus whose key headings are summarised in Figure 46.

The IPA Vision, or long-term goal, was stated as follows: 'To be seen as personal trainers, mental sparring partners, negotiators and spokespeople for the world's best advertising and marketing communications agencies so that we achieve respect, credibility and continued relevance within a fast-changing market.' These were ambitious, indeed visionary terms for what might be thought of from the outside as a rather dry, dusty civil-service-type organisation, even if it was in the business of serving the needs of the leading advertising and media communications agencies in the UK. However, when presented to the collective

The IPA focus: key elements

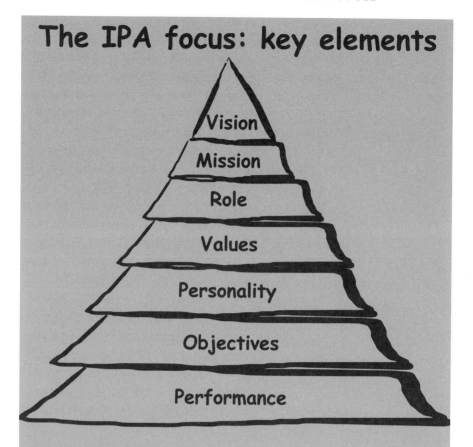

Figure 46 *The IPA pyramid diagram.*

employees of the IPA there was no real surprise or concern, just a reinforcement of all their own input. These were their words coming back to them. There was also a commitment to greater electronic communication, the need to move 'further, faster', and to back up revisions to the corporate identity with real organisational change.

The same was true of the IPA Mission, or what the organisation actually needed to do. This was defined as: 'To serve, promote and anticipate the collective interests of our members and in particular define, develop and help maintain the highest possible standards of professional practice within the advertising and marketing communications business.' Again the familiar ground of the IPA's Role, or what the model trade association does for its members was comfortably received: 'Negotiating, lobbying, demonstrating the value of advertising, providing training and development, defining and promoting best practice, providing advisory services and creating a forum for debate.'

In this context the IPA Values, or things it holds dear, were more emotional aspects which perhaps had always been present, but which had been drawn out and articulated more fully and rewardingly. These Values were defined as 'continuity, stimulation, authoritative thinking, integrity and neutral ground'. Similarly, the IPA Personality, or how people needed to 'be' was generated anew: 'member focused, professional, enthusiastic, well-managed and visionary'. Again, this could have been potentially threatening for some people who perhaps did not feel their own character fully reflected some of the more ambitious of these attributes, but since they had had full authorship and involvement in the process, worry gave way to aspiration.

The company objectives, or what the IPA does as a result of all this, are simple to say, but less easy to achieve. In essence its goal is to fulfil the annual agendas set by all the individual Committees, such as Media Policy Group, Value of Advertising, Training and Development, and the Creative Directors' Forum. From this follows the need for Individual Performance, or what each person in the IPA can to do to help achieve this collective goal. A key tool in doing this is the setting of individual objectives within each person's annual Mapping sessions. 'Mapping' is the IPA appraisal process whose primary task is to enable constructive and continuous personal development through training and education, all set in the context of the IPA Focus described above.

The net result of this exhaustive process is a more closely aligned organisation. It is one which is now fully prepared for the expansion of membership, the challenges of providing 'your IPA' to as many as 13,000 individuals, and the provision of the support needed to help keep the UK's leading advertising and marketing communications agencies on top of the world.

People prefer to have a dialogue, than be simply 'informed', particularly when the matter is dear to their heart. Deciding when to 'consult' and when to 'inform' needs to become a core skill in delivering the brand manners. Other suggestions for improving the listening capability of the organisation include:

1. Train the whole organisation on how to listen effectively. Make 'powerful listening' a part of the brand manners of the corporation, and use it to get the most out of personal interactions. Ask people about benefits (what they liked), as well as their concerns. Be explicit about

expectations – start and finish every meeting with an exchange and review of these.

2, Create recurring opportunities for top management to experience this listening regularly with customers and employees. Learn from the listening and prepare responses to the problems raised. Use it to bring out and harness the creativity that's in everyone.

3. Use advanced data mining techniques to really listen hard to what customers are saying to the corporation through their various interactions with it, and then provide employee brand ambassadors with the tools to react most appropriately to what they're hearing.

23

The Power of Customer Pledges

A very simple thing can be one of the most effective components of a system of brand manners for a corporation. This is the idea of the 'customer pledge'. It's surprising how few organisations have these, and yet so often the ones that do seem to be rather successful.

The Chief Executive and the top management team who are responsible for setting out the company dream and then planning how to achieve it, have to get to the point where they have synthesised in the clearest and most unequivocal terms exactly what the brand promise to customers is. This should then be translated into the 'customer pledge' as well as the other key components that form the basis of the brand manners such as vision, mission, values, roles and objectives.

This core definition becomes the jumping off point for both internal and external communications such as advertising, point-of-sale, direct marketing, public relations, sponsorship and many other channels to market.

The customer pledge can often be forgotten in the rush for the sexier media such as advertising. Perhaps this tool also gets overlooked because it is a very public guarantee against which the company must deliver, and therefore carries significant risks in the case of non-performance. Once a charter is made it is hard to be withdrawn, and therefore it has to be very carefully researched and have the full force of the board behind it. These customer charters are the rational underpinning of the visionary elements of the corporate dream. Whilst the latter can be communicated in language that is often poetic, the verbal statements that comprise an effective customer charter have to be weighed in the balance with legal precision. Indeed, the more accurate the statement and the more black and white it is, the less likely there will be miscommunications and misunderstandings. If the language can also be aspirational, then the charter or pledge becomes truly powerful.

Customer pledges are a key tool in managing customer expectations and setting benchmarks for internal procedures and quality management. They create a baseline from which the self-confident organisation can excel by taking risks on behalf of the customer to over-deliver on the promised minimum. They also give an objective basis upon which employees may use their discretion in customer complaints situations. Perhaps one of the reasons why we respond so well to charters is the deep involvement of their spiritual or political analogies in our religious and social cultures. For example, consider how durable the Ten Commandments have been. Many nations have also striven to produce Bills of Rights – perhaps the USA is the most famous of these. Whilst the United Kingdom has never had a similar document for the protection of its citizens it has relied instead on the accumulated body of Common Law and this has afforded the individual the same protection. John Major in the last Conservative Government in the UK introduced the concept of service standards presented as Citizens Charters.

The point of all this is that customers of Governments and public services are increasingly having targets set and their expectations managed by the publication of charters and league tables. These rankings have always existed in the commercial world – we love 'top tens' and star ratings, Michelin for food and Parker for wine – and the likelihood is that they will increase in popularity. Thus the customer population is living in a world in which charters, pledges, benchmarks and ratings have a pervasive influence on the way they shop and the social choices they make. Corporations and their brands that lack a formal customer pledge are missing a key element in their brand manners.

Perhaps one of the oldest commercial customer charters is that of the John Lewis Partnership. This is summarised in the famous advertising copy line 'Never knowingly undersold' and is supported by the following statement:

> Our buyers are required to set prices our competitors are unlikely to beat. If we find a local retailer selling the same goods at a better price, we will reduce ours to match it. Even if their goods are in a sale. If you buy goods from John Lewis and then see them for a better price elsewhere, we will refund the difference. We employ people who do nothing but monitor our competitors' prices to make sure we remain competitive. Partners are paid a £2 bonus if they spot the same product cheaper elsewhere. We have been never knowingly undersold for over 60 years.

The unequivocal and comprehensive nature of their statement is truly impressive.

Supported by their distinctive partnership status John Lewis, Peter Jones and a number of their other department stores around the UK have continued to thrive relative to many of their peers in the embattled department store sector. This has seen giants like Storehouse, M&S, and Arcadia stumble, and indeed fall in the case of C&A which announced it was closing all its UK retail outlets in May 2000, in the face of the polarisation between the discounters such as Matalan and Primark, and the newer more fashionable brands such as the Gap and H&M.

UK tyre and exhaust repair retailer KwikFit's Stop'n'Steer's approach is based on fixed-cost servicing. Whatever the technical need – service, cambelt, suspension, steering or brakes – this means no hidden extras, plus explanations in plain English, firm quotations, and work carried out only with the customer's permission. KwikFit's customer charter consists of the following key promises:

- Treating your vehicle with care and always fitting protective seat covers.
- Ensuring that your vehicle is inspected by a technically qualified staff member.
- Examining the vehicle with you and giving an honest appraisal of the work required.
- Giving you a binding quotation that includes all associated charges prior to work commencing.
- Ensuring you are aware that any non-exchange part or component removed from your vehicle is available for you to take away.
- Ensuring that all work is carried out in accordance with the company's laid down procedures and informing you immediately of any complications or delays.
- Ensuring that all completed work is checked by a technically qualified staff member.
- Offering to inspect the finished work with you at the time of delivery.

Another market where customer knowledge is likely to be far outstripped by rapid advances in technology is that of mobile telephones. In the UK the market has been complicated from the start because of the separation of network providers and handset manufacturers. Add to this successive waves of product innovation, 'tied' and independent retail distribution, plus subsidised handsets to achieve airtime sales contracts and you have a perfect recipe for customer confusion. In this arena, one UK retailer in particular has made use of customer pledges and an innovative advertising campaign to establish its brand position most successfully.

Case History: **CARPHONE WAREHOUSE**

In 1989 at the young age of 25, Charles Dunstone set up the Carphone Warehouse (CPW) with just £6,000 in the bank. In its first year, he turned over an astonishing £1.5 million and employee numbers increased from two to fourteen. Today CPW is Europe's largest independent retailer of mobile phones; there are 462 stores in the UK, 833 in total and the company employs over 4,000 people. In July 2000, in order to raise capital to finance European growth, Dunstone floated his company on the London Stock Exchange and it was valued at £1.3 billion.

Carphone Warehouse has created its distinctive positioning in the highly competitive and volatile retail market for mobile telephones by offering impartial advice to customers trying to pick their way through the minefield of special tariffs and new technologies. CPW has remained independent of any particular manufacturer or network provider in order to maintain its reputation as the customer's friend and ally. Through organic growth, takeovers, and technical innovation, CPW have worked hard to stay ahead of the game. For example, in December 1998 they launched their own e-retail centre, carphonewarehouse.com and became the first independent retailer to stock all four networks and a range of mobile phones and data products provided through the Internet, as well as offering their trademark impartial advice on buying a mobile phone.

But it is the company's very public commitment to customers that has given the Carphone Warehouse its competitive advantage. Dunstone has developed five rules that he believes encapsulate the company's passion for delivering second-to-none customer service. These appear across many areas of the day-to-day workspace, on screen savers and business cards:

1. If we do not look after the customer, somebody else will.
2. Nothing is gained by winning an argument but losing a customer.
3. Always deliver what we promise. If in doubt, under promise and over deliver.
4. Always treat customers as we ourselves would like to be treated.
5. The reputation of the whole company is in the hands of each individual.

Perhaps it's typical of the founder's attitude to these customer pledges that on the back of his own business card is the first of these pithy statements: 'If we don't look after our customers somebody else will'. Their commitment to customer service is well known in the UK industry.

In 1999 CPW won three awards in the retail and customer service fields: the Retail Week Customer Satisfaction Excellence Award, the Retail Week Employer of the Year Award and for the sixth year running the Mobile News Award for best large retailer. The Carphone Warehouse's original aims still hold true: 'To put the customer first and to ensure that all employees share in the company's success.'

Clearly recruiting and training the right sort of employees to be appropriate ambassadors for their brand is an absolute priority. The CPW invests around £1,500 per member of staff on training and this is more than eight times the average retailer. All staff undergo a two or three week intensive training course which covers both the structure of the communications industry and also the company's customer care initiatives. 'Why can't we?' forums are regularly held and encourage different departments to discuss improvements and new ways of working across every aspect of the business. A formal suggestion scheme receives about 1,000 entries per year and successful suggestions are rewarded with £25 by way of thank-you.

All employees receive regular annual appraisals whereby key objectives are agreed; these are reviewed after 6-month periods. From these meetings parties work together to develop programmes from a series of training schemes that will best meet the needs of the individual. After the appraisals, the employee completes an action plan which details what he/she learned and what they will do differently, and this is reviewed two months on to ensure that the plan is on course. All this is geared to the CPW sales philosophy that is to give the customer the knowledge that they need to make an educated choice as to the best network, tariff and handset for their particular needs.

However, the company also offers staff over 200 books and tapes that are designed to allow for every aspect of individual development. Should an employee wish to embark upon an educational course, then CPW will pay for up to half of the fees. For instance, an employee who has been with the CPW for 12 months can expect to receive a 50% contribution toward an MBA course. Every year the CPW produces a 25-page internal market research document that is sent to every employee in the organisation. This covers many aspects of the business such as management style, career development, pay and benefits and understanding the company goals. The results of the most recent questionnaire revealed the following:

- 92% of employees said that they enjoyed their jobs.
- 90% of employees said that they were proud to work for CPW.
- 46% of staff joining the CPW were employed as a result of existing employee recommendation.
- 90% agree that customer service is the number one priority.

Staff turnover is at 18% that is considerably less than the 39/40% retail average.

New customers also receive a survey that is designed to determine service levels and to explore the reason for choosing CPW. Results from the last quarter were as follows:

- Nearly 90% of customers rated CPW as excellent or good on its quality of service, value for money, product choice and product information.
- 90% of customers rated CPW as excellent or good by comparison to the competition.
- 88% of customers would definitely recommend CPW to others.

These are impressive figures, both internally as regards employees and externally for customers and is a testament to the effectiveness of the Carphone Warehouse in committing itself to concrete pledges in customer service. They have also been forthright in making these commitments in public and have been a consistent user of advertising communications to convey their brand promises. The Carphone Warehouse has been a long-standing enthusiast for radio as its prime advertising medium. In the early days of mobile telephony there was an obvious logic to using commercial radio because of its cost effectiveness and appropriateness in editorial context terms, i.e. addressing the prime target audience during drive time in their cars.

CPW used radio from its early days, when it was a medium that commanded only 3% of total UK advertising expenditure. They committed relatively large sums of money to it, with a regular media exposure and a consistent tone and style which enabled the Carphone Warehouse to establish a high degree of 'ownership' of the medium. It would not have achieved this had it spread its money across more media types or attempted to use television, with its far greater capital cost.

Most recently their 'True Story' campaign has attracted a good deal of attention in the media due to its effectiveness. In a sense this innovative radio campaign was the logical outcome of all the internal work that the

Carphone Warehouse does in terms of recruitment and training in combination with its public promises to customers. The idea was simple enough. Follow the progress of Carphone Warehouse trainees as they are inducted into the company over a two to three week period and use their experiences to convey to customers the deep-seated reality of the company's commitment to service and the provision of impartial advice. Executed in a naturalistic style using 'vox pops' of the young employees, the campaign had a wholly convincing effect and radio listeners, many of them potential customers, were treated to an engaging 'fly on the wall' documentary series. Not only did they get emotionally involved with the trainees as they went through their programme with its mini dramas such as product test examinations, but they also learned of the genuine support within the company for training designed to deliver the core brand promise. Another benefit of the creative approach produced by Radioville, CPW's agency, was the reinforcing effect it had on existing customers, staff and commercial partners -- everybody gained a deeper understanding of what made the Carphone Warehouse tick and how they managed to live up to their reputation.

Radioville attribute the True Story campaign's success to the fact that:

It WAS true. We didn't use actors; we didn't put words into people's mouths. We just let the CPW trainees talk. People can spend weeks chiselling and honing a script, crossing the 't's' and dotting the 'i's', but often an off the cuff remark or observation carries far more weight, because you know it's true. The Carphone Warehouse has a fantastic story to tell. All we did was let them tell it.'

Despite the Carphone Warehouse's phenomenal growth, it has never lost sight of its original aim, 'To empower people to make the right choice when purchasing a mobile phone'. Letting customers hear over the radio how new employees absorb this vision in training, warts and all, was a courageous move and one which paid off handsomely because CPW knew they were writing a cheque in public they always knew they could cash.

By making firm commitments to customers in support of the brand promise, corporations can inject discipline into service delivery and help manage customer expectations.

The CEO and the top management team should create customer pledges. This must be done in the context of competitive benchmarking and customer research. The customer charter is the rational underpinning of the corporate dream. It is separate from, but complementary to, the statement of vision, mission, values, roles and objectives of the organisation. It needs to be visibly displayed to customers; short enough to be actionable and detailed enough to be believable. It should be tested with key stakeholders, both internally and externally, including trading standards officers and any other relevant regulatory bodies. Make it a central part of the training programme. Ensure it is measurable, and then it will matter. Use the pledge in advertising and other marketing communications.

The benefits are linked to the delivery, or non-delivery, of each customer pledge and should be used to drive continuous improvement in the organisation. It also provides a compelling reason for the different functions of the organisation to work together. This 'horizontal' working should be harnessed to build organisation flexibility and capability.

24

Moments of Truth

The key purpose of this chapter is to highlight how often the lowest paid and most 'junior' employees are asked to deliver the most value in terms of the impact on customers, and usually how ill-equipped they are to do so. This is not just in terms of the training that they receive, but also in terms of their self-perception with regard to customers and their management 'superiors'.

Every day, every company of even a moderate size has literally millions of customer interactions through all the different channels of communication available in a modern economy. Each of these represents potential market research resulting from high-quality listening as has been described earlier, but they also represent an even more powerful series of opportunities for defining the brand values in the minds of customers: 'moments of truth'.

The Chief Executive and senior management of the company need to mobilise their 'front-line' troops (who may actually be in the back office), who are at the customer interface, and create a brand manners culture which enables every employee to be an effective ambassador for the organisation, and to add value through their behaviour, particularly in 'moments of truth'.

One can define a 'moment of truth' as being an instance where a company representative has the opportunity to reinforce powerfully the brand's values at a point of customer contact and rises successfully to the occasion. Clearly, if the employee concerned is acting in their normal role, this should be relatively easily achieved but so often this is not the case. Because of the hierarchical or pyramidal structure in nearly every company, the vast majority of customers meet relatively junior employees at their first point of contact with the brand (Figure 47). With training, they will be

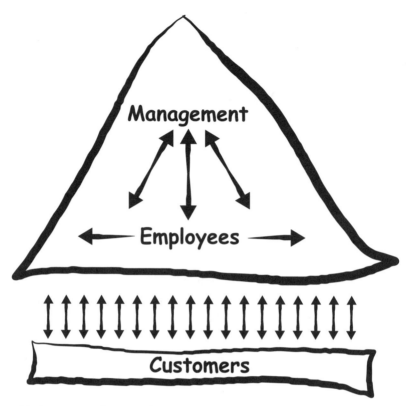

Figure 47 *Customer–employee interface.*

able to act appropriately in familiar situations but they are unlikely to have the experience to field enquiries or solve problems beyond their normal sphere of influence. Not only that, it is quite often the case that the employee in question is not officially meant to be dealing with customers, and finds themselves doing so by some accident or special circumstance. Psychologically, this can put them at a disadvantage and make them reluctant to 'take a risk' for the customer. Because corporations are organised into operating companies, divisions, departments, and other sorts of organisational silo, there is a natural tendency for an employee to be limited, and self-limiting, in the scope of personal responsibility. An individual in department A will be disinclined to deal with the customer issue that they perceive to be the domain of departments B or C.

Given the profit responsibility of the managers in operating division, their behaviour in trying to maintain their budgets and achieve their targets will militate against their team members being encouraged to go beyond their defined roles. Thus an overriding concern with personal agendas and politics will act against the common good. This problem operates at all levels; the Labour Government in the UK has coined the phrase 'joined up government' as an expression of their desire to get the Civil Service departments working together rather than in their own separate interests.

The problem with all this, of course, is that customers are oblivious to the internal organisational niceties of the companies they're dealing with – all they care about is the service they receive. When they meet, have a phone call with, receive an e-mail or letter from anyone within a company, their natural working assumption is that the employee speaks and acts for the brand. Every time a customer inquiry is ineffectively or inappropriately passed off to a colleague, there is a diminution in the authority of the person at the first line of contact. This lessens the strength of the brand in the customer's mind. Quite obviously the employee is aware of this relative customer service limitation and their lowly status within the organisation is reaffirmed in the process. It's hardly surprising that the 'job's worth' syndrome has developed over the last couple of centuries as a refined defence mechanism in the face of this. The employee who says 'It's more than my job's worth to do that' asserts a veneer of responsibility and authority in defining their limits in this way, but for most customers it comes across as a smug stubbornness and is simply infuriating.

Another challenge that faces companies and their employees, at the sharp end, is that many customers they come into contact with will actually represent a whole series of other customer relationships and be able to impact reputation by word of mouth. Failing to recognise this may completely miss the possibility that the same person is also the owner of a business as well as being a private customer, or is married or related to someone who is, or representative of a syndicate, club or interest group. Very few people in modern times live a singular life. The individual who has a bad experience with a credit card company may also be the decision-maker responsible for the assignment of the corporate credit card account. The person who books a cab through a cab company which then proceeds to let them down badly through cancellation or late arrival of the car, may similarly have the power of decision on whether or not that firm should be fired from the company account. The customer treated badly at the counter of a retail financial services company may also be the club secretary of an organisation with significant funds on deposit at the same place.

If one assumes that for a hypothetical retail organisation with 500 branches and 750 million customer interactions per year, of which just 1% per cent represent 'moments of truth' and then you multiply that number by a factor of 10 to indicate the potential influence that they may have on others through positive word of mouth, this would add up to a phenomenal number of potential brand building interactions. All of this represents a very big challenge to the company. Effective listening can enable a significant proportion of the desired response, but this does not go far enough if the corporation really wishes to make a powerful branded impact on customers. The real test of a system of brand manners occurs when employees come into contact with customers who are unexpected, angry, frightened, lost or in some other way in an unusual frame of mind, position or context. It is at these points, typical 'moments of truth', when the customer is at their most vulnerable and volatile that appropriate behaviour can create an incredibly positive and indelible impression on the customer. As we have seen, the problem really can become a part of the solution.

Mary Spillane, Chief Executive of Image Works and author of the book *Branding Yourself*, quotes research from the University of Toronto in Canada that gives a fascinating insight into the power of human beings to make accurate personal judgements almost instantaneously. In a controlled experiment the University asked executive search professionals to interview 500 candidates. They were instructed to stop after fifteen seconds and note their opinions and conclusions on whether or not to hire the person. The interviews then continued for 30 minutes and at the end another appraisal was made. Astonishingly, 97% of the impressions were the same at 15 seconds as they were at 30 minutes. This sort of information is put forward as advice to the individual who is in the 'selling' position with the clear indication that they should take steps to address their skills in each of the key areas that affect the way in which the communication is received by the 'buyer'. Essentially form matters much more than content.

But usually this advice is largely reserved for more senior management, and especially those who are formally designated as having a sales role, and is relatively rarely given to 'ordinary' members of staff. But obviously the skills are invaluable wherever there is an interface between employee and customer. Surely then these skills should be deployed where there is most customer interaction? The key point is that this instant recognition and appraisal takes place within fifteen seconds, and it's a two-way street. The customer is instantly getting a 'fix' on an employee (who often may not think they're selling, or realise that the customer is buying) and meanwhile the employee is getting a similar 'fix' on their potential client. It's essential that every employee has an appreciation of this interpersonal dynamic in order to even begin to be able to deal with 'moments of truth'.

Assuming that the employee has been given some training in these aspects of communication, and has been imbued with a motivating understanding of what the brand values are, then what is required is a sense of alertness to the potential for moments of truth and to recognise them when they happen. A skill that sales people are taught is to build on their instant assessment abilities and to 'get on the same level' as the person with whom they're dealing as quickly as possible. This entails 'reading' the demeanour of the prospect, appreciating their body language, absorbing the pitch, pace and power of their speech and responding in a way that mirrors their behaviour, thus establishing rapport. All employees who have even the slightest chance of getting involved with customers need to understand these dynamics and to learn to put them at the brand's disposal. They need to have the self-confidence born out of good training, and nurtured by a supportive management style, to take the first and most basic risk on behalf of the company for the benefit of the customer and the reputation of the brand. This 'risk' is taking ownership of the customer in all circumstances and especially when the customer's needs are apparently outside the remit of the particular employee at a particular time.

Because corporate behaviour is increasingly understood, customers fully appreciate the division of labour for powerfully good reasons of efficiency and focus within companies. They understand that someone in the cosmetics department doesn't necessarily know anything about bakery nor should they expect that someone in duty free should know anything about departure gates. But therein lies the power of dealing with the moment of truth. The unexpected response of someone rising to the occasion, stepping outside his or her particular 'box' and solving a customer problem is so powerful just because it's so unusual. For the employee who achieves this, it can be the most extraordinarily rewarding personal experience. It's an affirmation of their individuality, because they will have had to react very quickly, instinctively and without reference to superiors. To have made a sale when their real job was in administration, to have calmed an angry customer when they normally deal with technology, or to save someone's life by identifying a serious product fault with a minimum of maintenance experience are all examples of self-expression and improvisation at their best. Moreover, although relatively rare, successfully confronting moments of truth and controlling them is a reaffirmation of an individual's power over their working environment and a great contributor to long-term job satisfaction.

Whilst careful research into the nature of the interactions between the brand and its buyers can prepare the company for many frequently occurring types of interaction, obviously it's impossible to anticipate every single scenario in which moments of truth may occur for employees and their customers. Therefore there needs to be a culture and set of brand manners that creates the context in which employees can have the inclination and the self-confidence to deliver for the brand. An outstanding example of a culture change was orchestrated within Vauxhall Motors, the UK operating company for General Motors.

Case History: THE 'VAUXHALL DIFFERENCE'

Vauxhall, like many other motor manufacturers with a dealer network primarily composed of franchise owners, constantly battled to establish common standards of excellent customer service across its retail network. They appreciated that quite often the first person a prospective car buyer might meet on the dealer forecourt could be a trainee washing cars on display, rather than a qualified salesperson. They understood that customers booking a vehicle in for a service might quite naturally phone their original salesperson to organise it, rather than appreciating that they should properly call the Service Receptionist. They knew that customers coming to collect their new car in a state of enthusiastic excitement would very likely be brought down to earth in a hurry by a 45-minute delay whilst paperwork was completed and the car finally prepared for handover.

Accordingly, building on some key elements of the Saturn programme in the United States, Vauxhall developed a massive cultural change process, called the 'Vauxhall Difference' (Figure 48). This did not just entail retraining, but the building of partnerships as well. The heart of the programme lay in developing the relationships with dealers and all other key parties involved in a strategy designed to improve customer focus and processes across Vauxhall Motors.

The 'Vauxhall Difference' was a multi-phased programme that started in the UK in 1994 and rolled out to become a pan-European culture development. Vauxhall committed very significant resources to it, employing five full-time people to run the project who in turn sub-contracted some of the work to many freelance trainers. As an indication of the scale of the 'Vauxhall Difference' a specially designed training ground was purpose built in Jerez, Spain. Impressively, and in an early indication of the attention to detail and commitment to excellence that typified the culture development project, the site was chosen as a result of detailed analysis of weather records and satellite photography. This analysis identified the sunniest place within a two-hour flight of Luton airport – the nearest one to Vauxhall! It was also well positioned for Opel, General Motor's European arm, who took over from Vauxhall's UK pilot and used it

Figure 48 *Vauxhall Difference logo.*

across their operations. The specially designed and built Jerez site was rigged with a whole series of climbing/mountaineering structures which revealed some macho sales types to be scared of heights and some accounts clerks to be as agile as monkeys at 40 feet above ground! (Figure 49). This was a great leveller and the crux of the team building and self-discovery elements of the 'Vauxhall Difference'. In order to succeed as teams in the various exercises many individuals had to confront their own personal 'moments of truth', encouraged and coached to do so by their colleagues.

In all, over 20,000 people have been through the 'Vauxhall Difference' process: about one thousand Vauxhall people, two thousand supplier employees, and seventeen thousand retailer management and staff. Thus all stakeholders in enterprise Vauxhall were brought into it. Everybody went through the experience, right down to car cleaners in a six-phase plan that was extraordinary considering the cost to retailers of sending them. The Vauxhall Difference is standards driven at both retail and wholesale levels. Within each Vauxhall department and sub-department there is someone responsible for looking at the particular standards that apply to their piece of the operation. At the outset, standards were set for Vauxhall at the wholesale level; in order for retailers to perform it was essential that Vauxhall supported them with such essentials as parts on time, cars on time, and standards of excellence in terms of the delivery process. Warranties also had to be fully supported, with technical resources to get repairs or replacements right first time.

Figure 49 *Climbing rig in Jerez.*

These internal task forces who are responsible for their own wholesale standards remain *in situ* today. The commitment to a total culture change was the reason for bringing in Vauxhall's suppliers as well as bringing in internal customers. The transporter company is an integral part of the delivery process and if the driver blocks off a street, scratches the cars, or is rude, then this does not live up to 'Vauxhall Difference' standards. A committee consisting of representatives from within Vauxhall's key departments, their retailers and supplier companies formulated the standards. The standards were fully discussed and agreed upon, in a demonstration of Vauxhall's commitment to open management.

The 'Headline' phase took place in Spain and lasted three days for people in leadership positions such as retailer operators, departmental or regional managers, senior supplier representatives and retail facility key managers. A primary purpose of the leadership course at Jerez was to communicate and get commitment to a whole range of retail standards and to emphasise the importance of attitude and behaviour in successful customer relationship management. For example, the standard that was set regarding the follow up after a service is that a retailer should call the customer within three days and ascertain whether the experience was okay, the car is okay and if not to fix it. This may seem very obvious, but prior to the 'Vauxhall Difference' beginning in 1994 in excess of 50% of Vauxhall retailers did not do this as a part of a regular business process. Best practice in this key area is vital to a retailer's business. Service retention in the first year of new-car ownership, when the vehicle is under warranty, averages between 70% and 80%. This drops to 60% to 70% in the second year and then down to 30% to 40% in year three as people often feel the franchised retailer is more expensive. Any improvement in these percentages makes a big impact on profitability and on the potential for future new car sales. The 'Vauxhall Difference' was essentially an early example of customer relationship management; the goal was not only to have enthusiastic customers at the point of purchase, but loyal ones too. Service is key to retaining a customer in the loop and getting them back as a new-car customer in future. Retailers may write letters, send brochures and make calls, but there's nothing quite like having the physical contact that is naturally created by a regular car service. This is when the opportunity for fulfilling 'moments of truth' can so often arise and if successfully managed create true bonds with the customer.

Apart from the Jerez course, a great deal of the work was done in the UK at one-day events designed to communicate the key cultural message. Once everyone had been exposed to the concepts at the retailer level through Vauxhall training the programme took on a life of its own through dealers' own development of it, creating retailer self-help and best practice infrastructure. And this still continues, where it matters. Never described as a 'programme' but as an on-going process, the 'Vauxhall Difference' goal was always to integrate the new behaviour and attitude into day-to-day thinking and business planning. Six years later it's true that the Vauxhall Difference is not as high profile as it was, when there were big slogans on the walls reminding them of the key messages and exhorting people to deliver on them. But where it matters, that is in the way people behave and relate to each other and the general culture of the organisation, it's become institutionalised. Therefore Vauxhall no longer actually need the big machine to keep it going because it's become what they do – the best possible sign of success.

The retail standards that were rolled out in Spain were turned into a customer questionnaire used to survey people just after the point of sale and after the point of service experience. This was important in order to have measurable results and to be able to monitor key trends to see how effective the culture change process was being. They are asked the precise questions relating to the service standards that were set out in the Vauxhall Difference. Feedback is tracked and standards have improved with a measurable improvement in customer care as related by customers themselves. They also take polls to see how they, Vauxhall, are living up to 'Vauxhall Difference' wholesale standards in their retailers' eyes. Again these have been improving significantly as retailers have held Vauxhall to account – the mutual commitment that was cemented in Jerez, Spain.

The company did not rush to use elements of the 'Vauxhall Difference' in its advertising because of the serious risk of over-promising and under-delivering. They needed to make significant improvements first. Indeed, customer expectations have moved forward massively since the 'Vauxhall Difference' started. Therefore inching up the customer satisfaction figures is painfully difficult, because the brand is swimming against a tide of rising consumer expectation. Around 1998, Vauxhall felt that enough real progress had been made and that the time was right to have some external embodiment of both the brand and the ethos that goes behind it. They researched some direct translations of 'Vauxhall Difference' into customer communications, but it didn't work. When presented with a series of internally focused standards and goals, customers responded with: 'So what's in it for me?' This is a classic example of the 'political' dimension, and led to an intensive period of brand re-discovery or marque redefinition. This eventually resulted in a new brand proposition encapsulated in the copy line: 'Raising the Standard'. This positioning clearly mirrors 'Vauxhall Difference' themes and it embodies and embraces the concept of continuous improvement, the key idea they are driving towards. There is also a link to the Vauxhall logo with its heraldic motif of a griffin and flag (Figure 50). This line has become a rallying call and an external statement of all that Vauxhall have been doing over the last six years.

Figure 50 *Vauxhall Griffin logo.*

Ian Coomber, Executive Director for Sales Marketing and Customer Care, and one of the key drivers of the 'Vauxhall Difference', expressed his view of the culture change process as follows:

> The 'Vauxhall Difference' has been unusual in its longevity and it's still very much alive and well. It's not been supplanted by the next flavour of the month as so often happens with these sorts of initiative. In terms of sales results, it is difficult to point to direct cause and effect, but certainly our customer satisfaction results are going up and therefore if you apply common sense to those sorts of factors you believe that you are selling more cars as a result of it. Some of the internal work has without doubt taken cost out of our operations; in finding best practice, you end up doing things more efficiently and that's also true at the retailer end. We have definitely kept pace with a rising consumer demand on our organisation and on our retail franchises that we certainly wouldn't have done if we hadn't created the 'Vauxhall Difference'. Therefore we are more likely to be talking about the avoidance of loss of share over the whole six-year period, rather than gain. As it happens, in the last two years our market share has increased; there are many factors which lie behind this success, and the 'Vauxhall Difference' is definitely a significant one.

The main point of the Vauxhall case history is that for an organisation to be truly successful in identifying and dealing with customers, and especially customers' moments of truth, it must have a genuine sense of team spirit and a commitment right from the top. This is key to its success. Further, each individual has to be aware that their particular skills in one area are quite likely to be matched by weaknesses in another, and that they therefore need reinforcement and support. This is the only way to make the whole greater than the sum of the individual parts.

Finally, the scale and longevity of the 'Vauxhall Difference' in itself created its own success. The quality of the Jerez leadership experience, the numbers of people involved, and the expenditure committed by manufacturer, supplier and retailer together created a powerful bond between business partners and an exciting sense of *force majeure* that would over-ride any minor difficulties along the way.

The car industry is regarded as a very tough, competitive and 'hard bitten' one and it's a testament to the vision of General Motors and the 'Vauxhall Difference' that a culture change process that depended as much on emotional commitment as rational standards, has worked so well for them.

It is the job of management to ensure that employees are equipped to make the very best from each 'moment of truth'. This is best done by simplifying the work process, making the systems user friendly and teaching people core skills on the job, which will improve the customer experience. There also needs to be a corporate mindset which recognises that those employees dealing directly with the customer are the most important people in the organisation for the delivering of brand manners.

The CEO needs to ensure that all employees with the potential for customer contact are trained in presentation and recognition skills. The level and duration of the commitment to this and the resources deployed will themselves send a powerful signal to the company. Team building exercises should be used to break down inter-departmental barriers and internal politics. They should be designed as parables for 'moments of truth', put very senior and very junior people in positions of reverse ability and confidence and rely on team dynamics to create mutual reinforcement and compensation for varying skill levels. In parallel with the emotional experience of team building in this way, there must be a fully worked out set of rational underpinnings in terms of measurable, repeatable behaviours or brand manners. These should be linked to appraisals, incentives and customer market research. Employees who experience 'moments of truth' with customers should be encouraged to report them, good or bad, in order to add to the learning pool.

Section Five

'Feeling Good'

Having created 'Happy surprises' in customers' experience, the improvement cycle turns to bringing 'Feeling good' to life through: outstanding customer service, under-promising and over-delivering, enabled employees, and recruitment for the brand.

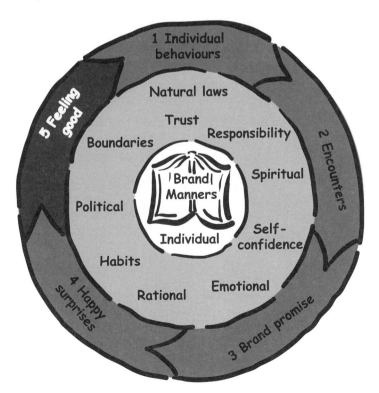

Figure 51 *Section Five: The Brand Manners Improvement Cycle – feeling good.*

25

Defining Outstanding Customer Service

The key purpose of this chapter is to define one of the most important concepts in brand manners. This is what counts as an outstanding customer service experience. There has been a great deal of discussion of the notion of giving customers more than just average service. For example, people talk about 'delighting' their customers, but so often it is unclear what this actually means in the day-to-day reality of a business.

A central thesis of brand manners is that the managing of expectations is one of the most crucial aspects of making people feel good, not only in business, but also in life. Politicians such as Margaret Thatcher have managed to push through radical programmes through the shrewd use of expectation management. Announcing a controversial initiative well in advance and holding the line in the face of critical attack enables the debate to be had and for people to become accustomed to the new idea. By the time it becomes a legislative reality much of the heat has gone out of the issue as it has been assimilated into the political consciousness.

The same process operates in business and in interpersonal relationships. It seems to be a fundamental aspect of human psychology that we can discount information in a systematic way, as a self-protective process, given some warning. We don't like sudden shocks to the system, but the same shock can become little more than a gentle frisson should we have plenty of notice of its arrival. We are creatures of habit and are uncomfortable when our habits are disturbed. However, we can be managed out of these routines, customs and practices over time, given a clear direction and convincing leadership.

The creation of a brand manners system provides the means to manage the expectations of those inside the business, its customers, its investors and indeed all its stakeholders. If the company can do this systematically then it's possible to manage success in, and failure out.

It's obviously the case that different industries or different market sectors have different service standards. Indeed, even within a particular area, service may vary according to the channel of distribution, the time of year, or some other variable. Nevertheless, human beings do seem to have an uncanny ability to conceive in their minds what would count as 'good service' in virtually any situation, even the absolutely new. To take a couple of futuristic examples, even if commercial space travel or videophones become a reality it seems likely their customers would embark on the first shuttle ride or videocon with a pretty good idea of what would make a good one or not.

It's also true that service standards cannot be easily compared between one industry and another. A good experience on a train doesn't immediately relate to a good experience in a cinema. A phone call to a helpline doesn't necessarily have the same quality parameters as an e-mail or a letter. What seems to happen is that we construct for ourselves a notion of good service for each of these individual situations. Another dimension is that of individual perceptions in each of these cases. What counts as good customer service for a disc jockey or a duchess may not be

Cartoon 6 *'Difficult choice'.*

the same at all for a dustman or a designer. The point of all this is to demonstrate that there are no absolute objective measures of good customer service; all we can deal with are relativities and draw broad conclusions within particular industries and for fairly general target groups.

If a customer were to imagine that they were going on a shopping trip intending to buy some shoes, they would immediately bring up the construct in their mind as to what such a shopping customer service experience might be. This will be based on their past experience of this activity, and will be very much conditioned by their own personality and physical attributes and preferences in relationship to shoes. The price point that they shop at and therefore the types of outlet that they will visit will also affect it. No doubt they would also have an idea of the likely shopping conditions on a Saturday near the end of the school holidays or in a sale, as opposed to during a period of full-priced trading in the middle of the week. Out of all these instinctive considerations they will have synthesised a generalised idea of what 'good service' might be, and off they go on their shoe-shopping trip with this in their mind.

However, sadly, they know only too well that the notion of good service that is in their mind is very rarely fulfilled in reality. Years of indifferent or even poor service experiences in shoe shops puts them in a frame of mind that expects less than 100% fulfilment of their ideal of good service. It's much more likely that they walk into their first shoe shop expecting perhaps 80% at best (Figure 52). The same semi-conscious process of measuring personal expectations against reality takes place in every service experience. If the brand ambassadors and the architects of brand manners for the company fully understand this, then the opportunity for delivering outstanding customer service on a regular basis is there for the taking.

If the brand has done its research it should be aware of all this. The shoe retailer will have a good idea of the contributory factors to and the parameters within which good and bad service exists in their trade. In other words, they should have gone through exactly the same process as the customer has, on a mass-market basis. The learning from these researches should have been conveyed to all the managers and employees who face customers at store level, but also interact with them by other means. Thus the first goal for the company is to ensure that their service levels live up to the 100% ideal that exists in their customer's mind. Given that the majority of customers have entered their outlet with an expectation of relative disappointment against their ideal, it's actually relatively easy to exceed their expectations by simply closing the 20%

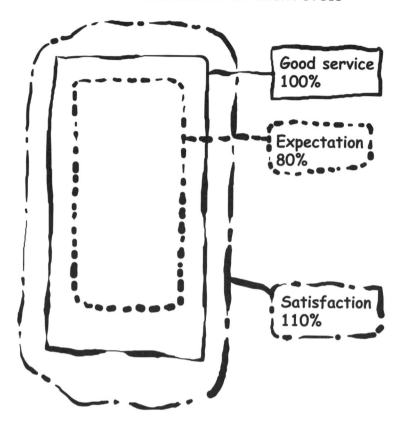

Good service
100%

Expectation
80%

Satisfaction
110%

The brand ambassador breaks the rules in the customer's favour and achieves
110% of the ideal in 'good service' – true customer satisfaction.

Figure 52 *Customer satisfaction.*

'ideal to reality service gap'. The precise percentage will vary depending
on the industry, segment and brand, but can be established as a norm
through market research.

The really exciting thing that comes out of using brand manners and the
management of expectations is that it is possible to over-achieve
systematically on the ideal of customer service and deliver an outstanding
experience. It is not possible, or indeed desirable for every single customer
that enters every single shoe shop in the brand's chain to receive such
service, because by definition it is a question of relativity. If every customer
were to receive an outstanding service experience every time they visited
the shop, this would become the norm for them within that shop and
therefore the brand would be on a never-ending treadmill to find ways of
exceeding the level again. Since there is an expense attached to over-
performance, this is unlikely to be a cost-effective strategy.

The power of word of mouth is such that a relatively small percentage of all customer visits which result in an outstanding personal experience will generate, through the word of mouth multiplier effect, a very much bigger impact on brand reputation. Experience suggests that an average of between 10% and 15% of all customers affected in an extraordinary way will open up significant competitive advantage in a given market place. Look how quickly Virgin Atlantic managed to establish this kind of reputation when they had only one transatlantic route and relatively tiny passenger numbers. Equally, look how much damage has been done to the Virgin brand through its less than successful involvement in railways. It is better to position the level of service and the ratio of outstanding experiences at these levels, observe competitors closing the gap, and then move to new service standards which come to represent the higher level of 100% for the brand's customers.

Qualitative research amongst a wide range of demographic groupings reveals a remarkably similar pattern of reactions in the service situation. It is also relatively easy to discern the key common factor that unites a very large proportion of outstanding customer service experiences. When customers are asked to recall their best and worst experiences, they can do this remarkably easily. Descriptions of the worst experiences are peppered with phrases such as: 'they treated me like a number, not an individual'; 'I needed help badly, but their attitude was simply couldn't care less'; 'I had to speak to six different people in three different departments before I made contact with anyone who seemed to know anything about it at all'; and 'I had been a loyal customer to them for years, but I might as well have just turned up for the first time for all the difference it made'.

By contrast, when describing their most positive service experiences, customers report being treated absolutely as an individual and at the time feeling as if they were getting very special attention from the person with whom they were dealing. The descriptions are not unlike those that surround charismatic leaders. People who have met them report that they were made to feel as if at that time they were the most important person in the world. The customer's desire for acknowledgement is very powerful, as is the sense of empathy and appreciation created by another's recognition of one's own situation and personal needs at a particular time and place. However, on top of these deep human needs, the single most powerful thing which creates an outstanding service experience, is the preparedness of the brand representative to break the rules in favour of the customer.

Over and over again, customer anecdotes describing their great service experiences return to the theme of them being made an exception to the rule. Typical examples would be the extension of a guarantee which expired only a few days before the appliance broke down; the fully booked aeroplane which miraculously produces a vacant upgrade seat or the traditional high-street grocer who throws in a couple of extra potatoes in the pound. These little discretionary favours granted by the representative of the brand in a situation where the customer is often distressed, not only solves the problem to their relief but also makes them feel like very special individuals who are being treated better than the average person. This does wonders for their self-esteem and has an enormous impact on brand reputation. At the same time it is enormously empowering for the employee, firstly because they have the freedom to render outstanding service and secondly because of the positive feedback they get from their customer and their manager who can see a potential problem averted and turned to advantage.

In order to make these brand manners work and to manage expectations effectively two things need to be in place. Firstly, and most obviously, in order for customers to feel that the rules have been broken in their favour, they need to know what the rules were in the first place. Thus it is incumbent on the brand to have established its customer pledges, brand positioning, and a brand promise and to have communicated these and the overall brand dream effectively to its public. Secondly, the brand representatives who interact with customers have to have clearly defined parameters within which they can operate in breaking the company's own rules. This requires a carefully researched and managed system which enables concessions to be made to the benefit of the brand, and in relationship to an overall appraisal and incentive scheme which governs the whole process. Training is essential in order for employees in the front line to be able to recognise moments of truth that can be capitalised upon and turned into outstanding examples of customer service and brand experience. In the very act of breaking the brand rules they must in fact be reinforced by clear communication of all they are normally and what they have become in his special customer situation.

A UK brand, Pret a Manger, which is just embarking on its USA launch, makes an interesting example of this responsive approach to customer service.

Case History: PRET A MANGER
Pret a Manger is a UK chain of sandwich shops founded by Julian Metcalfe and Sinclair Beecham in 1986. Their first shop in Victoria, London had a kitchen in the basement and the values and methodology that were in

place then have remained firmly in place today. All the suppliers who provide the ingredients used by Pret a Manger were selected first-hand by the owners, who scoured the streets of London in search of the finest quality foods, refusing to compromise profits for quality. All chemical additives and preservatives are avoided and ingredients within ingredients are closely monitored to ensure that they are kept as natural as possible.

This enthusiasm at the beginning of any venture is not surprising but fourteen years on and one hundred shops down the line Sinclair Beecham, the founder and co-owner has spent the last six months carrying out the same process in the USA. They opened their first shop in mid 2000. In refusing to compromise quality for profits, establishing Pret in New York has not been easy. For example, sliced granary bread in the UK doesn't exist in the USA. The option of importing the bread was rejected due to the effects on quality, so instead of settling for second best, Sinclair has hired a small, Brooklyn baker to bake the bread for Pret fresh every day; this way it is almost identical to the bread used in the UK. Another hurdle has been the difficulty in finding fresh food in America that matches the quality to which Pret a Manger adheres in the UK. The cost is high as a lot of the food produced in the USA is genetically modified or contains many preservatives, which Pret strive to avoid. Once again they have refused to change their beliefs and insist on finding fresh foods, which is both time and cost consuming, but in their view is also essential to the integrity of their brand.

Adhering to these core beliefs has clearly been central to the brand's success, but given that Pret a Manger does not advertise, it's interesting to consider how it communicates with its customers and the role this has had in building the business. Like any other retail brand Pret relies on its shops, its employees and its packaging to convey its brand proposition. But perhaps it's the ubiquitous availability of the co-owner Julian Metcalfe's name and phone number, which is printed on all serviettes and packaging, that is the biggest symbol of Pret a Manger's customer service, and is a particular brand strength in the after-sales situation.

For the first few years customers calling his number would indeed get straight through to Julian, but now the scale of Pret's business means that they speak to the customer service team. However, if a customer were to specifically request to speak to Julian they will be put through to him or in the event that he is unavailable he guarantees to call them straight back. Pret a Manger use this customer feedback very actively in their business.

Perhaps the best example of the power of the customer voice is the story of the egg and bacon croissant. In early 2000 Pret decided that this product line was not consistent with their image and that it was time to take it off the market. The impact of this decision could never have been predicted. The degree to which Pret a Manger's core London franchise of 'City' traders had come to rely upon the Pret croissant was unbelievable and the consumer backlash phenomenal. Hundreds of anguished customers sent faxes with drawings of the croissant saying 'Bring me back' and threatening never to visit Pret again unless the croissant was relaunched. Within six weeks of the product being taken off the market it was back on the shelves again. As well as relaunching the product Pret wrote to all the customers who had complained and informed them that because of their comments the croissant had been reintroduced. In these sorts of ways Pret a Manger managed constantly to reiterate their brand and turn negative instances in their favour.

When a product is out of stock they explain why, by saying that they do not wish to compromise their standards by substituting the norm with poor-quality ingredients. This attention to detail and the transparency of the company constantly reinforces the brand image. Pret's popular pastries, a likely option for a City breakfast, are delivered in a glossy waxed bag. This, we are told on the back of the bag, is because one of their customers complained that the pastry stuck to the old paper bags. It is this sort of action, which makes Pret the successful and respected company that it is, they do listen to customers and change their processes in reflection.

Their transparency is both reassuring and convincing. Many companies claim to use healthy ingredients but few go to the lengths that Pret a Manger do to educate and inform customers exactly how they do this. Their 'Passion Facts', which are available in all stores, detail the source and make up of all the foods used. For instance, Pret Passion Fact No. 2: 'Pret ham comes from Freedom Farms approved by the RSPCA who guarantee the pigs are reared outdoors on a vegetarian diet. The colour, texture and taste of our ham is a world apart from the shiny slippery square stuff commonly found in most kitchens. All our hams are hand-glazed with honey and cloves and then baked in the oven.'

Pret have clocked on to the fact that people do care about what they put in their bodies and that there is a real advantage to be reaped from keeping customers informed. As new processes are discovered or ideas improved Pret informs the customer what they have done and why. For instance, recently they changed their sandwich containers to paper instead of plastic. There is an explanation for this on the box: Pret believes that as the shelf life of their sandwiches is only a day there is no need to have a container with any longer life. Thus the fresh food and environmental card is played in a completely appropriate manner.

There are endless examples of Pret a Manger's provision of exceedingly good customer service, but the overall theme is that they stick to their promise and crucially, everything that they claim to do, they actually do. This is a very powerful tool; after-sales customer service such as this is the mechanism that generates the volume of repeat customers that Pret has managed to attain. The walls of the head office of Pret a Manger are covered in customers' letters commenting on the popularity of the company. In this way the staff who are not directly at the customer interface are kept in touch with the success of Pret in terms of customer satisfaction and this keeps them motivated to provide a good service in return. Every Monday a newsletter circulates around the head office, which details all of the issues that have been raised, from new products to customer complaints, and this allows for great communication with everybody in the organisation being kept well informed.

Within stores there is an opportunity for customers to comment on the service or products by filling out a card which is always available. These comments are discussed by all the staff every morning and anything that cannot be dealt with in store is then passed back to head office for Julian to deal with. The benefit of having these regular meetings cannot be overemphasised as they allow each store to be in control of their own problems and to celebrate their own victories. Seeing these comments first hand ensures that all staff can see clearly their role in the organisation and their impact on the customer. Often, such a system reports back to a central communications centre, which often results in a loss of accountability and thus effectiveness.

Pret a Manger's openness to customer communication, embodied by the visible accessibility of the founders, has been a powerful component of its success. Unlike many other fast-food brands Pret have focused a good deal of attention on the after-sales process and this provides a useful lesson in brand manners.

Outstanding customer service doesn't just happen. It results from an understanding of brand manners and the creation of a self-confident organisation to deliver them. Management needs to ensure that the organisation really does understand customer behaviour and expectations in respect of the brand's market sector, its competitive set and the relationship with all the key variables that may affect the customer experience. In particular, the marketing, communications and human resource functions have to establish the brand manners and then convey them effectively internally and externally to create the climate of expectation for the product or service brand.

Brand ambassadors, who interact with customers through whatever channel, need to be trained in the understanding of what expectations of customer service are in their particular context, and how to respond accordingly. They need a system within which brand representatives have the discretion and defined degrees of freedom to take risks on behalf of the customer and the company. The company needs to have a monitoring process to track levels of customer satisfaction for the brand and the key competitors.

The sad reality of everyday life is that good customer service is the exception rather than the norm. The electronics shop with high-priced items that expects customers to serve themselves as the staff can do no more than read the label is an example. Further examples would be the bank or post office counter where the employees look as if they are probably somewhere else; the transportation company whose employees blame their employer to customers; the passport queue at the airport where staff tell you: 'write to the government'; the shambolic queuing for taxis at many major airports, and so on. The good news is there is lots of room for improvements! So, review every aspect of the communication of the brand at the point of purchase to ensure it is aligned with the brand positioning and promise including:

- front of house and back office
- product or service packaging
- window presentation
- staff dress and personal presentation
- tone of voice/verbal style
- written style in letters and e-mails
- serving knowledge and style at point of purchase
- retail theatre
- advertising and marketing communications.

26

The Importance of Under-promising and Over-delivering

As we have seen, an outstanding service experience is almost entirely subjective, conditioned by delivery against expectations. This chapter builds on the idea of how to create outstanding customer service experiences on a more systematic and regular basis.

The creation of expectations in customers' minds is fundamental to establishing the psychological framework within which the brand can deliver. All brands must communicate to their target audiences what their promises actually are in order to establish their benchmarks and expectations against which the product or service brand should be judged. If this is done well, and if the customer service process, acting through the brand's representatives, can consistently over-deliver against these publicly established standards, then a sense of outstanding service will result.

Elsewhere in *Brand Manners*, we have shown the degree to which we are all creatures of habit and how we gain comfort and security from structure in our lives. We seem to be naturally resistant to change and usually unhappy about unexpected surprises. The same feelings apply to interpersonal relationships including those involved in vendor to customer interactions. We therefore gain great comfort from having our expectations fulfilled. A missed appointment with a service engineer can be an extremely upsetting experience. Not only is this because of the time wasted waiting for someone to arrive. Nor is it just the opportunity cost entailed in being away from money-earning work. Neither is it the irritation that the faulty appliance still does not function. As much as any of these things, it is the simple uncertainty of not knowing whether the engineer is going to arrive or not. This is an anxiety and a frustration which could so easily be resolved by a telephone call notifying of progress but which, curiously for nearly every home service company, never seems to come.

Over and over again, one can see the same thing happening in situations where there are delays on trains, at airports and in traffic on motorways. If the customer information is frequent and well informed, then human beings can be remarkably resilient in the face of delays. What they seem to be unable to bear for more than ten minutes or so is the lack of information about the causes, the likely resolution of the delay and its forecast duration that leads to a sense of loss of control and increasing anxiety. One of the rules of all brand communications is to establish a level of goodwill in the minds of customers that builds up a bank of credits against which the company can draw in future should it at any time run into difficulties. Branding is like growing asparagus, one should have started five years ago! In many ways the sheer longevity of a branding campaign is one of its greatest strengths and the cause of the reassurance that this gives customers through its consistency and familiarity.

In developing a branding campaign, communication must build upon the key components we have discussed elsewhere namely the rational, the emotional, the political and spiritual. Naturally the company wishes to make the strongest possible claims that it can for its brand, within the constraints of the product and service performance and the regulatory framework. Occasionally marketers over-claim, nearly always with adverse results. For example the recent introduction by Procter & Gamble (P&G) of a radical new toilet tissue was intended to take the UK marketplace by storm. Charmin, the best selling lavatory paper in America, was introduced in Britain in January with a £27 million marketing campaign. However, evidence subsequently emerged to suggest that usage of this new stronger paper technology may cause problems and P&G has agreed to halve the 'temporary wet strength' of Charmin paper after water companies and rival manufacturers warned that it could block the sewerage system. As a result, Charmin has had to be re-formulated to a lower specification, with consequent loss of credibility at the trade and customer level.

P&G's great rival, Unilever, had previously run into similar sorts of problems with its new detergent, 'Persil Power', that contained manganese. This miracle new cleaning ingredient was removed in 1995 after it was found to rot clothes, a fact that Procter & Gamble was at pains to point out following rigorous testing of its own, to demonstrate the problem to the regulatory authorities and the media, which revelled in Bart Simpson-like headlines of the 'Persil Power ate my shorts' variety!

The skill in communicating the various dimensions of a brand to its actual or potential customers is in pitching it at a level which gives competitive advantage but still leaves room for the product or service brand to outperform in practice. In the world of sales promotion, it's often better to avoid a straight money-off discount because this literally does put a new price point on the brand and tends to lead to a downward spiral of successive price promotions with damaging effects on profitability. Added-value promotions, in which extra product is given free, or Brand A is banded with Brand B, or a BOGOF promotion (Buy One Get One Free) are better for the brand promise. In the service arena, 'introduce a friend', extended benefits, and fringe benefit promotions have the same appeal. In using these strategies there is a sense in which the brand still retains its self-esteem and believes it's worth giving more of itself to the customer at the price, rather than the same of itself at a reduced one.

With respect to the nature and type of advertising communication to be used, there is still a belief in the minds of many marketers that the 'hard sell' is more effective than the 'soft sell'. In confirmation of the complex nature of modern branding techniques, Tim Ambler's analysis of the winners of the 1998 IPA Advertising Effectiveness Awards (Figure 53) has shown that the combination of rational, emotional and other complex psychological factors was the most commonly successful branding approach used. Strategies which rely on purely rational approaches were in a very small minority.

This shows pretty clearly that in fact a mix of the rational and emotional is rather more likely to be effective than one based on the rational alone. Adding the political and spiritual dimensions would make this even stronger. In practical terms this means that the overly bombastic banging on the brand drum, shouting benefits and plugging giant logos, is unlikely to be as successful as a rather subtler, more engaging approach. While this may seem to some to be under-promising, in fact it is creating the potential for over-delivery. Two famous American brands, both of which have often been cited as case histories, used the strategy of under-promising and over-delivering in building their businesses. Federal Express became famous for guaranteeing that it would deliver packages before 8 a.m. to over 5,000

How did the 1998 entrants to the IPA Advertising Effectiveness Awards think their campaigns worked?

Rationally only	4%
Emotionally only	22%
Persuasive combination of the rational and emotional	22%
Reinforcement of existing behaviour	6%
Complex of the above factors, or more	46%

Source: IPA Data Bank.

Figure 53 *IPA advertising statistics.*

USA postal zip codes by the next day. Domino's Pizza used the promise that their pizzas would be delivered within twenty minutes of ordering or they would be free of charge. In both these cases the organisations had done their research, discovered that timeliness of delivery was a crucial factor in customer satisfaction, and then set publicised targets that they knew their business processes could beat systematically. They designed over-delivery into their customer pledge.

An example of another company that has made a very public virtue from under-promising and over-delivering, is the UK brand Ronseal. The charm of this case is that success has been achieved on relatively small marketing communications budgets in a highly competitive marketplace dominated by a handful of multiple retailers with enormous power over distribution.

Case History: RONSEAL 'DOES EXACTLY WHAT IT SAYS ON THE TIN'

Sheffield-based Ronseal Limited operates in the UK paints and decorative products business, specialising in the wood-care sector. The company has had a number of firsts in the market over the years, from wood dye in the 1930s to the first water-based exterior woodstain (Ronseal Quick Dry Woodstain) and the first water-based wood graining product (Ronseal Paint & Grain) in the 1990s. It was in 1956 that the first Ronseal varnish entered the arena. Over the years, they have continued to progress, and they are now the acknowledged leaders in both market share and technological advances. The American coatings corporation Sherwin Williams acquired Ronseal Limited in 1997.

Penetration of home ownership in the UK is high and prices in the late 1990s and into the new century have been moving up steadily ahead of inflation. As a result 'Home owners are improving not moving' in the view of Paul Barrow, Managing Director of Ronseal. 'Accordingly consumers are spending more and more of their disposable income on DIY (do it yourself) products as opposed to clothes and holidays and as increasingly harried, time-pressured consumers look for labour-saving products, quick easy application is becoming more important.' The challenge therefore in this market is significant and Ronseal is embracing it wholeheartedly, investing substantially in R&D and consumer marketing to ensure they are able to respond to these demands. Ronseal firmly believe that these changing consumer characteristics impact on every aspect of their company and throughout it people have to be well trained, motivated and capable of responding to the needs of both end-users and trade customers. As a result of this, Ronseal have adopted a philosophy of continuous improvement and created the infrastructure to support and achieve it.

Paul Barrow defines the brand positioning as follows: 'Ronseal is about simplifying techniques and processes to make the consumer's job quicker and easier with the guarantee of an excellent finish.' New product development has played a key part in the brand's success and the variety and consistent quality of products offered by Ronseal are perhaps demonstrated by the following. In 1998, Ronseal Paint and Grain achieved a rare DIY trade accolade. The 1.5 litre kit became the best-selling line in all wood care, and won the coveted Prince of Wales Award for Innovation. This product's success continued and in 1999 won the Best New International Product at Australia's National Hardware Show in Melbourne.

Perhaps the most impactful element in their marketing mix has been Ronseal's advertising campaign through The Advertising Brasserie agency. At first sight, a range of wood-care products might not seem the most auspicious of creative tasks for an agency to take on, and on first reading the scripts might have seemed straightforward to the point of dullness. In essence, the campaign is composed of a remarkably similar series of presenter commercials wherein the product tin is shown to camera and the finished results pointed out (Figure 54). Production values are simple and professional – no exotic location shoots or fancy set builds for this brand! Indeed, the distinctiveness of the Ronseal approach is that it has eschewed most of the technical gimmicks and special effects which have led much modern UK advertising to be a triumph of form over content. In reverting to one of the earliest types of TV advertising – the presenter to camera – and doing it almost as a parody of the genre, Ronseal have created a cult classic. 'Most people assume that all DIY adverts were about presenters talking to camera when in fact this wasn't the case – so we decided to make this style our own' says Marketing Director Ged Shields.

Ronseal are renowned for the frankness of their advertising; there are no complex messages, just very matter of fact sentences delivered in a very matter of fact, even understated manner. It says that the product is straightforward and no nonsense, and that all that the consumer has to do is to read the tin. They describe their advertising as follows: 'It tells them what the product is, tells them what the product does and tells them again.' Using this straight-talking, no-frills approach, which exploits the classical

Figure 54 *Ronseal ad still.*

rhetorical 'law of three', Ronseal portrays a simple, clear message. This reinforces the ease of use of their products and gives the customer the reassurance that they will be able to get the desired decorative or protective result. Presented in this way, Ronseal achieve a motivating and persuasive selling proposition and their advertising contains a powerful call to action, without resorting to exaggerated claims.

For example, one could imagine alternative strategies wherein the creative approach could have focused on the aspirational lifestyle change or property value increase that would result from using the Ronseal brand. Although the enhancement of the home through DIY may well achieve this in reality, it would very likely come over as something of an over-claim for a wood-care product. In essence, Ronseal's deadpan communication demonstrates the power of under-promising and over-delivering. ' "Does exactly what it says on the tin" has been phenomenally successful for us, because it is straight talking and gets straight to the point' comments Marketing Director Ged Shields. The campaign has now been running since 1990 and in 1999 Ronseal spent more than any other wood-care firm on their national advertising campaigns. The most recent iteration of the campaign, which is consistent with the very matter of fact advertising of the past, featured women for the first time and saw Ronseal raising their spend to £3 million.

Whilst this budget is the largest in their sector, Ronseal's spend is dwarfed by the overall level of UK advertising expenditure. Nevertheless, the creative approach is achieving cut-through. In an ADWATCH survey conducted for *Marketing* magazine in 2000, consumers were asked which TV commercials they had remembered seeing recently, and the response revealed that 49% said that they recalled the Ronseal advertising. In 1999, Ronseal's campaign reached over 80% of their core target audience, and Ronseal's own research figures showed that over 60% of this target population could describe their advertising. The research also showed that the Ronseal brand is associated more with wood care than any other, which implies that Ronseal's campaign is extremely well branded. In addition to media the brand has used new product development, packaging innovation, and consumer exhibitions to ram home the 'Does exactly what it says on the tin' message.

The results in the marketplace have also been significant. Their dedication to product innovation and commitment to marketing communications has led to a 34% share in the wood-care market, this figure being a third better than Ronseal's nearest competitor. In 2000 Ronseal had a 66% market share in varnish and was still growing ahead of general market trends.

The advertising campaign has in effect become central to the Ronseal company philosophy, and their claim of 'doing exactly what it says on the tin' does not just relate to the product itself but also to the service offered. Paul Barrow summarises the company's policy as follows: 'Ronseal are committed to living up to its claim through substantial investment in people, equipment, technology and training.'

This chapter complements the previous one on customer service.

Management needs to ensure that the organisation makes promises on behalf of its brands that are realistic and clearly broadcast to the marketplace and internally within the company. Again, under-promising tends to allow more potential for over-delivering.

Wherever possible, clear action standards should be included in the brand promise or customer pledge so that customers and employees can see that they are achieved and occasionally exceeded. In service industries, tell customers where they stand when things go wrong – enlist their understanding, rather than their fury.

Managing expectations and then exceeding them is one of the most powerful ways to achieve outstanding customer service experience.

27

How Enabled Employees can Deliver for Customers

There is great power in having enabled employees acting according to an agreed system of brand manners when they interact with customers, both internal and external. If they have discretionary budgets and parameters for deploying them, customer problems can be solved before they become relationship threatening.

Not only is there greatly increased efficiency as a result of this, there is also much greater impact on customers. As the pace of life increases and the number of transactions per employee per day grows due to the advances in information technology, the ability to get things right first time becomes paramount in containing costs and maintaining profitability.

At the same time, employees who are enabled take control of themselves, as well as taking control of the customer relationship. In doing this they gain much greater job satisfaction and a sense of security and self-esteem. Their personal and professional goals fit more closely together and reduce the dissonance between work and family. As a result of this, employee churn is minimised, absenteeism can be reined in and long-term loyalty rewarded.

Management must aim to get as many employees as possible to act as if they were the owners of the brand. In other words, to get as many people as possible into positions of responsibility and discretion over decisions that need to be taken to foster the relationship with customers. At the same time, there needs to be a good level of confidence that the downside risk of doing this is contained, and that there is a fluent process whereby an employee can delegate upwards easily and effectively, should the necessity arise.

For example, assume a company with 1,000 employees and that each of them has ten customer interactions, both internal and external, per day.

"Now we've out-sourced, down-sized,
re-engineered, up-graded, relocated and
contracted-out, I can't remember what it is
we actually do"

Cartoon 7 *'What do we do?'*

Roughly speaking, this would amount to 2.6 million interactions per year, given a five-day working week, and assuming that each interaction is self-contained and does not need to be referred to anyone else. One can immediately see that if even just a third of these transactions – say 30% – were problematical and required referral to one other person, then 50% referred it to another and 75% referred it on again, the number of transactions would increase by 50% overall. The negative impact of this process of onward referral on productivity, due to the lack of an early resolution is clear, let alone the customer frustration and brand alienation caused. CEOs and top management need to examine employee-customer interactions in detail in order to discern the nature and volume of 'not-right-first-time' incidents and then create appropriate degrees of freedom required to minimise them.

For example, in the UK the average cost of handling and fulfilling a mail order purchase is about £8, no matter what the item. In the clothing sector, the level of mail order returns runs at up to 30% of all orders. This percentage is likely to rise as customers become more and more used to shopping in this way and lose their embarrassment at ordering two or three sizes or colour variations of an item, keeping one (hopefully) and sending the rest back. Think how expensive it is if on top of these inherent costs, if employees involved in direct mail, including many of the newly emerging dotcom companies, get an order wrong!

One of the positive benefits of the Internet era has been the rapid growth of the website convention of posting frequently asked questions, or FAQs. This is an iterative process whereby the brand owner, building on successive customer questions, is able to discern patterns in the lines of enquiry and produce relevant answers that can save both the customer and the company a significant amount of time. This database of customer enquiries can also produce an enhanced personal response from a brand representative, because they can be forewarned about most of the issues with which they are likely to be faced. Nationwide Building Society in the UK have already conducted a successful branch trial of iris recognition technology and the likely increase in the use of biometrics at branch level in order to increase protection against fraud. These new identification processes will also increase the ability of staff to recognise their customers in a positive sense and enable them to be greeted and dealt with in a more personalised manner without loss of efficiency in transaction time. But no matter how good the systems are, there is still the inherent unpredictability of human interactions. Employees can not be given the 'script' for every encounter; they need to feel sufficiently empowered and confident to ad lib and improvise within the overall scenario that has been created for the brand.

The ultimate extension of employee empowerment with respect to the brand is the concept of the brand franchise where there is the delegation of operational responsibility from the brand owner to an entrepreneur. This combines the benefits of a proven brand vision and service or product delivery, supported by operational systems and infrastructure, with the energy and drive of an 'owner-driver' business. There have been many examples of extremely successful companies built on the franchise model. For example, Pizza Express in the UK, Kentucky Fried Chicken in the USA and of course nearly all of the car marques around the world.

However, there seems to be a pattern in the growth of many franchise operations. Once the brand idea is established, then franchising can create a very rapid growth and geographical expansion through the capital and management resources acquired via franchisees. After that has been achieved, it is often the case that the brand owner is faced with some very powerful multi-franchisees, who are often difficult to control and may have divergent views on the direction of the brand. As a result, one or two things usually happen – the brand runs into trouble, as has happened with KFC and Burger King, or all the franchisees are systematically bought out by the brand owner and control is repatriated.

Interestingly, Abbey National in the UK announced their intention in June 2000 to trial franchising their branches as a response to the 'over shopped' situation in financial institutions on British high streets. It will be very interesting to see whether this strategy will lead to improvements in customer service in a sector that has had a poor reputation for some years and how effectively Abbey National will be able to maintain its brand authorship. It's an experiment which has come just in time as it is at last coming under real pressure to improve through the combined effects of Internet banking and significant changes to the ease with which bank accounts can be switched from one provider to another.

Brand owners can also give their ambassadors bits of behaviour or 'business' in theatrical terms, that enhances the brand proposition whilst giving them a greater sense of participation and making them and their customers feel good too. People talk a great deal about 'retail theatre', and it's surprising how little of it there is to be seen on our high streets or in our shopping malls. A good example of a new retail concept, which has built this idea into its brand proposition, is Girl Heaven. This niche retailer aims to give 'a young girl everything she could dream of' and is targeted at two- to ten-year-olds and their mothers, aunts, grannies, and indeed anyone who might like to indulge them with a pink fluffy sparkly treat!

Every hour outside the store the staff line-up and perform a dance routine to the latest pop hit, enlisting young customers where they can and teaching them the steps (Figure 55). This is a showstopper in the major shopping malls such as Bluewater in Kent where Girl Heaven launched and has been an important ingredient in the publicity achieved for the brand and the enjoyment of customers and employees alike. The retail theatre theme continues in store with the 'Princess Makeover Studio', where young children can have their faces painted and their hair plaited, and then be photographed instantly on the 'Princess Throne' (Figure 56) to complete their fantasy dressing up experience.

Employees at the retail level can be imbued with the brand's values to a significant degree simply as a result of the environment in which they work, which can manifest the corporate identity of the brand all around them. This can be taken further. For example, Ralph Lauren's offices are decorated in the same total look and style as his shops which enhances the

Figure 55 *Girl Heaven dancing staff.*

feeling of belonging and alignment amongst the staff. Whilst this may be commonplace for a fashion brand, which is very conscious of these aesthetic considerations, why should it not be true for all companies who are in the business of marketing a brand and enlisting the maximum possible support from all their people to do so? Call centres, back offices and factories need to be decorated too. For instance it's sad that the UK company, Thornton's, whose brand is summarised by the words 'Chocolate heaven since 1911', has modern factory buildings which completely lack

Figure 56 *Girl Heaven throne.*

any visual evidence relating to this promise and are rather utilitarian and uninspiring as a result.

For most businesses, the ideal solution is to achieve a situation where they maintain absolute control over their brand and enable their employees to behave as much like entrepreneurs or franchisees as possible. An example of a brand that has gone some way toward achieving this in the UK, is the Hong Kong & Shanghai Banking Corporation or HSBC.

Case History: HSBC

Jessica Gorst-Williams, writing in the *Daily Telegraph* on 30 October 1999, gave a fascinating insight into her mailbag. She counted the number of letters she had received from readers complaining about various financial institutions. Bearing in mind the effort it takes to commit pen to paper, paper to envelope, and stamped envelope to a post box, most people see letters to the press as the tip of a pretty large iceberg. Figure 57 shows the results for the year to date and features most of the major high street banks or their equivalent. There are some differences between the most and least written about amongst the top six, and it is clear that the likes of the Halifax, and NatWest in particular, have got something to worry about in terms of the way they deal with their customers.

What was very striking was the remarkably low number of letters of complaint attributable to HSBC (including First Direct, their direct banking subsidiary). Just three in the year. Curious as to why this should be the case, Gorst-Williams made enquiries with the bank and gained a fascinating insight into how HSBC and First Direct organise themselves to achieve such a minimal level of letter writing by irate customers.

She talked to Carole Gibbs, Head of Customer Relations at HSBC, who had told her about the measures their bank takes to produce excellent

Financial institution	Annual no. of complaints
Halifax	150
Nat West	120
Lloyds TSB	100
Barclays	100
Royal Bank of Scotland	80
Abbey National	60
HSBC	3

Figure 57 *Annual number of complaints for banks.*

customer service. In simple terms, they enable their employees to solve as many problems themselves at the first point of contact. To achieve this they empower staff to make instant decisions whereas other banks require staff to consult with managers before correcting a mistake. This freedom to act on their own initiative, combined with the constant flow of communication when issues have to be dealt with by somebody else, were cited as the main reasons for success.

HSBC give their staff set amounts to grant as compensation in circumstances that are clearly defined. If there is a complex problem that has to be referred to someone else within the organisation, then HSBC prides itself on keeping in touch proactively with customers on the progress of the resolution of their complaint or issue. There is also a dedicated customer helpline to HSBC head office designed to resolve disputes that cannot be tackled at branch level though, HSBC always tries to resolve complaints locally.

Building on Gorst-Williams's original article, we have dug deeper into the bank's customer relationship management culture and have learned more from Carole Gibbs about what makes it tick. She summarises the bank's philosophy as follows: 'We welcome complaints, we make it easy for customers to voice their views, we say we are sorry and we put things right as quickly as we can.' For example, HSBC investigates every single customer complaint regardless of how it arrives. 'We have some letters typed on fine note paper, others are written on scrap paper, but each is taken as seriously as the other' she reports. 'Often it is the simplest comment that represents the most serious problem, and the key to it is to treat all customers as individuals.' HSBC promises to acknowledge every letter or call within 48 hours, but if they can, they will do it quicker. There is a process which has to be followed, but the imperative for HSBC is the belief that the sooner the problem is sorted out, the sooner they will have the customer back on their side. Each of the responses made by staff at HSBC is personal and they do not have standard replies. They simply inform the customer *what* they understand the problem to be, *who* will be dealing with it and *when* they think they will arrive at a solution. In doing this, HSBC employees 'own' the customer problem and manage their expectations – key themes in living the brand through effective brand manners.

Carole Gibbs describes the HSBC techniques for establishing rapport and creating empathy:

> We always try to get a sense of how the customer is feeling. There is no textbook way of dealing with complaints; the trick is to treat each one individually and to remember that the clock is always ticking. There are only nine people in the core Customer Relations team and so they all know what each other is doing; between the team there is over 200 years experience in the company. Yes, we are always stretched but this just means that we don't leave things lying around, things just get done.

The attitude of the HSBC team seems to confirm the old adage that 'if you want something done, ask a busy person to do it'.

According to her, it is often the little things that can defuse a situation. 'The first thing that I say to a customer is "Can I call you back – it's bad enough that you have had cause to complain and we wouldn't want you to pay for the phone call too." Often when the customer is extremely upset and agitated, we just say "What can I do to make this better?" Showing this concern and admitting the problem is often the solution in itself.'

In many companies, complaints are feared by those dealing with them, but at HSBC they are not scared of them, and though it may seem a relatively insignificant point, this mindset has a massive impact on the manner in which they deal with customers. HSBC have a strong 'no blame' culture. When customers complain, the bank is not afraid to say sorry, and brand representatives always end the conversation by saying 'thank you for taking the time and trouble to tell us about this problem'. After all, if people didn't complain, then they would never know how they are performing and how to make things better for the customer. However, it is not all bad news – HSBC receives many heartening compliments too!

Keeping the customer in the picture is crucial; if staff cannot deal with a certain complaint then they ensure that whoever is dealing with the issue is doing so in an appropriate manner. Within every department at HSBC 'Complaint Owners' have been assigned and these people provide a specialist extension to the customer relations team to prioritise complaints and deal with them as and when they arise. Having such customer representatives all over the company ensures that complaints are taken seriously and are not lost in the plethora of other day-to-day tasks. It's Carole's view that 'we all make mistakes from time to time; it's how we deal with the consequences that sets us apart from our competitors'.

An example of HSBC's constant attention to changing trends and amending processes accordingly, is the manner in which deceased customers' relatives are dealt with. HSBC had noticed that there had been several complaints under these circumstances and so looked at the process more closely. One of the complaints detailed a situation whereby the wife of the deceased customer came into the branch to request an account closure, and the cashier immediately reached for a form, rather than saying 'Oh, I am sorry to hear that'. HSBC looked at the interactions in this situation and constructed ways of dealing with this that would not upset the customer any more. Responses along the lines such as 'You don't have to do this today if you don't feel up to it' were encouraged and as a result the problem was alleviated.

Another change was the leaflet in every branch entitled 'How to complain'. This was replaced with 'Listening to your comments'. Staff in branches used to be worried if they saw a customer picking up a leaflet but now they feel empowered to ask 'Can I help you at all' when they see it happening, and strive to turn this interaction into a positive experience. People on the front line constantly call the Customer Relations team seeking guidance on how to deal with certain aspects of the business, either with difficult customers or just more general complaints. Importantly, there is a culture in the bank in which no one is afraid to do this.

The Customer Relations department holds one-day workshops on a quarterly basis for the front-line 'complaint owners' to come and talk about the common problems and solutions to issues that they face each day. These sessions are all on a 'no holds barred' basis, which means employees feel free to express their concerns without them being noted or attributed specifically to them. Impressively, the Chief Executive will always find time to join these workshops for a while. HSBC also has a training programme called 'Leap', an appropriate name for a corporate culture in which 'taking a risk for the customer' is so deeply embedded. This is presented in the form of books and videos, and there are modules such as letter writing and dealing with difficult customers. This gives an opportunity for employees to improve their skills, and these training courses are an ongoing initiative within the bank and are at the pace of each individual member of staff.

HSBC have a firm belief that if an individual can't work out the best solution to a problem on their own, then they must feel able to have a chat about it with colleagues, and try to sort it out together. In Carole Gibbs's view, 'It isn't about who's to blame, it's about who's making it better', and in the Customer Relations office they have a poster saying, 'Not one of us is better than all of us'. Some people say that 'It isn't about what you say it's how you say it', but HSBC take this one step further, 'it isn't about what you say or how you say it, it's all about what the customer hears!'. This really sums up the way that HSBC works and goes a long way to explaining their substantial competitive advantage over the other banks listed in Gorst-Williams's league table.

HSBC send out customer surveys to named personal customers at a rate of 100,000 per month, and 120,000 surveys to business customers every quarter. For example, one question is: 'Have you ever complained or felt like complaining?' This information enables branches to telephone customers in response to their complaints or comments, hence personalising the service further.

A good indication of how seriously HSBC takes the issue of enabling employees to really listen, understand and deliver for customers, is the regular contact between Customer Relations and the CEO, Bill Dalton. Carole Gibbs confirms that 'I see him most days and we chat about customer issues and how we can improve our services. He is very involved in the whole process and takes a keen interest in everything that goes on'.

Creating an environment where employees have the freedom and initiative to deal with customer feedback is essential to brand manners. Trying to get a sense of how the customer is feeling is a good example. Beyond the rational, the emotional (feeling) and political (was it a good deal?) come into play. Encourage teamwork in problem-solving and create a 'no blame' culture in which brand representatives feel enabled to take risks for their customers.

Analyse the transactional behaviour between the company and its customers and discern the patterns that exist, the bottlenecks that occur, the frequently asked questions and the common problems that arise.

Map the progress of complaints and do a cost-benefit analysis of them in terms of their value to the customer and the value to the company depending on various levels of resolution internally.

Establish the trade-off between a front-line solution and delegation upwards to two, three or four more senior levels of management with the time cost that that involves. On this basis generate discretionary budgets for brand representatives to deploy.

Monitor problem resolution regularly and in detail and make it part of employee training, assessment and remuneration.

Explore the options of franchising where this is feasible. Where it is not, try to create the type of motivational environment which would exist if employees felt like real owners.

28

Recruiting in Line with the Brand's Values

As a key move in ensuring that customers get the maximum of good feeling about the brand, we're advocating that companies should be as exacting in their recruitment of people as they are in defining the target audience for their brand communications. By doing this they can align their internal and external values and reinforce the power of their total brand presentation to their customers.

Typically a company will spend very large sums of money on market research designed to tease out the precise attributes of their brand in the customer's eyes. This will be done in terms of rational and emotional benefits and increasingly political and spiritual ones. At the same time they will also define their customer typologies and segments in great detail to ensure that the communication of the brand's benefits will be as precisely tailored as possible to the needs of those people. However, when it comes to recruitment of people, i.e. those who are actually charged with the responsibility of supporting and delivering the brand experience to customers, often relatively little special attention is paid to the criteria on which they are hired.

Most companies recruit for skills and competencies, but pay relatively little attention to personality types and attitudes beyond a generalised assessment of 'personal chemistry' and 'fit'. It is very difficult to change people's natural behaviour and force-fit them to a situation that they do not occupy comfortably. It would be much easier to recruit people who have a basic natural affinity with the brand and its values, so they can behave normally and deliver against the corporate dream in a free, expressive and interpretative way without the need for excessive policing, rules or regulations. They'll feel better, and so will their customers.

The corporation should develop tailor-made recruitment questionnaires and diagnostic techniques which seek to match people to values and relevant behaviours. This does not mean that the company should hire only one type of person, clearly this would be limiting, as there are many dimensions to an organisation and its operations. But certainly those people who represent the brand to customers should have the appropriate intrinsic values so they support and reinforce them more effectively.

One of the great strengths of the smaller, more personal company or partnership, is that the leader of it often has a very important, if not decisive say in the type of people that the organisation recruits. The Chairman who favours graduates who have been to a particular school or university (perhaps his own); the senior partner who smiles upon candidates who share their passion for rowing, and the managing director who identifies strongly with those who prefer classical music, all tend to recruit in their own image. A great benefit of this personal culture is that by definition it is aligned with the leadership and if the core skills and competencies are there too, then this can deliver powerful competitive advantage, especially in professional service organisations.

However, during the last quarter of the 20th century this 'old boy network' approach to recruitment became increasingly unfashionable. It was deemed to be elitist, snobbish and anti equal opportunities. As a result it became increasingly politically incorrect and potentially illegal to focus on the 'soft attributes' of the personality aspects of a CV and so much greater impetus was placed on the technicalities of qualifications and skills. Meanwhile, in larger companies, where the task of recruitment is delegated to human resources and management levels far below the Board, the cohesiveness of selection was inevitably much diluted.

The net result of this is that companies struggle to achieve a sense of culture within their organisations. A disparate group of employees, recruited for largely rational reasons and in the absence of acceptably discriminating background or character-based criteria, is unlikely to exhibit of itself a collective spirit or personality. The chances of this heterogeneous human pool being aligned with the brand values of the products and services that the company produces are remote. A fundamental part of creating a distinctive set of brand manners for a corporation is to grasp the nettle of recruitment and impose a new set of criteria on top of those of skills and competencies. This approach will deliver a stream of employees who are much more naturally aligned with the character, personality and aspirations of the corporation as expressed in its brand dream.

When you approach a Rolls-Royce franchise such as H. R. Owen in Berkeley Square, London, it is highly likely you do so with a very clear picture of the sort of customer experience that you're about to enjoy. You also have an expectation of the type of person, their demeanour, their dress and their tone of voice that is likely to greet you on crossing the threshold. It is likely that the adjectives and descriptors that would apply to the customer experience and the brand representative's behaviour will be almost the same as those that would apply to the Rolls-Royce vehicle and the driving experience.

In the case of Rolls-Royce, it may appear to be relatively simple to achieve the best fit between employees and brand. But that's just because the brand has been so clearly defined for so long and, under the guidance of the manufacturer, dealerships such as H. R. Owen have painstakingly recruited appropriate people to match over the years. The contention of this book is that any company or organisation should take the trouble to do the same in their own particular case and reap the benefits that result from having totally aligned people and brand promise.

Some brands succeed in doing this on an intuitive basis and through the mechanism of their recruitment process. Majestic Wine for example relies very heavily on its existing employees to recruit new ones. Assuming that the incumbent staff are appropriate representatives of the brand, then if they are part of the recruiting process and are empowered to hire people that they like and they feel will fit into the team, there will be a self-replicating personality type drawn into the business.

Another example of a company which relies very heavily on its existing employees to find its new ones, is Digitas, a high-tech company with its origins in California. Their commitment to quality of people and their working environment is such that they have a 'Chief People Officer', currently Rob Galford, who has the rank of Executive Vice-President, one of only four in the company. This role is in stark contrast to so many companies where Human Resources is aligned with group services, with the most senior HR person often reporting to the Chief Financial Officer. In these environments, the CFOs are so often seen as 'no' people dedicated to containing and cutting costs, rather than someone key to building the culture and aligning employees with the company brand values. One of the key brand values of the Digitas company is 'trailblazing', but interestingly they do not currently have any formal tests for this policy but are actively considering creating them at the moment. In the meantime, they rely on role modelling by senior management and a philosophy of giving employees the freedom and security to be trailblazers on behalf of their customers. Control is exercised by a 'three strikes and out' procedure within a culture which encourages calculated risk.

The Digitas culture is clearly an attractive one: 40% of their new hirings come from introductions by existing employees who are encouraged at the level of $5,000 per referral. In the world of high-tech companies, where competition for key talent is intense, Digitas's people culture is a major advantage. The Digitas approach supports our thesis in that its employees can behave naturally in the workplace and be more relaxed, have a greater sense of self-control and be more self-confident. Because they do not have to adjust their normal behaviour to fit an alien culture all their energies can go into supporting the brand values to which the company aspires and on which their delivery to customers depends.

To achieve this, a company needs to analyse its branded offering to customers in terms of the image values and attributes that it has constructed in their minds. There are many dimensions by which a brand can be described. For example, low price to high price, high quality to low quality, commodity to premium, harsh to caring, young to old, male to female, high involvement to low involvement, sexy to workaday, innovative and modern to traditional and more established, hand crafted to high-tech, niche to mass market, durable to ephemeral and considered purchase to impulse purchase, to name but a few.

Each individual brand can be represented by their particular mix of these sorts of attributes put together in a distinctive way. Having drawn the picture of the brand in these terms and with these descriptors, the company is in a position to do two things. Firstly the internal and external communications programme can convey and reinforce these aspects of their brand. Most modern companies have the intention of doing this and many succeed pretty well. But the second application of the analysis is very rarely, if ever, applied to the recruitment criteria of employees – have you ever seen a recruitment procedure which looks for anything like this richness of data about a candidate? This is an exciting new area for the development of brand manners.

People will still need to be employed as a result of their skill sets and competencies and techniques such as the situational scenario-based exercises popular in the USA, plus psychological testing using techniques, such as Myers Briggs, will always have a role to play. In France, up to 90% of companies use graphology as a part of their recruitment process, and in the UK the British Institute of Graphologists suggests that up to 3,000 British companies use it too, but do not like to admit it!

An example of a company doing interesting and potentially very powerful work in the area of values-based recruitment is the SHL recruitment consultancy which operates in over 40 countries and has

2,500 clients, large and small, private and public. They are currently developing a very interesting new way of recruiting people. As others do, they have already developed a cross-company audit on company culture and values that involves talking to a whole variety of people in the company and extracting specific behavioural characteristics and values that are a core part of the organisational ethos. They are now in the process of developing an individual questionnaire that complements this, to try to extract from an individual what their own personal values and expectations are. Their tool has already been tested in 63 countries, and when it is supported by a behavioural interview, creates a much richer recruiting procedure. This allows employers not only to match an individual's skills to the job, but also to match the individual's values to the organisation. This ties in nicely with the brand manners goal of achieving a 'win win', for both parties, and satisfying people's four key needs of the Rational (have the right skills), Emotional (have the same values), Political (have the same agenda), and Spiritual (doing something meaningful).

The recognition of, and recruitment for, this new layer of personal values attributes, over and above competencies and skills, will fit the employee to the brand values that the corporation is determined to deliver to the marketplace. This is going to become a powerful leveraging of the people assets employed. Implementing this brand manners recruitment strategy, managing its implementation and then coaching the company team in training and appraisals thereafter, must be the responsibility of a key senior executive within the organisation. The more the corporation realises the benefits of continuous communication to its employees, and the power of an aligned army of brand representatives in turn communicating the core brand values at the customer interface, the more the roles of Human Resources Director, Communications Director and Marketing Director will have to come closer together in support of the CEO and line management.

Case History: BOASE MASSIMI POLLITT

A good example of the power of this approach can be seen at London advertising agency Boase Massimi Pollitt (as it was known in the days before its acquisition by Omnicom and the merger with Doyle Dane Bernbach to become BMPDDB). Martin Boase and Stanley Pollitt created their new agency in the late 1960s based on the revolutionary idea of Account Planning. Much has been written about this concept elsewhere, and it's well worth reading *Excellence in Advertising*, edited by Leslie

Butterfield and published by Butterworth Heinemann in association with the IPA, in order to get detailed insights into its theory and practice, as well as important related areas. In essence, Account Planning entails bringing the world of consumer market research into the heart of the creative development process. This was achieved through the creation of the new role of Account Planner and partnering that person with the traditional one of Account Manager (or Account Executive in American terms), creating a new core team analogous to the pairing of a Copywriter with an Art Director in the creative department.

This powerful new duo even shared an office in another radical piece of territorial innovation – the research people were previously kept very much out of the way on another floor or way down the corridor. Together, Account Manager and Account Planner would liaise with the client and co-ordinate the internal service departments of the agency to deliver for the client. This would include strategy, plans, creative ideas, qualitative pre-testing research, advertising production and then quantitative assessment through tracking studies, usage and attitude surveys, market sales and distribution data and consumer purchasing research.

The very earliest Account Planners were actually transferred from the Media Planning department because these were the only available people who were sufficiently numerate for the task and who also understood the quantitative databases such as Target Group Index (TGI) and appreciated the fundamental importance of communications in marketing. However, Stanley Pollitt quickly realised that in order to ensure that his radical idea of Account Planning survived and thrived, he would have to grow his own people in the absence of a ready supply in the marketplace. He had to do this in the face of what at the time was fierce opposition mounted by the old style 'robber barons' in Client Service or Account Management, who saw their authority vis-à-vis the client being threatened by the voice of the consumer in their midst.

His strategy was a simple one: go to the very best universities and recruit the cleverest people who believed, in Martin Boase's words, that 'good advertising doesn't have to be bad'. This summarised the BMP creative ethos and its reaction against the USA-style formulaic, hard-sell advertising that still dominated the market on both sides of the Atlantic, despite the pioneering efforts of agencies such as Doyle Dane Bernbach.

BMP promised its clients advertising which would reward creativity in order to persuade. Since it would primarily be seen by customers in the context of TV entertainment, it had to fulfil the goal of being the 'relevant and unexpected'. To achieve this BMP preached the revolutionary gospel of mandatory qualitative pre-testing by their Account Planners of all proposed TV commercials, using 'animatics' or filmed storyboards to convey the creative idea to consumers in focus groups.

Many of the graduates who endorsed this philosophy had first-class degrees from Oxbridge or other top universities, and many were left of centre politically. Most shared Martin Boase's laid-back self-confidence and Stanley Pollitt's intellectual curiosity, with several sharing the latter's endearing eccentricity. Most importantly BMP has religiously recruited graduate trainees every year without a break, even for the severe recessionary periods of the early 1970s (oil crisis), early 1980s (Thatcher v. unions) and the early 1990s (consumer credit squeeze). BMP then put them through a rigorous training programme, run for many years by Planning Director, David Cowan that had at its heart the discipline of understanding all the media and customer research databases and, key to the philosophy of Account Planning, the techniques of qualitative research. BMP was and remains highly protective of these planners such that they became known as 'Stanley's strawberries'. He literally kept them under wraps in the graduate trainee programme for at least six months and always supported them throughout their careers in the agency.

There are four main testaments to the strength of Stanley Pollitt's original idea. First is the fact that the agency is today managed by a core team of people, James Best, Group Chairman, and Ross Barr and Chris Cowpe, Joint Managing Directors, who were graduate trainees respectively 25 and 28 years ago. BMP is renowned in the volatile UK advertising industry for the continuity, cohesiveness and creativity of their culture. Second is the outstanding creative work it has produced over the years. Their 'Martians' commercial for Cadbury's Smash was voted no. 1 in the leading UK advertising trade magazine, Campaign's, review of the 'Best 100 Ads of the Century in December 1999 and they were voted 'the world's most creative agency' in 1999 according to the Gunn survey. Third is their reputation for advertising that works, as evidenced by their dominance of the world-renowned IPA Advertising Effectiveness Awards. Now in their twentieth year, BMPDDB have won the Grand Prix three times out of a possible ten in this biennial event, and 15 top prizes in the shape of First, Gold or Five Star Awards. On an informal calculation of overall prizes won in this demanding competition, BMPDDB leads a top-quality UK agency field by some considerable margin.

Fourthly, it is apparent that the BMP diaspora has spread throughout the UK advertising industry to the extent that there is hardly an agency which has not been touched by Account Planning and indeed the way in which the British advertising practitioner operates is essentially based on the Pollitt model. Account Planning has also made very significant inroads into the United States through agencies such as Chiat Day, whose first Planning Director was Jane Newman, herself a Pollitt 'strawberry'. Her pioneering move to America was followed by the likes of Jon Steel who joined Goodby Silverstein, and Damian O'Malley who went to DDB in New York. In fact, the Account Planning discipline has by now spread into most English-speaking advertising markets around the world and strongly influenced the global industry. In the USA the annual Account Planning Group Conference attracted 950 delegates. The combination of a compelling brand idea, Account Planning, allied to a consistent and highly specific recruitment strategy has literally changed the way advertising and marketing communications are done throughout most Westernised economies.

We recommend a threefold process to interview a potential recruit. Firstly a 'fit' interview to ensure individuals have values in line with the brand and culture of the company, secondly, a 'content' interview to assess capability and thirdly, a 'trajectory' interview to assess where the person would best fit and what the best career path should be. The process should be adopted and augmented to test for brand manners fit and ability.

Management needs to reappraise the importance of human resources within the organisation. It's essential that the people assets in the company are optimised and led by a director of line management or of human resources who sits at the highest levels of the organisation and has the authority to recruit for and speak for the brand.

Tailor-made recruitment questionnaires and interview techniques need to be developed such that the people the company hires have intrinsic characteristics and value systems and attitudes which are aligned with the product or service brand that the corporation delivers to customers. These criteria should be applied to all new recruits and they should also be applied to existing ones in order to structure any necessary retraining and, at the limit, counselling and exit management.

So far, we have set out the Brand Manners Book of Life, and Way, illustrated by the Tesco and Orange Stories. We then went further by developing the brand manners improvement cycle, including practical examples, anecdotes and further case histories. We now move to pull all of this material together, in summary form, through 'How-To' guides, tailored to each of the main actors: the CEO, the Marketing Director, the Employee, the Management and finally but most importantly – the Customer. Each of these has a Brand Manners agenda, to provide a focus and suggest key priority areas.

PART IV
The Brand Manners
how-to guides

29

The Chief Executive Officer

The Chief Executive's Brand Manners Agenda is set out below, as a practical set of ten action points.

1. Vision, will, capability

The key tests of an organisation's determination to develop true brand manners are in these three areas. Firstly, the CEO and the top team need to have, or be prepared to develop, a higher-order vision for the organisation that goes well beyond the standard 'mission statement'. This must be customer orientated and practical for the business, while developing the potential inherent in the spiritual element. 'Will' is a difficult one to test, in advance. Management can give the impression of being prepared to tackle tough topics, but it is not until individuals are asked to make sacrifices in the interest of the common good that the true strength of the corporate will can be assessed. Brand manners will not be developed without the daily will, at all levels of the organisation, to see improvements through. Finally, the state of readiness of the organisation must be assessed so that brand manners programmes can be realistically achieved, through the building of the capabilities necessary to create the 'self-confident organisation'.

2. Action learning leadership

'Keep movin'!' Organisational momentum is difficult to build and needs nourishment to be sustained. The 80/20 rule should be applied to both decision-making and action ... think, act, learn ... think, act, learn.

Analysis should be no more than a third of the effort, at most. Sensible risk-taking should be rewarded. The ability to turn the organisation on a pinhead means that one has the flexibility to respond with lightning speed to opportunities, while still building capability. Remember the great Compaq advertisement? 'We never give a rival time'. This sums up the world we are now in. Speed is at a premium over excessive accuracy. In an increasing number of situations, companies should rely on alliances, built on trust, to extend their capability and their speed of response. If Tesco come on the line and ask you to reply within two days if you want to join a venture, there is no time for fancy analysis, nor to consult all of the non-executives ... it's showtime, potentially every moment of every day!

3. Design guidelines for the 'self-confident organisation'

We have set out ideas on this type of organisation that lies in the space between bad old 'command and control', and open-toe sandals *laissez-faire*. The self-confident organisation has clear boundaries, accountabilities and authority levels. People know what the CEO would want, or say, without asking. The presence is felt everywhere, and it is all about delivering brand manners, all the time – by taking measured risks for customers, by reaching for one's own potential, by participating in an exciting corporate drama, and by never accepting mediocrity. The organisational jigsaw fits together and the pieces – work, systems, skills, measures, rewards – are designed to work and feed off each other. This holistic approach is key to self-confidence. When a company breaks into this space, it puts blue water between itself and its competitors, Tesco being an excellent example. There is no going back, as the rewards are there and people like the self-confident way of working. Welcome to the world of 'could be'!

4. Unlocking the real potential of customers

Being close to customers may seem obvious but it is difficult to achieve. Think about being close to someone else – it is not always easy. Superficially, yes; in depth, no. Even if you know what customers want today, they may not know what they want, tomorrow. So anticipation and insight are essential.

Many companies do not talk directly with their customers, and rely on outside researchers to interview and calculate. The result is lots of reports, with some verbal commentary, often received by folk in the Marketing Department, who then interpret and communicate upwards. By the time the message gets to the Marketing Director, let alone the CEO, it has been 'interpreted' several times, with several splashes of politics added. The message is talk directly to your customers, frequently. The more senior you are, the more you should do this.

Increasingly, firms are looking at the opportunities presented by loyalty card data and 'data mining'. This can yield valuable insights, but is no replacement for direct discussions with customers, face to face. In dealing with customers, some firms even effectively sub-contract out the creation and evolution of what we call the 'dream' or the higher-order vision, to advertising agencies. As a result, the insight and much of the data remains outside the firm and executives eat what they are fed. This can work well until Marketing Directors change and decide to 'go out to pitch' for a new advertising campaign, so often they can make a name for themselves – the politics of self interest which can be so damaging to the grand asset. With the average tenure of both Marketing Directors and, indeed, CEOs declining, there is a real danger that firms will fall out of touch with their customers, and we have cited several examples of this earlier. The answer lies in the crucial customer-related processes which need to be designed into the 'self-confident' organisation.

The people with the most contact with customers need to be equipped to engage in dialogue in a friendly and fun way and communicate constantly what they are learning back to their colleagues in buying, marketing, sales and merchandising. No-one owns customers – they are an asset to be cherished and grown so that their lifetime loyalty can be sought. The economics of loyalty are well known – loyal customers, staff and shareholders create huge amounts of shareholder value. If you are not paying your staff top quartile, you are likely to be pushed into the commodity end of your business. Competing solely on cost is unlikely to be the way to maximising shareholder value, let alone providing a rewarding experience for your customers or your staff. So, pay your employees well – reward them handsomely for delivering brand manners, and make sure your sources of customer insight are direct, connected and operating in real time.

5. Unlocking the real potential of employees

Many management teams are taking to the notion that 'happy employees make happy customers'. This is ground zero, as it treats the symptoms without unearthing the causes. The true potential of employees lies in

**"You realise, Timpson, that thorough decency
is a sacking offence?"**

Cartoon 8 *'Decency'.*

helping each individual understand what their place is on this earth, and
helping them to be true to themselves. By discovering who they are and the
effect they can have on others, individuals can become hugely motivated.
Sumantra Ghoshal tells a great story to illustrate this.

> Every summer, I take my family to Calcutta to visit our relatives. Although
> this is an enjoyable and rewarding experience – it's always great to see the
> family – the combination of the heat, some 40 degrees C, and the humidity,
> at around 100%, results in my having almost no energy and not wanting to
> get out of bed. I contrast this with working at INSEAD Business School,
> outside Fontainebleau, south of Paris. There, it is almost impossible to go for
> a quiet stroll in the forest in the springtime. The combination of
> temperature, light and the trees makes you hop and skip!

The point of Ghoshal's story, is that most employees are in the equivalent
of Calcutta – imagine the effect of helping them move to Fontainebleau!
This, for us, captures brilliantly the image of the opportunity that could and
should be made available to employees to lead more rewarding lives by
serving customers better.

6. The role of the CEO in creating and delivering brand manners

Lead and coach! People rise to a leader: they like to be associated with a winning team and this raises their overall game. Sumantra also compares the role of a building in a Scottish village, one which is empty most of the time but has a huge impact on the community, with the CEO's job. The building is a church. The CEO's presence should be felt in the same way. Charles Handy once described leadership as going into the 'lonely space around the job'. Leadership is about people knowing what you would want, even when you are not present. It is about the why, the what and increasingly, the how. Much of the value of brand manners lies in the 'how' they are delivered. There are good ways, there are better ways, and there are plain bad ways (call centres generally being an example of this). Which leads us to the next key role, that of coach. Being coach should involve tough love, to be prepared to provide honest and constructive feedback to people you may have grown up with professionally and know well. Being a good coach means that those around you should be able to blossom, with your encouragement, guidance, and occasional chastisement! It does not mean abandoning your fiduciary duties as CEO, such as financial probity, responsibilities to customers, staff and shareholders and corporate strategy. It is additional to the traditional accountabilities of management. You should be constantly leaving behind a legacy which is not dependent on you.

7. Direct contact with employees and customers

This one is simple. Be close to your customers and your people. Spend proper time talking with them, and constantly try to understand them. Second-hand is no good. You must connect with them directly.

8. The top team, coaching and leaving a series of legacies

We have covered the topic of the choice of the top team in the brand manners way. This choice is critical to achieving brand manners – the CEO's immediate and extended team must drive vision, demonstrate will and make the additional effort necessary to build future capability. An athletic organisation can change direction tactically while still moving towards achieving its higher-order vision. The days of setting a linear strategy and then implementing are over. Capability increasingly drives strategy; the two need to be connected in a continuous, virtuous circle. The process of leaving a series of legacies can be a nourishing experience for the organisation and its people. Going beyond, but in no way abandoning, operational performance, creates brand manners.

9. The never-ending and repeating 20-month agenda for continuous improvement

Building capability for tomorrow and making today's organisation more athletic requires hard work. The attraction of the 'single driving issue' is that one can engage a broad spectrum of the organisation around a vital topic and see it through to completion. Once an organisation understands that horizontal working across the different entities adds real value to the vertical operation of the businesses, a thirst develops to continue to improve, and people will always be asking the question: 'What's next?'. So, in addition to running the company day to day, the CEO can and should create a series of single driving issues which will continuously catapult the organisation into new space, ahead of the competition. The core linkage in all of this is the customer, and the determination to improve brand manners for them, continuously.

In moving the corporation forward, stay out of the Ditch! It is widely recognised that, as firms grow, they will move from early profitability, usually based on domination of a 'local' market, through a period of relative danger when they are neither small and nimble, nor big enough to compete with global players. This is called 'The Ditch'. Move through it quickly and build the scale necessary to succeed in the next competitive space (Figure 58).

The same holds true for organisations. Two systems of management cannot survive too long together in the same company; natural law indicates that one will suffocate the other. So, moving beyond 'command and control' will require you to move quickly through The Ditch. The 'self-confident' organisation is fragile early on as only a minority of the employees will have embraced it fully. The rest will still be asking themselves: 'Why should I abandon the old tried and trusted ways which have formed the basis of my success all of my life?'. As CEO, you need to lead the people through change into the promised land of brand manners. A truly self-confident organisation will never want to return to the old, fear-laden ways. So, factor this into your development through your waves of never-ending continuous improvement.

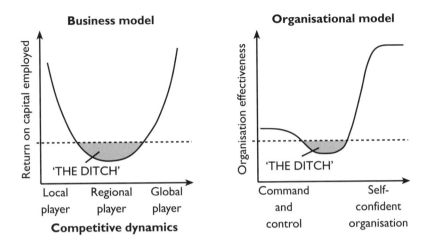

Figure 58 *The Ditch.*

10. Corporate spirit

The never-ending agenda needs to be part of the overall corporate drama which attracts and excites customers and staff alike. CEOs need to break out beyond the left-brained, rational mode to develop a higher-order vision and create a corporate drama which provides enjoyment and satisfaction. The best of the dot-com world has shown what this can look like. Companies are moving at previously undreamed of speeds, with daily instalments in the corporate soap.

A friend of ours, an Italian scientist, spent most of his life studying the stars. He even built a tower on an island in the Grenadines in the Caribbean on which he mounted a computer-controlled telescope of great magnification. The last time we saw him, he had almost abandoned his life's previous love, the stars, and was studying books on the human brain. 'Guido, what's going on?', we asked. 'I have calculated that there are as many connections in the human brain as there are atoms in the known universe', came back the reply, with the habitual broad and warm smile. 'Now, every time I see a human being, I am in complete awe, as it feels like I am looking at the entire cosmos!'. This is reinforced by the views of James Kelly, friend, author and businessman. 'You cannot hope to build a relationship with someone if you do not deeply respect them. People sense whether or not you respect them. If they sense you do not, this will shine through, in subtle ways, and you will never be able to build trust with the person in question'. These are not trivial points, in our view. The corporate spirit must embody them, along with other fundamental truths, such as deep respect for human beings; strengths, fatal flaws and all. The biggest potential on the planet lies in releasing the natural power of the human brain. We know that today, only a small portion of it is used fully.

30

The Marketing Director

The nine-point brand manners agenda for the Marketing Director is shown below.

1. Direct customer contact

You, personally, must be accountable to the Board, and indeed all of the stakeholders, for understanding and anticipating the needs of your customers. You should be the custodian of what brand manners should mean in the customer experience. This is not an activity which can be delegated, either within the company or outside. Indeed you should encourage, if not insist, that each member of the main board spend time talking directly with customers and subsequently discussing the implications of what they have heard, taking ownership of what they each need to do differently (the vertical), as well as together (the horizontal). The good work of marketing services firms, both above and below the line, should be used to validate, support or synthesise the direct customer experience of yourself, the members of your team, the members of the board. The key point is that this insight is invaluable and should not be overtly sub-contracted to outside agencies valuable as they are.

An equally important opportunity to understand customers better occurs at the interface between the employees and the customers, whether directly engaged in sales, or dealing with receipts or complaints. The danger lies in depending too much on technology and systems, without gaining the insight which comes only through direct customer interactions. You should ensure that those employees who are in the front line of the customer experience are skilled in active dialogue with, and powerful listening to, customers. There is a fine line to be struck in engaging with customers without them feeling uncomfortable – the trick is to have adult-adult interactions, and avoid being intrusive. The front-line management supporting these employees should be skilled in customer psychology and realise their major value-added is in developing those who work for them, primarily through continuous coaching. Simple tools like root-cause analysis, and plan-do-review can really help. The insight, information and experience gained by customer-facing employees needs to be connected to other customer data coming from other parts of the organisation, including buyers, merchandisers, complaint handlers, suppliers and alliance partners. Customer understanding is the primary source of nourishment for brand manners.

2. Creating, sustaining and evolving the dream

While the CEO and the board have the accountability to develop the higher-order vision for the organisation, the Marketing Director has a vital role to play in creating what we call the dream, which embodies the actions implicit in the pursuit of the vision, and captures people's imagination. Increasingly, it is becoming possible to achieve feats previously considered impossible in the business world – the Internet being a key contributor to this. Even some ten years ago, it was becoming feasible to transform the capability of an organisation through improvements in processes, systems and people skills ... making dreams come true. One Managing Director asked us 'How can I be sure that it is the right dream?' The question is spot on. The Marketing Director should drive the creation of the dream, based on customer understanding gained through direct contact, and supplemented by secondary data. Marketing services firms can play a vital role in firing the imagination of the organisation through creative and analytic input. The marketing role is to harness these talents external to the firm, and connect them to the organisation, often in real time. Sustaining the dream requires the mobilisation of the organisation in such a way that information is communicated with the minimum of distortion and embodied in the core processes of the company. Just as CEO tenure is declining, that of Marketing Directors is following the same trend. Resist the temptation to make a name for yourself and move on. You owe it to yourself, your customers and, indeed, the whole organisation to ensure there is excellent management succession in marketing and that there is continuity of understanding passed between the organisation and the marketing firms it works with – and also between these firms. It is a natural phenomenon of the competitive world to husband information and not share it. Knowledge management is therefore a critical part of the marketing role. Evolving the dream goes back to the cycle of continuous improvement inherent in series of Board-led single driving issues which build the capability required to deliver increasing brand manners performance.

3. Living what customers experience – in real time

'Spend a day in the life of your Customers' appeared in the *Harvard Business Review* many years ago. Yet few senior executives engineer the time into their diaries to spend a full day with a single customer. While you might argue that understanding a customer does not necessarily require a full day, we would propose that you need to understand the world in which your customers live in order to be able to anticipate what they may want in the future. Deep understanding only comes with quality time. Which means time to build trust with customers, and the same factors we have mentioned before come into play – credibility, intimacy and risk. As the organisation evolves, and capability improves, stay close to your customers – particularly as you make the transition from 'command and control' into the self-confident arena.

4. Driving change into the organisation and making it stick

The never-ending series of single driving issues must always be fed from the customer. Marketing must make sure that changes, irrespective how far away they are from the customer, improve, and do not detract from, the customer experience. Organisations of any size generally have a whole plethora of initiatives going on. The programmes which flow from each single, driving issue must embrace existing momentum in the organisation and provide both focus and direction to initiatives. Indeed, it is often helpful to have a 'list' of mission-critical projects which should be managed with the rigour required to make horizontal working successful – clear deliverables and expectations, adequate resourcing, appropriate governance and fair human resource processes. This is the way to drive change in the organisation and make it stick.

5. Marketing implications of brand manners – advertising, below the line and beyond

Marketing service firms should be natural alliance partners. This means that they need to really understand the higher-order vision, the 'dream', and how the customer experience, in the form of brand manners, should evolve. Advertising spend should be structured to be mutually reinforcing with below-the-line activity – the classic thesis of 'integrated communications'. This gets into the rational, emotional and political arenas, particularly as the marketing world is generally not short on egos and opinions. Communications should aim not only at the customer, but at other key stakeholders, including employees, shareholders, and suppliers. Marketing service activities need to feed seamlessly into the technology systems which underpin effective marketing, such as data warehousing, data mining, supply chain and customer relationship management systems.

6. Brand manners capability and the role of the Marketing Director

The ability to improve the customer experience with an organisation which thrives on delivering improved manners, depends heavily on the skill base in the organisation. Make sure marketing is not only about the activities associated with marketing – market research, advertising, sales promotion, public relations and data management – but also about contributing to the virtuous strategy development and capability building cycle. Make sure that people in the organisation can think for themselves, and not be overreliant on outsiders to do their thinking for them! Make sure the skills necessary for brand manners, from the front line, back up to the full length of the value chain are in place. Work with both line management and the human resource function to make this happen. Insist on training on the job, which is evaluated by those concerned to help them do their jobs better. Otherwise, raid the off-the-job training budget and re-deploy it in the service of customers, whether through more front-line staff, or through tailored training and development. Use the increasing power of computer simulators to help develop people in a fraction of the time it would otherwise take, by creating virtual, action-learning environments where judgements are made and actions taken in simulated real-life situations.

7. Technology as a customer-experience-enriching servant to brand manners

Technology is still in its infancy, compared to where it will be in even five years time. Do not let this be an excuse for letting it become the master rather than the driver of customer enhancements. It is crazy to spend millions of dollars on a gee-whiz IT system, designed by people with PhDs, to be used by modest, but equally worthy individuals who deal day-in, day-out with customers. An IT Director once told us that he had just realised that he had spent all of his life designing IT systems to a paper specification, rather than to be used by people! In our experience, this is, sadly, the rule – although things are getting better. So, when embarking on an IT investment which will affect the customer (and the majority do, in one way or another), spend more, not less in order to change the work processes and build the skills required to delight customers. We have cited call centres as a big opportunity here. Never cut yourself off from local contact with your customer.

Increasingly, technology is becoming customer-centric; hand-held scanners, palm-sized WAP-enabled devices which can compare prices for you on the high street before you enter a shop, and internet exchanges where you can get and see real-time customer feedback. Grab the opportunities afforded by all of this front-line technology before your competitors do. Marketing people have to be technology experts, too.

8. Front-line brand manners in customer service

The moments of truth for customers occur when they meet one of your employees, or interact with one of your systems, whether a call centre, simple switchboard, or Internet site. Constantly test what it is like to be a customer coming into contact with your own organisation. Get your employees to do the same. Unlike many telecommunications companies, make sure a director is available for a customer to speak to. Make sure customers feel that they can get action in your organisation when they need it.

Revisit what we have talked about with your people, in terms of the rational – 'Our product/service delivered against the brand promise', the emotional – 'I really enjoyed that experience!', the political – 'No-one lost out; it was a fair transaction', and the spiritual – 'I feel that dealing with this organisation enriches me as a person, and may even contribute to a better world'.

Focus on building trust between your company and its customers. Recognise that your staff, often the ones who are paid the least, are key to this. Reward them as well as you possibly can.

9. Brand Spirit

In a previous book, *Brand Spirit*, Hamish Pringle and Marjorie Thompson set out the case for brands to be deployed in a more ethical way. Social or cause-related marketing is a great step forward in this respect. Brand manners takes this a step further, by not only linking the rational through the emotional to the spiritual, but also setting out ideas regarding the practical politics of achieving a higher-order vision, and the 'dream'.

True brand spirit, in this context, should ignite the enthusiasm of customers and employees, alike. The key to this lies in 'speaking' to each person as an individual, whether they work for the firm or are customers. Brand spirit should be at the heart of the corporate drama, and of the higher-order vision, and thence the values and behaviour of the company.

31

The Employee

We have set out eight key points for employees below.

"You 'just want to be happy' – what kind of a pie-in-the-sky ambition is that?"

Cartoon 9 *'Just a pie in the sky!'*

1. What to do with your life – employee spirit

We can be fairly sure that two factors exist which shape our personality and behaviour: our genetic inheritance from our parents, and our experience of life, particularly at an early age. These combine to make us creatures of habit. An increasing number of people also believe that we arrive with both good and bad baggage from our previous lives – karma. Underpinning the notion of karma is the belief that we are responsible for what we do with our lives, and that we build up a sort of balance sheet over time. We are not going to debate the merits, or otherwise, of reincarnation, but we do believe that some of the lessons of the idea of karma are very relevant to brand manners.

Both employee and customer need to feel responsible for what they do. What each of us does affects the world we live in. So, one of our great tasks is to get to know ourselves – who we really are, and whether we believe we have a role to play in life. This does not have to be a vocation as such, but a deep understanding of ourselves is fundamental to achieving our potential as individual human beings. Most of us, the authors included, spend far too much time, and sacrifice too much energy on displacement activity – being busy for the sake of being busy. We each need to figure out how many lives we want to lead – personal, family, work, sport, art, music, travel, religion – the list is potentially very long, yet our ability to live more than three or four lives simultaneously, with any decent level of quality, is limited by the time at our disposal and the relative levels of energy we commit to each activity. So, channel your energy into the few areas you want to do well in.

Most of us move from dependency to independence. Few of us then go on to achieve interdependence, which is core to brand manners.

2. Where you came from – what really drives you

We are creatures of our past – this is what makes us creatures of habit. There are all kinds of ways of getting at who we are and who we might become. The key starting point is to try to find out, and understand, the dimensions which mould you most. First-born children tend to be more organised than those coming later – due to the obvious need to make their way in an unfamiliar world, without the help of older siblings. Our parents' background and outlook has an enormous impact on us, as can have other close family, teachers, role models, and our peers. Try to gain an understanding of these drivers and also try to learn how other people see you, and the impact you have on them. Remember that your non-verbal signals are much more powerful communicators than the spoken word. Facial expression, body posture, tone of voice, all of these have an impact that is easy to take for granted and thereby underestimate!

Try to figure out what is really important to you, and live your life accordingly. The saying 'where there is a will, there is a way', is increasingly true as people have choices to work for themselves, more and more, or to change jobs more often. How disempowering the notion of 'a job for life' was. Who wants to fall for the illusion of job security? There is no such thing in an increasingly meritocratic world where you have to earn the right to your job, day by day. Stepping up to this responsibility not only frees you, it offers you the chance of making a difference and doing something worthwhile. Potential should go hand in hand with fulfilment, right up to the level of spirit – the whither in life. Brand manners requires you to take risks for your customers, and also for yourself. Build your self-confidence in real, deeply held convictions, not on white-knuckled striving. Learn to let go: by giving more and more, you will receive back much more than you would ever have got by taking. Take pride in building a self-confident organisation, where the rules are based on giving of yourself, rather than on fear of others.

3. Understanding the benefits of being part of the Corporate Dream

The great advantage of working in an organisation lies in the power of teamwork – being able to achieve things you could never aspire to on your own. By contributing to the creation of a Corporate Dream, you may also earn the right to make it come true. The right dream must be rooted in your belief that the customer experience can be improved, given your own experience. Time and time again we see organisations where the front-line employees who work with customers know exactly what it would take to improve the firm's brand manners, but the company seems incapable of seeking out this information and acting on it. How many times have you come across fellow employees who say 'it is not my problem, it's my employer's fault. I can do nothing about it' (i.e. 'go away')? Do not ever allow yourself to be like them! Be active in the corporate drama. Inject fun and excitement into your job and it will catalyse others to do the same in a positively reinforcing way.

4. Making the world a better place for customers

There is a shop in London called 'Low Pressure' that sells surfing gear and the like. We love to visit this shop as the staff exude a natural warmth and happiness which is infectious. Making a purchase feels very un-pressured, and enjoyable. So here we have a fun product (all the attributes – the rational), wrapped around with a great environment (including fun brands – the emotional), where it feels like a fair deal (win-win – the political), and it feels worthwhile (sport, health and well-being – the spiritual). Think about these brand manners dimensions and how they could be applied to your job. Talk to your customers – as individuals, not as transactions or a means to an end.

5. Making the world a better place for you

Be kind as well as tough with yourself. This part of the book is about working on yourself. No-one can do this for you. We encourage you to keep an open mind – try to discover things one at a time, and then figure out how they fit together for you. You are the only judge of the worth of this effort.

Self-esteem, decisions, behaviour and competence

Start with your self-esteem, as opposed to ego. You cannot progress without first coming to terms with yourself. Work on your decisions, mixing your analytical capabilities with the judgement that lies deep within you – which lets you feel what is the right thing to do. 'The Inner Game of Tennis' makes the point that you cannot become a great tennis player by controlling the racquet with your mind – there are simply too many variables to control. You have to let go and trust your instincts; your subconscious can do a much better job than your brain ever can! Work on your behaviour. Bear in mind that there is always an element of this that cannot be attributed to brain processes – something exists beyond conscious thought. Finally, decide to work on your capabilities so that you are equipped as well as you possibly can be to take your rightful place in the world. So, try to make decisions and perform actions without being conscious of process. Open systems change as surrounding conditions change – they learn from experience; closed systems don't. Turn your behaviour into an open system where the learning rate is always greater than the rate of change.

The impact of behaviour

The nature and intensity of your behaviour affects others – be aware of this. Positive elements of behaviour include: interest, excitement, enjoyment, joy; negative elements are associated with distress, anguish, anger, rage, fear, terror, shame, humiliation, contempt and disgust. Neutral behaviours, in terms of their effect on others are few; surprise, startle.

Learn from the wisdom of others: some 40 points to think about

We have touched frequently on the rational, emotional, and political aspects of life in organisations. To really develop, take time to develop your spiritual side, in the sense we use the word in this book. Treat this as independent from any particular religious beliefs. Take each of the following points, one per day at a time, and spend time reflecting on what each could mean for you. You may want to make a few notes to help organise and progress your thoughts as they evolve. These points are deliberately not presented in a rational structure. They are there to help you by stimulating thought about your own process of personal discovery.

- Logic is a great deceiver – and therefore not necessarily the best way of doing things.
- This world needs more than anything else people who can make independent judgements.
- People develop a fear of taking risks due to the threat of sanction.
- Treat everyone as their own person.
- Recognise two worlds: the visible and the invisible – the latter is felt rather than known.
- Ingredients key to personal development include: trust, recognition, self-expression and individuality.
- Our behaviour is ruled by instincts, emotions and mind.
- Personal transformation requires balance and harmony of instinct, emotion and thought.
- There are faculties and powers latent in man but long buried under the weight of our logical thinking.
- It is not enough to know, one also has to be.
- Our capacity for work depends on the way we are connected with sources of energy inside us and beyond us.
- Knowledge is useless without being.
- Sense as well as think … without fear and without pride.

- True harmony is about being neither active nor passive but a third state which embraces such diverse qualities as love, freedom and order, reconciliation and truth.
- Without sacrifice, nothing can be gained.
- If you do not see yourself, it is impossible for anyone else to show you.
- You already have too much knowledge. It will remain only theory unless you learn to understand not with mind but with heart and body.
- Life is real only when I am.
- The unseen world is more truly real than the visible world.
- His thirst for survival makes him incapable of living in the present.
- Eastern laziness consists of sitting in the sun, drinking tea and doing nothing. Western laziness is cramming our lives with compulsory activity so there is no time to confront the real issues.
- Nothing has any lasting character in life. There is only one law of the universe that never changes; all things change, and all things are impermanent.
- We are terrified of letting go. Terrified in fact of living at all, since learning to live is learning to let go. Take a risk.
- If you are too clever, you could miss the point entirely.
- Everything is inextricably related, we have to be responsible for everything we do, say and think, as it impacts the world at large.
- Every action, even the smallest, is pregnant with consequences. Karma means our ability to create and to change.
- Negative action has one good quality – it can be purified.
- What you are is what you have been, what you will be is what you do now.
- A human being is part of a whole, called by us the 'universe', a part limited in time and space. We experience ourselves, our thoughts and feelings, as something separated from everything else – a kind of optical illusion of our consciousness. This illusion is a kind of prison for us, restricting us to our personal desires and to affection for a few persons nearest us. Our task must be to free ourselves from this prison by widening our circles of compassion to embrace all living creatures and the whole of nature in its beauty.
- Ego is the absence of the true knowledge of who we really are, and its result.
- Recognise the dreamlike qualities of life – practise good-heartedness towards all beings. Be loving and compassionate, no matter what others do to you.

- Mind is the creator of happiness and the creator of suffering. Four faults that prevent us from realising the nature of the mind: too close to be recognised, too profound for us to fathom, too easy for us to believe, too wonderful for us to accommodate.
- How we live now can cost us our entire future.
- Make haste slowly.
-
    'To see a World in a Grain of Sand,
    And a Heaven in a Wild Flower,
    Hold Infinity in the palm of your hand,
    And Eternity in an hour'
    William Blake.

- The teachings of all the mystical paths of the world make it clear that there is within us an enormous reservoir of power, the power of wisdom and compassion, the power of what Christ called the Kingdom of Heaven.
- Do what you do best.
- The fundamental emotions are love and fear – choose which one to guide you.
- No blame, no judgement.
- Things are what they are. 'When I eat, I eat; when I sleep, I sleep' Zen saying.
- Striving tends to produce more striving. Less striving creates more light.
- Faith, hope and charity. What does it mean to be charitable?
- 'As I am, so you will be' inscription in Italian church, referring to the Trinity.

Having worked these through, set out a diagram of what you feel is important to you, and try to live by it. An illustration of what this has meant for one of us is shown in Figure 59. It is up to you to provide your own questions and discover your own answers!

6. What the rational, emotional, political and spiritual dimensions mean for you

Try applying, in a very conscious way, these four dimensions to your working life and your personal life. We believe these to be natural laws which are potential sources of great benefit to you. When you have learned to make the best of them for yourself, you can apply them to the customer experience and

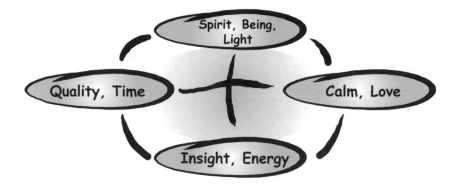

Figure 59 *Personal discovery – an illustration.*

so to brand manners. You cannot, alone, change the organisation in which you work, but you can show the way. The emphasis needs to be on showing, not telling. By making your experiences personal, they become non-threatening to others and will arouse the curiosity and interest of others. Combined with even a few of the other ideas in this book, you can change your life and the world for the better.

7. Making the corporate drama as exciting as the personal one – work as sport

Take the notion of the corporate drama to heart – try to create an excitement in your working life which makes it as rewarding as your other lives. Try the low-pressure, high-performance route; by taking work seriously, but lightly, you can turn your daily experiences into sport, especially when these affect your customers. Realise that you are the most important person in the organisation. If you follow some of the routes to personal discovery, we are confident that you will reap a strong dividend from your increased self-confidence. Turn this into continuous learning – if you are not learning, you need to change what you are doing. Trust yourself and build trust in others.

8. Why the individual is king (or queen)

We believe that organisations are only as good as their people, and the potential latent in each individual is largely untapped. This 'How-To' guide suggests ways for you to unleash a lot of this hidden talent. The organisation cannot do it for you. You have to take on the responsibility to do it for yourself!

32

Management

The brand manners way sets out guidelines for management to turn brand manners into reality. These should be taken in conjunction with the other 'how-to' guides. The brand manners agenda for management is set out in the five points shown below.

Underpinning the ideas in the brand manners way are the following;

1. Customer and employee potential

Brand manners come to life each time one of your employees comes into contact, directly or indirectly, with a customer. Having put in place the actions and processes necessary to understand and anticipate your customer, the role of management is to build and lead the capability required to over-deliver on the promises inherent in the brand, on an on-going basis.

Individuals can work at realising their full potential, but the organisation needs to help them. It is the organisation which should be the servant of those serving the customer, and the real dividend comes through creating the self-confidence which permits employees to take measured risks for customers, as well as for themselves. Dominic Houlder, from the London Business School, uses framework (Figure 60) to show how to run your life as if you were running a business.

Frames are defined as 'What I see in the world that is conducive to the realisation of my values'. This is all about having a brand manners mindset that also reflects the higher-order vision the individual has for his or her personal and working life – the rational dimension. Processes are 'How I lay down my own development path'. By aligning the personal agenda with the

Running your life as you run your business

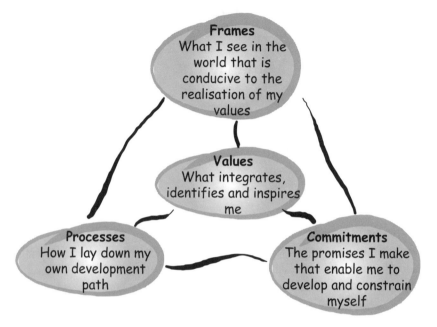

Figure 60 *Frames, processes, commitments and values.*

business agenda, you, as a manager, can generate enormous energy in the organisation. This can be harnessed in the cause of brand manners. Just as the processes need to be put in place in the organisation to improve the customer experience, individuals need to lay down their own development paths and it is your job to coach and help them – the political dimension.

Commitments include 'The promises I make that enable me to develop, and that constrain me'. These translate the corporate and the personal agendas into reality – the emotional dimension. Finally, values are 'What integrates, identifies and inspires me'. This is our higher-order spiritual agenda which we believe holds the key not just to personal fulfilment, but also to improved organisation working and a better world for customers and employees alike. By working through these, you can help align individuals with the organisation.

2. Your role as a manager

Help develop the dream which will deliver higher-order results and improved brand manners. Put in place the organisation processes, rewards, systems and behaviours to deliver them. Focus constantly on coaching your people. Never manage by fear – focus on the positive attributes of

"You lack initiative and ambition, Higgs, so
I'm promoting you to my deputy!"

Cartoon 10 *'Promotions'.*

behaviour, based more on love and integrity. Help individuals to discover themselves. Help them become brand ambassadors. Help create the corporate drama which will fire the imagination of the organisation.

Use neuro-linguistic programming techniques for managing interactions and in communicating. Take the non-verbal cues in managing people very seriously. What you say has less than a tenth of the total impact on the person with you – the rest being made up of your voice and body signals.

Recognise that people filter their experiences. Identify which of the three preferred thinking styles you are dealing with. Some 50–55% of people are 'visual' – they will say things like 'I see what you mean ... it looks good to me ... show me more'. They tend to look upwards or straight ahead when thinking (Figure 61).

With these folk, you need to use imagery to communicate effectively. Some 20–30% of the workforce are 'auditories' – who say things such as: 'I hear what you say ... sounds good to me ... tell me more'. They tend to look left to right (Figure 62).

They respond well to speech, and tend to make decisions on what they hear. About a quarter of the population are Kinaesthetes, who operate primarily in the feelings mode – both physical and emotional. So you will hear: 'I get what you are saying ... I feel good about this ... Fill me in on the details ...'. Eye movement tends to be towards the bottom left (Figure 63).

50% Population

Visual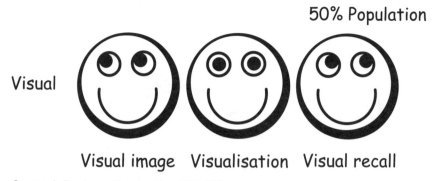

Visual image   Visualisation   Visual recall

Source: A. Bradbury, *Develop Your NLP Skills.*

Figure 61 *Visual image, visualisation and visual recall.*

25% Population

Audio

Audio image   Internal   Audio recall
dialogue

Source: A. Bradbury, *Develop Your NLP Skills.*

Figure 62 *Audio image, internal dialogue and audio recall.*

25% Population

Feeling (kinaesthesis)

Sensory recall

Source: A. Bradbury, *Develop Your NLP Skills.*

Figure 63 *Sensory recall.*

They tend to be empathetic and like time to work out how they feel about something before acting. Understand yourself and your effects on others.

We have set out these techniques, albeit briefly in summary, as we believe they can have a significant impact on the effectiveness of your own management skills and style.

3. Self-confidence vs. command and control

Management by fear is still the norm in most organisations as it is the easiest and often the most comfortable way to manage. Combined with the 'get someone who can' mentality, this can undermine brand manners completely, as fear flows down the organisation, paralysing individual initiative, stunting development and making people miserable. People may be operating at some 50% of their potential, or less.

In contrast, the self-confident organisation has the customer-facing employee at the centre, with the rest of the organisation in support, adding value. Authority flows up the organisation because the individual has it in their gift to give 80% or up to 120% of their potential. When individuals are self-confident, and the organisation is self-confident, the higher-order vision will lead naturally to improved brand manners. This does not mean there is no discipline – far from it. Authority levels and the rules of the game must be clear. However, people have a level of freedom which allows them to take measured risks and the firm learns better ways to serve customers all of the time.

Your role is to lead the transition from command and control to self-confidence, without falling in the Ditch! If your organisation is already operating in the self-confident space, your role is to focus on driving continuous improvement of the customer experience by mobilising, coaching and motivating your people. Focus on managing the rational, emotional, political and spiritual dimensions. Develop a management spirit that captures the essence of the dream and the corporate drama, built on leadership and trust. Build up positive corporate and personal karma.

4. Vision, will and capability

The three tests of success for following the brand manners way are vision, will and capability. Drive ahead with your interpretation of the vision that flows from the higher-order goals, the brand manners dream and the corporate drama. Demonstrate the will to drive change through and inspire others to do the same. This includes taking care of the political dimension, as well as the other three. These are necessary for you to help build the capability to deliver improving brand manners.

5. Technology as servant of the customer

Fully embrace technology but make sure that it is driven off the needs of the customer, and therefore off the needs of your employees. Ensure that technology focuses on the outputs necessary to improve customer satisfaction first, and only afterwards on cost reduction. Never run the risk of alienating your customers.

33

Customers

Our final 'How-to' guide is for customers, the agenda for which is set out below.

1. Making the world a better place

In Western consumer societies, the customer truly is king. With this privilege should come personal responsibility (rights normally imply duties). Much is already happening in this regard – from 'green' concerns through worries over child labour, and endangered species, and efforts to reduce the impact of war, famine and disease. What we would like you to do, as a customer is:

1. Be selective about what you buy and the impact it has on your family and friends.
2. Be very demanding when it comes to service and performance against inherent brand promises.
3. Show the way by role-modelling constructive behaviour so that employees you meet learn through adult–adult interactions.

So, stand up for the principles of brand manners and use some of the tips you may have learned in this book constantly to change things for the better.

2. Pushing back the envelope

Help organisations understand how you would like to live, so that they can anticipate your needs by continuously developing products and services that help you lead a more rewarding life. The exciting thing about new technologies is that they can help bring people together and communicate better, if used properly. Help to push back the envelope by stimulating the development of better lives for as many people as possible. Live life to the full.

3. Customer spirit

Think about what the rational, emotional, political and spiritual dimensions mean for you. Pay particular care to the forty or so pointers to spiritual development set out in the employees 'how-to' section. Because you drive most change, it is your responsibility to ensure that the resources of organisations are directed towards making things better. If you choose to follow the displacement activity route and be preoccupied with more and more meaningless gadgets, then more meaningful goods and services will never appear. In an increasingly global economy, what you do can have a greater effect on corporations than ever before, so use this privilege wisely and effectively.

4. Demand more; never accept poor

It is hard to make the effort never to accept poor service. However, it is getting easier, with the advent of the Internet and the possibility of sharing real-time information on product or service performance. Chat rooms are great for swapping experiences. And the banks and others will realise that their ghastly call-centres and computerised answering systems are not all you want! Increasingly, we are all customers, shareholders and employees, so we are not stuck in one role, and have the right to demand better. Don't let employees say it is not their fault, but rather their employer is to blame. We all need to be responsible for what we do.

5. How to get through to organisations – Naderism in the 2000s

Ralph Nader started the consumer movement in the USA in the 1960s. We need, as customers, to get through to poorly performing organisations in ways they will understand. Again, things are going in our favour, with increased privatisation and company scrutiny. The most effective way to get change is for you to switch suppliers. With customers abandoning them in droves, poorly performing firms will be forced to confront change. Not only that, we are entering the era of 'permission marketing' where increasingly you will have the power to decide which brands can communicate with you, and on what terms. This will galvanise companies like never before.

In dealing with organisations, engage the employees on an individual level – do not undermine their self-respect, rather try to build their self-confidence. Often it is better to use humour and try to find out how you can influence, rather than harangue them. Help the employee to help you.

6. Brand manners for life!

We hope that you have got some value from our thesis on brand manners. By concentrating on the individual and personal potential we have provided guidance for each person who reads the book to be an actor on this exciting and unfolding stage. From the brand, through the dream to each person playing a valuable part, we have sought to show ways whereby working life and personal life can be improved. And there is considerable room for improvement.

We all have the things which drive us nuts – like the walkways at Heathrow which are never all working, the computerised ordering system for the cab company that treats you like a number, the bank that used to provide good service and stops due to reorganisation, the employees who take a delight in saying no ... there is a never-ending list!

But this all represents a huge opportunity for improvement. We believe the crux of this is in the delivery, and in creating self-confident organisations where employees lead exciting and fulfilling working lives, resulting in a better experience for you, the customer. Your role in all of this, as a customer, dealing with self-confident organisations in which employees have a high level of dignity, should help us all lead better lives, realising that brand manners are for life!

Conclusion

Making the world a better place

Brand manners are for life, so that we can both enjoy and contribute to the world as customers, and lead more rich and stimulating lives at work as employees. By taking personal responsibility for our own development, and for our relationship with customers, across the four dimensions – the rational, emotional, political and spiritual, we can all increasingly feel good about the way we are living. For the individual, there is the prize of esteem, self-worth and satisfaction. For the corporation there is the prize of breaking into the management space of the 'self-confident' organisation, which will put blue water between it and its major competitors. Within society, the individual, the corporation and the customer should play more responsible and valuable roles.

Brand manners covers a rich and broad canvas, from the 'Book of Life', though the 'Brand Manners Way' and 'Improvement Cycle' to the 'How-To' guides – the brand manners diagram shown in Figure 64 summarises this. Each individual employee, customer and corporation is different on a host of dimensions. Some will benefit at the personal level, some will take out a few breakthrough ideas which will make a big difference to people's lives, and others may want to instigate a full brand manners programme or on-going process. We foresee the need for a Brand Manners Institute which helps to provide feedback to and from customers in support of their improvement journey. This would, unlike existing quality programmes, focus on output performance as perceived by customers, rather than input processes.

We do encourage you to read the whole book, rather than just 'cherry-picking' the sections that most obviously speak to your areas of interest.

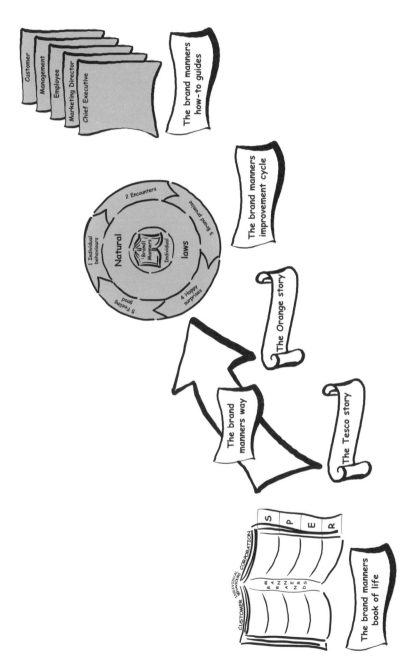

Figure 64 *The brand manners summary*

This is because brand manners require each of us to look at our lives in the round, to inderstand how all the elements fit together. We hope the book will appeal to at least four key audiences: management, marketing and communications professionals, academics and the many individuals who may be simply looking to develop themselves. We would welcome your feedback and further interest via our website: www.brandmanners.com.

That is happiness; to be dissolved into something complete and great.
Willa Cather

Bibliography

Access Survey, BMRBS telephone omnibus 1999.

Scott Adams, *The Dilbert Principle*, Boxtree/Macmillan Publishers Ltd (1997).

Julio Rocha do Amaral, MD and Renato M.E. Sabbatini, PhD, *The Sugar Pill*.

Tim Ambler, *Marketing and the Bottom Line*, Financial Times/Prentice Hall (2000).

Chris Agyris and Donald A. Schon, *Theory in Practice – Increasing Professional Effectiveness*, Jossey Bass, (1974).

B.P. Bapkin, *Pavlov*, Victor Gollancz (1951).

Michael Franz Basch, *Understanding Psychotherapy: The Science Behind the Art*, Basic Books, a subsidiary of Perseus Books (1988).

Michael Franz Basch, *Doing Brief Psychotherapy*, Basic Books, a subsidiary of Perseus Books (1995).

Warren Bennis, *Organising Genius: The Secrets of Creative Collaboration*, Nicholas Brealey Publishers (1997).

Eric Berne, M.D., *Games People Play*, Penguin Books (1970).

Susan Blackmore, *The Meme Machine*, Oxford University Press (1999).

Andrew Bradbury, *Develop Your NLP Skills*, Kogan Page (1997).

William Bratton and Peter Knobler, *Turnaround*, Random House (1998).

Tim Broadbent, *Advertising Works II*, NTC Publications (2000).

Stanley A. Brown, *What Customers Value Most*, John Wiley & Sons (1995).

Jeremy Bullmore, *Behind the Scenes in Advertising*, second edition, NTC Publications (1998).

Leslie Butterfield, *Excellence in Advertising*, second edition, Butterworth Heinemann in association with the IPA (1999).

Tony Buzan and Barry Buzan, *The Mindmap Book*, BBC Books (1993).

Robert D. Buzzell, John A. Quelch and Christopher A. Bartlett, *Global Marketing Management: Cases and Readings*, third edition, Addison Wesley Publishing Company (1994).

Robert Carroll and Stephen Prickett (eds), *The Bible: Authorized King James Version*, Oxford Paperbacks (1998).

Caviar Statistics on Films in 1998, 1999.

David Clutterbuck, with Dez Dearlove and Deborah Snow, *Actions Speak Louder*, Kingfisher (1992).

James C. Collins and Jerry I. Porras, *Built to Last: Successful Habits of Visionary Companies*, Random House (1998).

Co-operative Employee Survey, March 1998, Consumers' Association.

John Dalla Costa, *Working Wisdom*, Stoddart (1995)

Steven R. Covey, *Principle-Centred Leadership*, Simon and Schuster (1991).

Steven R. Covey, *The 7 Habits of Highly Effective People – Powerful Lessons in Personal Change*, Simon and Schuster (1998).

Steven R. Covey, *Living the 7 Habits – Stories of Courage and Inspiration*, Simon and Schuster (1999)

Hilaire Cunny, *Ivan Pavlov – His Theories*, Editions Seghers (1962).

Frank Dick, OBE, *Winning*, Abingdon (1992).

Charles Dickens, *Hard Times*, Penguin Books (1997).

Peter Doyle, *Marketing Management and Strategy*, second edition, Prentice Hall (1998).

Peter Doyle, *Value-based Marketing*, John Wiley and Sons (2000).

Tom Duncan and Sandra Moriarty, *Driving Brand Value*, McGraw Hill (1997).

Electronic Telegraph, *Marks and Spencer Sues Over Child Labour Claim*, 25 Feb. 1998.

Susan Estrich, *What's Driving New York's Crime Rate Down?*, Harvard Law School.

FAA Enforcement Actions – Violations of 14 CFR 91.11, *Unruly Passengers* – Quarterly Reports for Calendar Year 2000.

Future Foundation/Consumers' Association/Richmond Events, *What Do People Want From Their Ideal Company?* Richmond Events Limited (1999).

W. Timothy Gallwey, *The Inner Game of Tennis*, Random House (1974).

Howard Gardner, *Leading Minds*, HarperCollins (1996).

Malcolm Gladwell, *The Tipping Point*, Little, Brown and Company (2000).

Erving Goffman, *The Presentation of Self in Everyday Life*, Penguin (1959).

Francis J. Gouillart and James N. Kelly, *Transforming The Organization*, McGraw Hill (1995).

Lynda Gratton, *Living Strategy*, Prentice Hall (2000).

John Grays, *Women are from Venus, Men are from Mars*, HarperCollins (1992).

Charles Handy, *The Empty Raincoat*, Arrow (1994).

Charles Handy, *The Hungry Spirit – Beyond Capitalism a Quest for Purpose in the Modern World*, Hutchinson Arrow Books Limited (1997).

The Henley Centre, *Planning for Social Change*, The Henley Centre (1998).

James L. Heskett, W. Earl Sasser Jr and Leonard A. Schlesinger, *The Service Profit Chain*, Free Press (1997).

Howard League for Penal Reform fact sheets numbers 1, 2 and 29.

Dominic Hughes and Benedict Phillips, *The Oxford Union Guide to Successful Pubic Speaking*, Virgin Publishing (2000).

David Jobber, *Principles and Practice of Marketing*, second edition, McGraw Hill (1998).

John Philip Jones, *When Ads Work: New Proof That Advertising Triggers Sales*, Lexington Books (1995).

Charles Jonscher, *Wired Life*, Bantam Press (1999)

Debrah Kania and Beth Yaeckel, *Internet World Guide to One-to-One Web Marketing*, Cliff Allen, John Wiley & Sons (1998).

Jean Noel Kapferer, *Strategic Brand Management*, Kogan Page (1995).

Andrew Karmen, 'What's driving New York's crime rate down? Is improved policing responsible for the sharp drop in murder rates?', *Law Enforcement News* (1996).

Jon R. Katzenbach and Douglas K. Smith, *The Wisdom of Teams – Creating the High-Performance Organisation*, Harvard Business School Press (1994).

Nick Kendall, *Advertising Works 10*, NTC Publications (1999).

Charles Kingsley, *The Water-babies*, Puffin Books (1995).

Naomi Klein, *No Logo*, HarperCollins (2000).

Philip Kotler, *Kotler on Marketing: How to Create, Win, and Dominate Markets*, Free Press (1999).

Jesper Kunde, *Corporate Religion*, Financial Times/Prentice Hall (2000).

Karen Leland and Keith Bailey, *Customer Service for Dummies*, IDG Books World Wide (1995).

Brian MacArthur, *How the Express Stole the Mail's Star Man*, 7 Jan. 2000.

Chris Macrae, *The Brand Chartering Handbook*, Addison-Wesley (1996).

Thomas Maier, *Dr Spock: An American Life*, Harcourt (1998).

David H. Maister, *Managing the Professional Service Firm*, Free Press Paperbacks (1993).

Albert Mehrabian, *Silent Messages* (1971)

MORI Data on *Corporate Reputations – Familiarity vs. Favourability* (1999).

Ralph Nader, *Unsafe at Any Speed: The Designed-in Dangers of American Automobiles*, Grossman (1965).

Nicholas Negoponte, *Being Digital*, Hodder and Stoughton (1995).

Kjell A. Nordstrom and Jonas Ridderstrale, *Funky Business*, FT.com

NYSE – Press Releases and Quarterly Reports www.nyse.com

New York Times, 'Obituary of Dr Benjamin Spock' (1998).

Office of National Statistics – *Gross Domestic Product by Industry Groups at Factor Cost: Current Prices, 1991 and 1996: Regional Trends Dataset*.

Office of National Statistics Report (99) 78 1999, *Marriage and Divorce in England and Wales in 1996*.

Office of National Statistics *Labour Market Statistics: By Sub-region, 1997–98, 1998: Regional Trends Dataset*.

Wolf Olins, *Guide to Corporate Reputations*, Design Council (1990).

Richard Pascale, *Managing on the Edge*, Penguin (1990).

Tom Peters and Nancy Austin, *A Passion for Excellence*, Fontana (1986).

Tom Peters, *Liberation Management*, Knopf (1992).

Hamish Pringle and Marjorie Thompson, *Brand Spirit*, John Wiley & Sons (1999).

Proshare – London Stock Exchange Quarterly Dec. 1998 and Transactional Survey June 1998 www.proshare.co.uk

Julian Richer, *The Richer Way*, third edition, Julian Richer (1996).

Frederick F. Richheld, *The Loyalty Effect*, HBS Press (1996).

Matt Ridley, *Genome*, Fourth Estate (1999).

ROAR, *Trust a Little – Trust a Lot*, ROAR (1999).

Saatchi & Saatchi/Taylor Nelson AGB Omnimas, *Kid Connection – What purchases do kids influence* (1998).

Samaritans' Reports on *Young men speak out, Exploring the Taboo, Real People 1998–1999*.

Arthur K. Shapiro and Elaine Shapiro, *The Powerful Placebo*, Johns Hopkins University Press (1997).

Mandy Shaw and Ken Pease, Central Research Unit Report: *Preventing Repeat Victimisation in Scotland: Some examples of good practice*, Scottish Official Publications (2000).

Bernd H. Shmitt, *Experimental Marketing – How to get customers to sense, feel, think, act, relate to your company and brands*, Simon and Schuster Inc (1999).

Paul Southgate, *Total Branding by Design*, Kogan Page (1994).

Mary Spillane, *Branding Yourself*, Pan Books (2000).

Dr Benjamin Spock, *Baby and Child Care*, Simon & Schuster (1946).

Dr Benjamin Spock, *The Common Sense Book of Baby Care*, Simon & Schuster (1993).

Gordon R. Sullivan and Michael V. Harper, *Hope is Not a Method*, Broadway (1996).

Jeremy Swinfen-Green, *E-Media*, NTC Publications (2000).

Jim Taylor, Watts Wacker and Howard Means, *The 500 Year Delta – What happens after what comes next*, HarperCollins Publishers (1998).

Gillian Tett, *Japan's 'look before you leap' strategy to cut railway suicides*, published 12 May 2000, 16:54GMT – FT.com.

Edward Thorndike, *Laws of Psychology* (1910).

Robert Townsend, *Up the Organisation*, Fawcett (1983).

Sun Tzu, *The Art of War*, Hodder & Stoughton (1981).

US Census Bureau www.census.gov – *Frequently Requested Tables from the Statistical Abstract of the United States* (1999).

US News, March 15 1998, *Interview with Benjamin Spock*.

Watts Wacker and Jim Taylor, *The Visionary's Handbook*, Capstone Publishing Limited (2000).

Robin Wight, *The Day the Pigs Refused to be Driven to Market*, Granada Publishing (1972).

James Q. Wilson and George L. Kelling, 'Broken Windows', March 1982 in *Atlantic* monthly magazine.

Michael J. Wolf, *The Entertainment Economy*, Penguin (1999).

Webography

Companies

www.abbeynational.com
www.accenture.com
www.amazon.com
www.avis.com
www.bloomingmarvellous.co.uk
www.bpamoco.com
www.britishairways.com
www.bt.com (British Telecom)
www.burgerking.com
www.carphonewarehouse.com
www.cooperativebank.co.uk
www.daewoo-cars.co.uk
www.disney.co.uk
www.disney.com
www.dominospizza.com
www.euro.dell.com (Dell Computers European Website)
www.fedex.com (Federal Express)
www.gateway.com
www.genewatch.com (A genetically modified foods watchdog)
www.HSBC.com
www.john-lewis-partnership.co.uk
www.jrtr.net (Japanese railways)
www.kwikfit.co.uk (Kwikfit)
www.link.co.uk (The Link network)
www.mcdonalds.com
www.monsanto.com
www.music3w.com
www.nike.com

www.nikebiz.com (The Nike site detailing their policies)
www.pharmacia.com
www.pizzaexpress.co.uk
http://press.britishairways.com (British Airways Press Office website)
www.ronseal.co.uk
www.saatchikevin.com (Kevin Roberts home page)
www.saturn.com (Saturn Car Company, part of GM)
www.tesco.co.uk
www.thecoca-colacompany.com
www.virtual-office.co.uk (The Virtual Office)
www.walmart.com

The media

www.bbc.com
www.bizjournals.com
www.boston.com (Boston Globe online)
www.businessweek.com
www.dallasnews.com
www.forbes.com
www.ft.com
www.guardianunlimited.co.uk
www.latimes.com (Los Angeles Times)
www.lhj.com (Ladies Home Journal)
www.nationalpost.com
http://news.bbc.co.uk/hi/english (BBC News)
www.privateeye.com
www.smh.com.au (Sydney Morning Herald)
www.Sunday-times.co.uk
www.telegraph.co.uk
www.the-times.co.uk
www.thealantic.com (Magazine)
www.theeconomist.com
www.theseattlepost.com
www.theseattletimes.com
www.usatoday.com
www.usnews.com

Associations and bodies

www.adassoc.org.uk (Advertising Association)
www.bba.org.uk (British Bankers Association)
www.bma.org.uk (British Medical Association)
www.british-franchise.org.uk (British Franchise Association)
www.faa.gov (Federal Aviation Authority)

www.franchise.org (International Franchise Association)
www.gmc-uk.org (General Medical Council)
www.igd.com (Institute of Grocery Distribution)
www.ipa.co.uk
www.isba.org.uk (Incorporated Society of British Advertisers)
www.mrc.ac.uk (Medical Research Council)
www.samaritans.org.uk
www.smmt.co.uk (The Society of Motor Manufacturers and Traders)
www.spunk.com (Consumer anarchist site)
www.the-dma.org (The Direct Marketing Association)

Organisations

www.FARMSOURCE.com
www.forrester.com (Forrester Research)
www.henleycentre.com
www.liberty-human-rights.org (Liberty Protecting Civil Liberties)
www.mentalhealth.org.uk (Mental Health Organisation)
www.mori.com (Markets & Opinion Research International – the largest independent research agency in the UK)
www.mtr.org (Museum of Television and Radio)
www.nop.co.uk
www.olympic.org (Official Olympics committee site)
www.relate.org.uk
www.rice-research.org
www.the-fa.org (FA Website)
www.unicef.org (UNICEF Organisation)
www.ware.com
www.web.ukonline.co.uk/howard.league/index.html (The Howard League for Penal Reform)

Academia

www.ccir.ed.ac.uk (Centre for Communication Interface Research Group)
http://www.glenalmondcollege.co.uk/
www.hbs.edu (Harvard Business School)
www.hud.ac.uk/schools/human+health/research/acq/resapcbd.html (The Applied Criminology)
www.kcl.ac.uk (King's College, London)
www.london.edu (London Business School)
www.lib.ic.ac.uk/catalogue/cataccess (Science Museum Library Database)
http://library.wellcome.ac.uk (Wellcome Trust online library database)
www.lse.ac.uk (London School of Economics)

Government

www.dti.gov.uk (Department of Trade and Industry)
www.hm-treasury.gov.uk (Treasury Department)
www.homeoffice.gov.uk (The Home Office)
www.met.police.uk (Metropolitan Police Force)
www.open.gov.uk (Government main website)
www.standards.dfee.gov.uk (Government site on standards in education)
www.statistics.gov.uk (Government statistics webpages)
www.pub.whitehouse.gov

Other

www.amazon.com
www.berg.demon.co.uk (Berg Publishers)
www.bl.uk (The British Library)
www.brandmanners.com
www.britannica.com (Encyclopaedia Britannica)
www.btinternet.com/~alexandergrant/quotes/finquoteframes.html (Quote Finder)
www.encarta.msn.com (Encyclopaedia)
www.etiquettesource.com
www.glfanclub.com (Guiding Lights fan club site)
http://www.google.com
www.johnmajor.co.uk (Unofficial John Major website)
www.m-n.com (Dictionary)
www.maslow.org (About Maslow's work)
www.mrmanners.com (Manners Website)
www.o-bible.com (Online Bible)
www.randomhouse.com (Random House Publishers)
www.wiley.co.uk (John Wiley & Sons)
www.zimbardo.com (Philip Zimbardo's home page)

Index